THE Thirsty Land

THE Thirsty Land

THE STORY OF THE CENTRAL VALLEY PROJECT

Robert de Roos

BeardBooks
Washington, D.C.

TO MY MOTHER
WHO, AMONG MANY OTHER THINGS,
TOLD ME WHAT ISAIAH SAID

Preface

The aunt of a friend of mine, suffering possibly from idioglossia, has a perverse language of her own not related to any known tongue but which can be understood, within limits. This lady, for example, explains that she does not like movies adapted from books because, she avers, "they have a twinge to jeeper them up." I am not suffering as badly as this lady but I confess a general feeling of fag, five-o'clock shadow, and general apprehensiveness when suddenly confronted with such words as "multiple-purpose," "appropriation," "acre-feet, "kilowatt-hour," and "irrigationist." These words appear many times in this book. But apparently you can't build dams without them and you certainly cannot write about the Central Valley Project without using them over and over.

This book is not original research. It is a compilation of the history and sidelights, issues and policies of a tremendously important project. It is relatively objective as a compilation should be. But my bias has crept in from time to time. Although I do not say so in so many words, let me say here that I believe the Bureau of Reclamation is on the right track. I am opposed to the Army Corps of Engineers building irrigation and power dams and reservoirs. The Army, as Edward Hyatt has said, has consistently been on the side of "the interests." Naturally enough, I have a great respect for the Army. In this case, however, I wish they would go away and shoot their guns. I have no objection to state management and operation of the project if some way can be suggested to effect the change-over from federal to state. As you will see, however, no one has come up with any sensible plan for the change.

And certainly I am against the efforts of the Pacific Gas & Electric Co. to get control of the electrical energy generated by the project's power plants. Water is a vital resource in California and viii *The Thirsty Land*

from that water comes an almost inexhaustible supply of power. This power belongs to the people of California and of the United States. It should never be controlled by a privately owned utility, not even a utility regulated by a rate-making body.

It is well to bear in mind that this is a public project. That might seem an obvious statement. But so many people and special interests and corporations have been trying to muscle into the act that it is worth restating. The P. G. & E. could not have built the Central Valley Project—even if willing. The state of California could not build it. It was joyfully handed over to the federal government because the federal government was the only agency which *could* build it. As a public project, financed by the whole people of the United States—to the great benefit of California and its people—the highest policies of public good should determine its course and use.

This might be a good place to explain that an acre-foot of water is the amount of water which will cover an acre of land to a depth of one foot. It is 325,829 gallons. It is used to measure still water. Measurement for moving water is the number of cubic feet per second which pass a given point—which gives a measure both of volume and speed of the stream or canal.

I have many people to thank for their help. Marion Clawson and Mary Montgomery were most helpful, personally and through their important book, *History of Legislation and Policy Formation of the Central Valley Project.* Thanks are due, too, to Paul Taylor of the University of California; Norman Gallison, formerly information officer of the Army Corps of Engineers; Clyde Gorman of the Sacramento office of the Engineers; Alison Hawke Augustin; and Erma Celventra Fischer. And thanks go to Orman Lewis for the many hours he spent helping to prepare the Index—an exacting and difficult chore.

Some of the material herein first appeared in the *San Francisco Chronicle* and I have freely used the files of the *Chronicle* and the *San Francisco News.* I want to thank Larry Fanning, managing editor, John Bruce, city editor; and Stanley Mitchell of the *Chron-*

icle for their great help. Mrs. Marjorie D. Brown, the *Chronicle's* chief librarian, and her fine staff were very helpful and very patient with my sometimes irksome demands.

I want to thank Edward F. Treadwell for permission to use quotations from his book, *The Cattle King,* and Jon Frederic Stanton for his help with the photographs.

The Bureau of Reclamation men come in a special category. They were constantly helpful. I have a great admiration for the way they are doing their jobs; they are good public servants. Especially helpful were Phil Dickinson, Max Stern, Ben Glaha, and George Gideon.

And I find that credit of a sort is due to Isaiah. I had already chosen the name for this book when I discovered that old Isaiah had the same idea many years ago when he described the glory of the new Zion: "And the parched ground shall become a pool, and the thirsty land springs of water . . . ."

ROBERT DE ROOS

Contents

xi

Contents

The Thirsty Land

Ill fares the land, to hastening ills a prey,
Where wealth accumulates, and men decay . . . .

—OLIVER GOLDSMITH, "The Deserted Village"

I. Problems in Paradise

THE VIRTUES OF California are well known. The Native Son and his brother-in-boredom, the Californian by adoption, have sung its superlatives time without end. They sing of the California which has the tallest trees, the deepest valley, the highest mountain, the whitest snow, and the hottest sun. What other state has a genuine Golden Gate? Does California have oil? All over the place. It has the crispest lettuce, the most seedless grapes, and the orangest oranges. It's a natural scenic wonderland and it's an all-year affair and California here I come. Most of this talk is true—California is a fabulous land, a land of plenty and promise. It is full of good things—peaches and prunes, oranges and movie cuties, oil, gold, cotton, lemons, asparagus, grapes, artichokes, melons, airplanes, climate, and scenery. There are so many good things that it is hard to believe there can be problems in such a neon paradise.

There are real problems, most of them arising from the needs of the rapidly growing population—the needs for highways and houses and schools. But the tough, basic, all-important problem is water. California is a semiarid state. Without water it is not much. Water is its life force. Water is the limiting factor in the growth of its great cities and in the productivity of its land. Water produces cheap electrical energy in a land without coal. California's great struggle in its fight for growth and prosperity is to find ways to use every drop of the available water, to allow none to go to waste.

California's water supply is limited. It comes from winter rain and snow. The summers are rainless, long, hot, and dry. So it is necessary to find ways to store and conserve the winter waters for use in the cities and fields during the summer. The great volume of winter water frequently causes floods in its springtime rush to

3

the sea so it is necessary, too, to control the floods which damage the land and waste the water.

California is divided roughly into two parts. South of the Tehachapi Range of mountains lies southern California, famed in song and story, which has grave water problems. Its water supply comes from coastal wells, from the Colorado River, and from streams on the eastern face of the Sierra Nevada. Southern California has reached far and will reach farther for its vital water. North of the Tehachapi lie the great interior valleys of the Sacramento and San Joaquin rivers. They lie between the Coast Range on the west and the towering Sierra Nevada on the east. Together they are roughly five hundred miles long from north to south and about a hundred miles wide. The Sacramento Valley slopes from north to south and the San Joaquin Valley slopes from south to north. Their great rivers meet in the Delta region near Stockton and continue together toward the sea through the Golden Gate. In the spring, following the rain, the flat valley fields are green with wild grasses, and wild mustard turns the valleys to gold. But in summer, without water, the fields lie beige and desolate, unproductive deserts. Properly irrigated, they throw up jackpot yields of almost every known crop—the fruits and vegetables and fibers and nuts which have made California the most productive agricultural state in the country.

Nature, which delivers water only during the winter and spring, provides too much water in the Sacramento Valley and not enough in the San Joaquin. Two-thirds of the rain and snow of northern California fall in the Sacramento watershed, and the Sacramento Valley has only one-third of the arable land of the two valleys. And only one-third of the rain and snow reaches the San Joaquin Valley, which has two-thirds of the arable land.

Settlers were quick to recognize the richness of the soil. Even before the gold hysteria had worn off, men began to move into the great valleys; one-time miners became farmers. Over the years, these men built dams and complex irrigation systems. They fought floods with levees and dams and by-pass canals. They thrust wells deep into the earth and their pumps sucked the ground water for the land. Individuals, power companies, irrigation districts dammed the streams to catch the flood water, to store it for the summer months. It was a hard and never-won battle. Hard-working men and their dollars have not yet conquered a perverse Nature. In the Sacramento Valley the battle is lost to floods; in the San Joaquin the battle is lost both to floods and drought.

By 1920 it was apparent that all that men had done to get water on the arid land in the summer and to keep it from flooding their sodden acres in the spring was not enough. Floods still swept the land in the wet springs, swamping the valleys. In the San Joaquin, after a cycle of dry years, the water supply—the underground water table—was decreasing. In some areas, the water table dropped so low that farmers could not afford to pump the brackish water. Ranchers, for lack of water for their parched acres, gave up and left the land.

And all this time—while the sun baked the abandoned fields and vineyards and orchards in the San Joaquin Valley—the Sacramento River poured billions of gallons of unused water through the Golden Gate into the sea.

This book is about the Central Valley Project, a design and plan which proposes to do something about Nature's unequal distribution of rain and snow. The Central Valley Project takes over where almost-beaten individuals left off. It is a big plan to have the government do a job far beyond the means of individuals or corporations.

The Central Valley Project is the product of many years of careful water planning and study in California. It is a most ambitious—and expensive—undertaking. There are really two Central Valley projects: the authorized "initial" features which are now being constructed, and the ultimate development. If plans now on the drawing boards materialize into concrete and generators, into power lines, pumping plants, and irrigation canals, they will provide an integrated system of stream control and irrigation works for every stream emptying into the central valleys. This greater

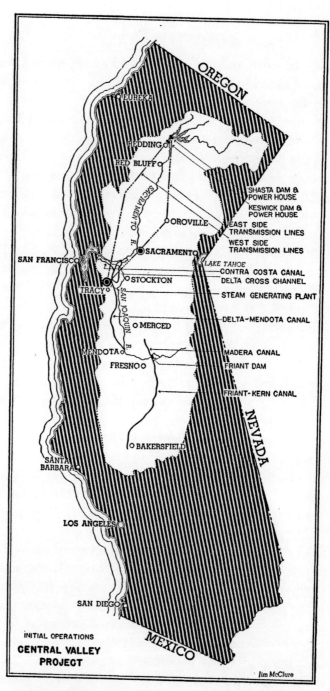

THREE DAMS, FIVE CANALS, POWERHOUSES, AND
TRANSMISSION LINES——THE BASIC ELEMENTS
OF THE CENTRAL VALLEY PROJECT.

Central Valley Project will cost more than $2,000,000,000. That one is for the future book, however. The concern here is for the authorized initial features of the Central Valley Project.

What finally evolved as the basic plan for the project had been dreamed about and studied for more than seventy-five years. In 1935, it came out of the dream stage. In that year, the federal government (after shameless wooing by California) took over responsibility for the project. The federal agency assigned to build the project was the Bureau of Reclamation, a division of the Department of the Interior.

Although work was retarded by the war, the Bureau already has spent more than $200,000,000 and the final cost of the initial features of the project will be about $384,000,000 at 1945 prices. This money will buy the following things:

1. Three dams.—Shasta Dam, north of Redding, the second highest and the second largest in bulk ever built, which impounds the water of the upper Sacramento, McCloud, and Pit rivers; Keswick Dam, nine miles downstream from Shasta, which forms a regulating afterbay for Shasta; Friant Dam on the San Joaquin River, twenty miles east of Fresno, which stores San Joaquin River water.

2. Five canals.—Madera Canal, which runs 37 miles north from Friant Dam to the Chowchilla River; the Friant-Kern Canal, which runs 160 miles south from Friant to the Kern River near Bakersfield; the Delta-Mendota Canal, which will carry Sacramento River water from the Delta 120 miles south to the Mendota pool on the great bend of the San Joaquin; the Contra Costa Canal, 58 miles long, conveys fresh water from the Delta to agricultural, industrial and urban consumers between Antioch and Martinez. A fifth conduit, the Delta Cross Channel, will carry Sacramento River water through the maze of waterways of the Delta to the intake of the Delta-Mendota Canal. Its design and route are under study.

3. Three power plants.—The biggest at Shasta Dam, where five generators will have a rated capacity of 375,000 kilowatts; Keswick powerhouse, which will have three generators with a

capacity of 75,000 kilowatts; a steam-generating plant to be located somewhere near Tracy—this plant will "firm" the hydroelectric power produced at the dams.

4. Transmission lines.—Three 200-mile high-voltage circuits, two on the west, one on the east side of the Sacramento Valley, running from Shasta and Keswick power plants to the steam plant; lines running from this junction to the Delta-Mendota Canal pumping system; a grid of transmission lines of lower capacity to serve wholesale customers in the two valleys.

These great dams and canals and the sizable power system have one objective: to shift water from the Sacramento Valley where there is too much, to the San Joaquin Valley where there is too little. Simply stated, the Central Valley Project is a north-to-south water exchange. The available water of the San Joaquin River, which normally flows north into San Francisco Bay and the sea, is diverted to the dry acres of the southern valley. Sacramento River water which ordinarily would wash out the Golden Gate, is shifted to the central San Joaquin Valley to replace the San Joaquin River water diverted to the south.

This is the way it will be done: Shasta and Keswick dams bring the Sacramento under partial control, make it possible to store the spring runoff and maintain a regulated stream. Friant Dam blocks off the San Joaquin as it emerges from the foothills and diverts a controlled flow of water into the Friant-Kern Canal which rims the eastern edge of the valley, carrying water as far south as Bakersfield. The short Madera Canal wanders north from Friant to provide surface water for irrigation and restore underground water supplies between the San Joaquin and the Chowchilla River. To compensate for this diverted San Joaquin water, Sacramento River water will be conveyed across the Delta and transferred to the San Joaquin Valley through the Delta-Mendota Canal. The Contra Costa Canal provides fresh water for San Francisco Bay communities which are faced with failing supplies of fresh water as well as for farm use. The Delta Cross Channel which picks up Sacramento River water and carries it through the Delta will provide fresh water to repel intrusion of salt water from San Francisco Bay into the rich Delta lands.

The project, as far as construction goes, is past the halfway mark. The war slowed the building but contracts were let as soon as possible for construction after the fighting stopped. Construction progress is dictated by Congress—which makes the appropriations. Work is almost finished on the three dams, on the Contra Costa Canal (which is near completion), on the Friant-Kern Canal, and the Delta-Mendota Canal, both well started. No work has been done, outside of planning, on the Delta Cross Channel which is still under study. The Madera Canal is complete. Work is under way on transmission lines and one, from Shasta powerhouse to Oroville, has been completed (on wooden poles). No funds have been appropriated for Delta steam-plant construction.

The physical facts of the Central Valley Project cannot be argued. Everyone agrees that the project is needed if California acres are to be exploited to the full. Everyone agrees that the plan and design are good. Everyone agrees that construction is a job for the federal government, simply because no other agency has the money to do it—not the state, not the irrigation districts, not the Pacific Gas & Electric Co.

And there the agreement ends. On policy matters of the Central Valley Project there is no agreement. There is a loud and continuous fight in California and the Congress practically every time the project is mentioned. President Truman, Governor Warren of California, Secretary of the Interior J. A. Krug, former Secretary Harold Ickes,* the California State Water Resources Board, the California State Chamber of Commerce, the California Water Project Authority, the Pacific Gas & Electric Co., the United States

---

* Even though he departed from the Truman administration in a custom-built huff, Ickes' policies—embraced by Truman and Krug at least to a great extent—lie at the bottom of many of the controversies. Ickes was Secretary of the Interior when the federal government took on the project and he has been its outspoken champion—at the same time providing a sporty, moving target for the opposition. Krug, his successor, also is proving a target—a somewhat slower-moving and bulkier one, however.

Army Engineers, the Bureau of Reclamation, farmers, labor unions, and war veterans are mixed up in this royal battle.

For the next few years the battle will continue. Great numbers of metaphors will be mixed. Perspiration will flow. Tempers will be lost. Philosophies will clash. Orations great and small will be made and tons of paper and ink will go into the fray. At least two versions of "the American Way" will be extolled. Monopolists will be castigated and bureaucrats attacked. Untruths will be sworn to. Palatable half-truths and bitter truths will be swallowed. The fight over the Central Valley Project is not new. It is merely entering its latest round.

The fight has been going on long enough now so that prejudices have hardened and tempers boil over on cue. Pat statements trot out at the sound of a bell. And almost everyone who has anything to do with the project, officially or unofficially, tells his pet lies, lies which have become assured through long mouthing. Everyone has his evasions and subjects which he won't discuss without the innuendo of lifted eyebrows and head-shaking.

Nevertheless, the issue of the Central Valley Project is clear: Shall the federal government, through the Bureau of Reclamation, maintain control over the use of irrigation water and electrical energy produced by the project? Shall the federal government, in short, operate the project under federal law for the benefit of the many after spending hundreds of millions in its construction? Or shall the federal government complete the project and bow out, leaving its operation to others, without regard to federal law?

The issue may be clear enough but the answers are complex. The project is being built with funds of the United States Government voted by Congress and the project is subject to the rules laid down by Congress—in this case, reclamation law. Briefly, reclamation law provides that costs of reclamation projects chargeable to flood control and navigation do not have to be repaid to the federal government. Costs allocated to irrigation, for storage reservoirs, dams and canals, must be repaid. Irrigation funds advanced by the government carry no interest. Costs for installation of power-generating facilities, including a share in reservoir costs, power plants, and transmission lines, must be repaid and carry interest at the rate of 3 percent.

There is no dispute over the necessity and fairness of these provisions. Financially, reclamation law is a bargain-basement deal. But reclamation law also provides for a limitation of the number of acres for which project water shall be provided. Project water will not be delivered to blocks of land greater than 160 acres—in California 320 acres—held in single ownership unless certain conditions are met. Reclamation law also provides safeguards against speculative gains on lands within projects. It provides that power generated by public plants shall be sold on a preferential basis to public, nonprofit agencies.

Because of these last provisions of reclamation law, many people are opposed to federal operation of a completed Central Valley Project. Naturally enough, the Pacific Gas & Electric Co. wants no part of federal management under reclamation or any other law. The P. G. & E., as it is universally known, is fighting and will continue to fight any threat to its power monopoly in northern California. Public power, publicly distributed at the lowest possible rates, constitutes a major threat to that monopoly. The P. G. & E. is a powerful foe of the Bureau of Reclamation, which is charged with the construction and operation of the project.

Large landowners in the project area object to federal operation of the project because of the acreage-limitation feature of the law. To qualify for project water for more than 160 acres, their large holdings would have to be broken up into units of 160 or 320 acres within a specified time. Owners of large acreage, and there are many in California, see this limitation as an un-American threat to their industry and welfare.

A variety of other people, whose motives are mixed, see great danger in federal control of the project. They are afraid of bureaucratic antics in general, afraid of "Washington control," afraid of the "socialization of California," afraid of Communists, and a number of other bogies. Before Ickes left the Cabinet they were most afraid of him. Oh, how they hated Ickes, the honest, tough administrator, who would not compromise with principle and who believed laws should be enforced. It is a three-to-one bet that already some of the loudest anti-Ickes men are missing their whipping boy. He was such a comfort to them.

Antifederal groups within California, headed by the California State Chamber of Commerce, are agreed that an ideal solution can be achieved if only the Bureau of Reclamation will just finish the construction job and then bow out, leaving management of the project to the state. People who like this solution are hopeful that the government, somehow, will find a way to write off its great investment—which is unlikely.

So many groups are opposed to the various policies governing the Central Valley Project that there is some room for wonder that it has been brought along past the halfway mark. The opposition can be misleading, and without doubt, some of the opponents make more noise than their strength and importance warrant.

The fight over the project is further agitated by undercover brawling between two federal agencies—the Bureau of Reclamation (Department of Interior) and the United States Corps of Engineers (War Department). Both agencies, dam builders and water men from 'way back, feel they have some kind of divine right to the Central Valley of California and both want as large a slice of the construction pie as they can wangle. Both have their eyes on the ultimate development of the Central Valley Project—that two billion dollars' worth of stuff on the drawing boards.

The same groups which are so violently opposed to federal agencies when they are talking about the Bureau of Reclamation usually find no fault with the Army Engineers. Their reason is clear. The Army Engineers pride themselves on their lack of philosophy. In the classic Army tradition, they "take orders" and "do the job" without reasoning why (they say). They simply want to build dams. They don't give a whoop about what happens to the water they impound. They are not interested in whatever power they happen to generate, not interested in who sells it, who buys it, or at what price. The Army men contend they are willing tools of the people and will do whatever is best for the people of a given locality when requested to enter the scene.

In contrast to the Army Engineers,* the Bureau of Reclamation carries its philosophy like a lance. The Bureau is evangelically interested in what happens to water and power. The Bureau believes in the "family-sized, family-operated" farm as an American way of life, if not *the* American Way. The Bureau believes (and so, incidentally, has the Congress) that power developed on federal projects should be distributed by public agencies and sold at the lowest practical price. The Bureau believes the land of America has been misused. It believes further that unless something is done about it, the economic base of the nation is in peril.

Both the Engineers and the Bureau have prepared long and detailed plans for the ultimate development of all of the streams of the Sacramento and San Joaquin River basins. Fundamentally, these plans have many similarities. Both agencies are trying to get go-ahead funds from Congress. The Bureau is deeply concerned (and so are a lot of other people) over the possibility of authorizations by Congress for the Army to build dams. The Bureau maintains that the streams of California should be controlled and integrated by a central, single administration, to the end that not a single drop of water shall be wasted. Patently, the Bureau regards itself the proper agency to achieve such administration and integration and it will fight any plan which would threaten integration and regulation of California's water.

Theoretically, it should not make much difference which agency builds the dams. Congress has ruled that, whether dams are built by the Army or by the Bureau, irrigation water and power shall be dispensed by the Secretary of the Interior under provisions of

---

* The term, Engineers, may be misleading. It will be used frequently to designate the Army's Corps of Engineers but it would be wrong to assume that the Bureau of Reclamation lacks engineers, engineering brains, and ability. Both agencies have excellent staffs and the record shows both to be efficient government tools. It is not in ability that they differ. It is only in approach and ultimate aims.

reclamation law. As Michael W. Straus, reclamation commissioner, puts it: "It just happens that we are a high-morale bureau. We happen to think we are the best damn dam builders in the world. We think we can build better and cheaper than anybody else."

There is no prospect of an early end to the Army-Bureau brawling. An uneasy truce has been forced by an Act of Congress and by presidential directive. Behind the peaceful front, however, the battle goes on.

The Bureau is our main concern here, because we will discuss principally the authorized initial features of the project for which the Bureau is responsible. The Bureau already has brought the tremendous project past the halfway mark. It has given California physical evidence of an attempt to solve its water problems in the interior valleys, an attempt of heroic proportions. Final policy decisions (if such decisions ever reach finality) will determine the ultimate place of the project in the state and the ultimate worth of the project to the people of the state. Unwise decisions which would deliver unwarranted benefits into the hands of the few could seriously weaken the original courageous conception and purpose of the project.

II. Project on Paper

BEFORE THE discovery of gold, there was no water problem in California. Every winter the rains came and soaked into the floor of the valleys until the ground became spongy and great swamps spread. While the rain fell in the lowlands and on the rolling foothills, snow settled in the 500-mile ridge of the jagged Sierra, its cold blanket packing many feet deep in mountain meadows and canyons and icing the peaks. In the spring, melting snows trickled into numberless rills which ran together building a thousand rivulets to sluice into the main streams which thundered toward the valleys. The mountain creeks became noisy torrents, rising rapidly, coursing through their narrow banks carrying a heaving raft of debris with them.

In the northern valley, the great Sacramento, a placid stream except for its annual binge, gulped water from its raging tributaries—the McCloud and the Pit, Antelope, Bear, Feather, Battle Creek, South Cow Creek, North Cow Creek, and Mill Creek. Midway on its course, the Sacramento, boiling full, muddy and churning, met the swollen Feather River and burst from its channel. For miles the valley became a lake of slowly flowing water, making its way south to the Bay of San Francisco.

In the southern valley, too, the mountains poured out the snow runoff. The Kings and the Kern, scouring their narrow canyons, struck the lowlands with explosive force. They spread out in sluggish lakes and dropped their silt. The San Joaquin, the main trunk of the southern river system, roiled from the hills and overflowed. It was joined by the Kings and flowed north toward the Delta, constantly swelling as the Merced, the Tuolumne, the Mokelumne, the Chowchilla, and Stanislaus rivers added their floods.

In a few days it was over. The floods receded, leaving behind

15

the rich sediment from the mountains. The rivers gradually found their banks and settled down to a summer of indolence. Many streams dried up completely during the hot months. The valleys, so recently lakes, became deserts. The vast valleys, ribboned at far distances by the winding green which marked the course of sluggish streams, turned a sere blond under the malignant sun and waited for the flood of the year to come.

Before the discovery of gold, this never-ending cycle of flood and drought made little difference. Northern California was thinly populated. There were tiny clusters of Spanish adventurers around Monterey and San Francisco, the few great families who ruled over the feudal ranchos on their crown grants, the clergy, spanning the coast with their adobe missions. The backward Indians of the country had little contact with the Spanish invaders except around the mission compounds where they served admirably as converts and farm labor.

There was intensive cultivation and some irrigation around the missions but the great ranchos almost took care of themselves. Lean cattle wandered the ranges whose boundaries were measured in miles—standing deep in the lush grasses of spring; later nibbling hungrily at the crackling summer feed. They were raised only for hides and tallow.

The Americans came in 1841. Only a few at first. Then the discovery of gold changed the historical pace of settlement. Against the gold-hungry thousands, the Mexican rulers of California did not have a chance. In 1850 California became one of the United States. And by 1850, water had become an important element in the life of the state. Water was of first importance to the gold miner who needed it for his gold pan and sluice box; water was the essential tool in hydraulic mining. Then, too, mining operations affected the streams, clogging them with debris torn from the hills by the hydraulic monitors. Of this, the first Legislature took notice. When it met in 1850, one of its first acts was to order the surveyor general to begin studies to improve navigation, drainage, and irrigation.

Far more important was another act of that first Legislature; it adopted the Common Law of England for California. Common Law recognizes the principle of riparian rights. The riparian principle entitles the owner of land bordering a stream to the right to a reasonable use of the stream's water; owners of land not contiguous to the stream have no right to its water.*

The federal government has been more than knee-deep in California water for many years. A commission headed by Lieutenant Colonel B. S. Alexander went out to study the Sacramento and San Joaquin rivers in 1873. In its report to President Grant, the Alexander Commission projected a system of canals which included the idea of a Sacramento-to-San Joaquin water exchange. The report also recommended that "Government, both state and national, encourage irrigation."

Five years later, William Hammond Hall, the first state engineer, persuaded the Legislature to grant $100,000 for studies "to provide a system of irrigation, promote drainage and improve navigation of the Sacramento and San Joaquin rivers." When this $100,000 was gone, the Legislature refused to vote more funds and the Hall studies were ended. A hundred thousand dollars was a lot of money in 1878 and besides, the ranchers seemed to be solving their own problem handily.

It was the time of the economic freebooter and California was a wide-open field for the land-grabber. Such men as Henry Miller of Miller & Lux, the land and cattle company which dominated the San Joaquin Valley, seemed competent to look out for themselves. Miller, greedily guarding his water rights, nevertheless was an

---

* No attempt will be made here to discuss California water rights. Without question, these rights are in a frightful tangle. As early as 1901, Dr. Elwood Mead in a *Report on Irrigation Investigations in California* declared: "Along with the remarkable ability shown by engineers and irrigators in diverting and using rivers has gone controversy over water rights in the courts and armed raids to destroy headgates or interfere with the use of canals . . . . Lack of certainty or stability in water rights has been a prolific source of neighborhood ill-feeling. The litigation is appalling . . . . Under the law, the record books of every county in the state have been thrown open to the entry of any sort of claim which need or greed might encourage. The aggregate of all water claims in California represent enough moisture to submerge the continent."

efficient pioneer in the development of California irrigation. He
built two major canal systems which did much to develop the barren acres.

Miller left an even deeper imprint on California. More than
any other man, he was responsible for the maintenance of riparian
rights in the state. Over a period of years, Miller acquired hundreds of thousands of acres in the San Joaquin Valley. He had
purchased Spanish land grants from the heirs, who were broke,
cheap swampland which he drained, and land scrip from Civil
War veterans and the railroads.

Miller bought along the rivers, principally the San Joaquin
and the Kern. His lands, lying astraddle the streams gave him a
vested interest in the water. Miller, among other people, had acquired a strip of land fifty miles long on the banks of the Kern in
the upper (southern) San Joaquin Valley near Bakersfield. A
great canal, one hundred feet wide and fifty miles long, was built.
A hundred thousand acres were reclaimed.

But farther up the river, a group headed by J. B. Haggin and
Lloyd Tevis of San Francisco, proposed to divert Kern River water
over the rich valley land. At the diversion point, only a small portion of their land was riparian to the river. Tevis and Haggin proposed to appropriate the water and sell it to settlers whose lands
lay far from the river.

Miller, seeing this threat to his downstream holdings, contended
that the river water properly belonged only to land along the river-
banks—the classic riparian interpretation. Miller was a strong
man. He was one of the wealthiest men in California. But Tevis
was no small farmer to be pushed around by the colossus. He was
a well-known financier. He had money and he knew where to get
more. The battle which was joined over the water of the Kern was
a fight between big men, well-armed with lawyers and money. Before the fight reached the courts there was some violence: flood
gates were ripped out, levees destroyed, and armed men patrolled
the stream.

Miller's lawyers defended the riparian principle: Miller was entitled to the full flow of the stream which passed through his lands. So said the Common Law of England which had been adopted as the law of California.

Tevis and Haggin contended that California, a semiarid state, could not be governed by the Common Law developed in England where conditions were so different. They argued that the Common Law was the law of reason and common sense and that common sense should rule in California. They pointed to the few acres which benefited from the stream under riparian rights as opposed to the large number of small holdings which could be watered if the stream was appropriated.

Those claiming the right of appropriation were fortified by the fact that during mining days, when no one owned the land, the right of appropriation was recognized. In other words, neither having any real title, priority or possession of land or water was equivalent to right. Then the United States Government had expressly recognized such right of appropriation as against the Government as owner of the public domain.

In the vicinity where this dispute arose, there were hundreds of persons to be benefited by the right of appropriation and only a few by riparian rights. Public sentiment was, therefore, strongly against the Miller claims. . . . . The great mass were against the "monopolistic" claim of the riparian owners . . . .*

Miller lost his suit in the lower court but won a reversal on appeal. A rehearing was granted and Miller and riparian rights won again—by a four-to-three decision—and riparian rights remain as basic California law. The courts agreed with Henry Miller who said the "water belonged where it had flowed from time immemortal."†

In 1887, the Wright Act, which empowered the formation of irrigation districts, was passed by the state Legislature. This act provided a spur to irrigation by making it possible for small landowners to pool their resources to build the costly works necessary for bringing water to their land. These districts were fought by Henry Miller and other large landowners. They feared their con-

* Edward F. Treadwell, *The Cattle King*, p. 83.
† *Ibid.*, p. 87.

trol of the streams would be jeopardized by the new districts. Miller carried a suit against the Madera Irrigation District to the United States Supreme Court on the contention that irrigation was primarily a private operation and should not be made subject to taxation. Selfish realism was behind Miller's move. Large landowners feared their "wet" lands would be linked with their neighbors' "dry" lands into districts whose object, in their view, would be to divide the available water and make their land subject to tax. Miller successfully staved off formation of districts affecting his lands but the district movement, a necessity for the small landowner, could not be stopped.

While the irrigation districts were solving, in some measure, their own problems, there was little governmental study of water. In 1905 an effort was made to obtain federal funds for a reclamation project in the Sacramento Valley but this plan fizzled because of its great cost. The project would have cost $40,000,000 and only $28,000,000 was available for reclamation in the entire West. In 1915, the state Legislature set up the State Water Problems Conference which held hearings on water in general in 1916.

"Foremost among the problems faced by the conference is the doctrine of riparian rights which has given the sanction in this state of court-made law and which retards progress toward the fullest utilization of the water resources of the state," the conference reported.*

During the early part of this century, Dr. Elwood Mead made an exhaustive report on California irrigation. Measurement of stream flow was begun. The Reclamation Service (now called the Bureau of Reclamation) made surveys of the Kings, Pit, and San Joaquin rivers before 1910 (as well as setting up a reclamation project at Orland, California), and later investigated the Iron Canyon Dam site on the Sacramento, and continued studies on the Pit and the Kings.

A major contribution to state water-planning was made in 1919

---

* As quoted in *History of Legislation and Policy Formation of the Central Valley Project,* by Mary Montgomery and Marion Clawson, p. 17.

by Colonel Robert Bradford Marshall, chief hydrographer of the United States Geological Survey. Marshall outlined his plan in a letter to Governor William D. Stephens and details were published later by the California State Irrigation Association. The Marshall Plan proposed a series of storage reservoirs on the Sacramento River system. Two large canals were to carry water on both sides of the Sacramento Valley into the San Joaquin Valley. Marshall also proposed diversion of the Kern River into the Los Angeles area. The Marshall Plan generally is credited with being the master pattern for the present Central Valley Project, although many changes have been made in Marshall's original conception. Chief value of the Marshall Plan was that it stirred an active interest in the state's water problems and suggested a daring solution.

In 1921, an attempt was made to get legislative approval for the Marshall Plan. The Water and Power Act which authorized the plan was passed by the Senate but killed in the Assembly. The next year, on initiative action, the Water and Power Act again was defeated. The 1922 defeat and subsequent defeats of the Act were credited to efforts of the Pacific Gas & Electric Co. and other utilities which opposed the power sections of the proposed Act.

The Marshall Plan also stimulated new studies by the state. The 1921 Legislature ordered investigations into the available water and determination of how it was being used. This marked the start of twelve years of intensive and expensive research into all phases of the water problem. Between 1920 and 1932 at least fourteen reports were made on water flow, drought conditions, flood control, and irrigation problems.

While the state was amassing a really imposing quantity of information about its water resources, another investigation was undertaken by the Federal-State Water Resources Commission (usually referred to as the Hoover-Young Commission). This commission was set up by President Herbert Hoover, Governor C. C. Young, and the state Legislature to report specifically on the feasibility of a dam at Boulder on the Colorado River and the Central Valley Project. It recommended construction of both projects.

Said the Commission:

It is not too strong a statement to say that in the neighborhood of 200,-000 acres of highly-developed land, worth more than $50,000,000 and now producing crops of an annual value of more than $20,000,000, must largely go back to desert condition unless the supply of water is increased. It is not a case of providing water for the development of more land, it is a case of providing water to save lands already developed and which have demonstrated their value.*

The Commission recommended that the Central Valley Project be constructed at federal expense. Under the Commission plan, the completed project would have been operated by the state and the state would have been bound to repay construction costs. It was a good report but it provoked no action. It was added to the great file of water information already compiled. And filed, too, was a report of a legislative committee to the 1931 Legislature. This committee, after conferring with President Hoover, declared the Central Valley Project could be constructed on a sound economic base if money could be obtained at not more than 3½ percent interest. There was only one place where money could be had at such a low interest rate: the United States Treasury. This report also recommended construction by the federal government and operation by the state.

Despite the pious recommendations, there was little hope that action could be expected very soon. By 1931, however, the great mass of reports and studies had jelled into a "State Water Plan" compiled by Edward Hyatt, state engineer. The state plan included the principal features of the Central Valley Project. By 1931 it was apparent that California's water ills could not be cured by piecemeal schemes. What was needed was an over-all approach to the problem, a daring and expensive solution. California had a great need. California had a great plan to answer that need. All that was lacking was the money. They figured it would cost $170,000,000—and $170,000,000 is a great deal of money.

* As quoted in *History of Legislation and Policy Formation of the Central Valley Project,* by Mary Montgomery and Marion Clawson, p. 38.

Financing was the great rub. It was terribly apparent that only the federal government could finance the project. President Hoover had encouraged Californians to believe that the United States would find some way to provide the cash. More than promises and encouragement were needed, however. After 1931, several events occurred. For one thing, President Hoover, who had pursued a business-as-usual policy when business itself was behaving most unusually, was defeated as President in 1932. This was discouraging at first. For Hoover was a Californian, familiar with the project and friendly toward it. It did not seem then that any other president could be as familiar or as friendly. President Roosevelt, however, brought a new policy and new philosophy into national affairs. A great program of public works was inaugurated. Unprecedented sums of money were to be spent—and it seemed likely that California would get its share.

California got a new governor, too. James Rolph, Jr., "lifetime" mayor of San Francisco, had gone to the Statehouse. And although Rolph knew very little about agricultural, or for that matter, legislative affairs, he had at least been told about the state's water problems and made brave statements. In August of 1931, in a message to his constituents, he cited the necessity for a quick solution of the state's water problems. He advocated federal assistance in financing as a matter of course. And in the years between Rolph's inauguration and 1933, when the New Deal opened its purse, chances for federal financing improved immensely.

In 1933, the Central Valley Project Act, which authorized issuance of $170,000,000 in revenue bonds for the project, was passed by the Legislature. Its passage was a surprising event. Looking back more than ten years it is easy to assume that the Water and Power Act was the chief issue before the Legislature. It was not. Had it been, it is probable it would not have passed. In 1933, the chief concern of the state was finance. The state was almost broke; its school system was endangered. The big taxpayers, notably the railroads and public utilities, had their lobbyists busy on the tax issue. Utility lobbyists paid very little attention to the

Central Valley Project bill. The Legislature did, in fact, overhaul the tax structure of the state—passing the Riley-Stewart tax plan—and that was considered its major work.

The fact is, passage of the Central Valley Project Act was as near a one-man job as such a thing can be. The man who did the job was John B. McColl. He got the votes for the Act. And later on, he saved the Act when it was threatened by referendum. Of course, many other men helped. To understand the wondrous part played by McColl it is necessary to backtrack a little. "Sunny Jim" Rolph was elected by a landslide in 1930. On his coattails there rode into the Legislature a new group of men unhampered by old political ties and obligations. They called themselves "Tin Pan Alley" in the State Senate. They were out to get what their home folks wanted and they voted enthusiastically and in a solid block. In the Senate, Tin Pan Alley had 21 members—a majority. John McColl was the Tin Pan Alley Senator from Redding.

McColl, a naturalized Nova Scotian and a Canadian veteran of the first World War, had set himself up in Redding as an ice-cream maker and soda-fountain owner. Coca-Cola set McColl to thinking. His fountain sold 800 glasses of the stuff every day—far more than any other fountain in town. McColl realized that people came to his store for Cokes, not alone for the drink which was available all over town, but because they liked him. Popularity means votes. So McColl decided to try for the Senate. In campaigning, popular John McColl found out that the only thing Redding wanted from the Legislature was a dam on the Sacramento River at Kennett. Redding wanted the dam because Redding merchants wanted the prosperity that dam payrolls bring. McColl promised to get the dam. He was elected on that promise and took his place in Tin Pan Alley. And McColl went to work. He had nothing on his legislative mind but the Central Valley Project bill. He was not interested in tax revision or anything else before the 1933 Legislature except that dam Redding wanted. He traded his votes and he rolled his logs with great care.

The Central Valley Project bill passed the Assembly. This did

not particularly worry the public-utility lobby. They were certain
the bill would be killed in the Senate. Then, too, the bill as it passed
the Assembly was not harmful to the power companies. The lob-
byists' surprise came when the Legislature reconvened for an un-
usual third session in July. Then the Senate wrote into the harm-
less Assembly bill four important new sections: a provision calling
for construction of power transmission lines; provision for financing the project through revenue bonds; a recapture clause which
made it possible for public districts to obtain electric power for resale even though it had been contracted for by individuals or firms;
a clause guaranteeing respect for existing water rights. At this
point, the bill normally would have been voted down resoundingly
by the conservative Senate. But the bill passed the Senate 23 to 15
—Tin Pan Alley, pledged to McColl, voted as a block—and was
signed by Governor Rolph.

If passage of the bill by the traditionally reactionary Senate
was surprising, inclusion of its liberal provisions was astounding.
It should be understood, however, that the good Senators had their
eyes cocked on the possibility of a federal handout. They were sure
that the Roosevelt administration would not come through with the
needed cash unless the Central Valley Project Act provided public
distribution of publicly generated power. It was a case of having
to let down the Pacific Gas & Electric Co., their old, old friend,
simply because no other course seemed possible.

As passed, the Act provided for the issuance of $170,000,000
in revenue bonds. This money was to be administered by the State
Water Project Authority, set up in the Act, which consisted of the
attorney general, the state treasurer, the state controller, the director of finance, and the director of public works. The money was
to build: (1) a dam and power plant on the Sacramento River at
Kennett (site of Shasta Dam); (2) a dam and power plant on the
San Joaquin River at Friant; (3) a transmission line, including
substations and other works, between the Kennett dam and Antioch;
(4) the Contra Costa, Madera, and Friant-Kern canals.

Instead of providing for the Delta-Mendota Canal, the Act

called for a system of dams and pumping stations on the San Joaquin River. Sacramento River water was to be pumped up the San Joaquin—a plan which literally would have reversed the flow of the San Joaquin. In addition, as noted, the Act provided for a power plant at Friant, since eliminated.

Authorization for the revenue bonds was limited. The total of $170,000,000 was to be reduced by the amount the federal government might contribute and by the amount of any contribution from the state treasury. Thus, if the United States pungled up $50,000,-000, the Water Project Authority would be allowed to issue only $120,000,000 in revenue bonds.

Such was the Central Valley Project Act. It incorporated the results of long study and planning by the state and federal governments. As of July 1933, the state had a paper project at least. The outlook, however, was still unpleasing. It was certain that the public utilities, sparked by the Pacific Gas & Electric Co., would challenge the will of the Legislature—a referendum, designed to repeal the Act, was believed inevitable, as Governor Rolph indicated when he signed the Act. Governor Rolph declared:

I will not stand for any sideshows on this serious matter. If any special interests try to block this measure or delay it in any way, I am prepared to fight them to the last ditch of my executive authority. And if we are forced to go into a campaign to establish this plan by a vote of the people, I am positive we shall meet with success.

III. How the Cow Helped

W ITHIN A FEW weeks after Governor Rolph signed the Central Valley Project Act and came out flat-footedly against sideshows, a referendum against the measure qualified for the ballot.

The referendum forces were led by one Fred G. Athearn of San Francisco, an attorney for the Pacific Gas & Electric Co. He acted, he said, as a citizen, property owner, and taxpayer, not as an agent of the P. G. & E., and perhaps he did. He said he was financing the circulation of petitions for the referendum out of his own pocket. Later, the P. G. & E. was shown to have contributed $30,000 toward Athearn's expenses. At any rate, the referendum qualified and a special election was set for December 19, 1933. And the fun began.

Things were not good in California in 1933. Effects of the 1929 stock-market crash had been slow to reach the West, but by 1933 no doubt existed: there was a "depression" and California was mired deeply in it. Franklin Roosevelt's heroic measures against economic suffering—the bank closure, mortgage moratoriums, the National Industry Recovery Act, complete with General Hugh Johnson and Blue Eagle, and the vast program of public works— had not yet beckoned prosperity. Farm prices were low. Farmers were being urged and bribed not to grow cotton and corn and wheat. There was discouragement in the great valleys of California. For lack of water, farms were being abandoned. Power bills were a heart-breaking problem for irrigationists. The people hoped and searched for a panacea which would cure their ills. The farmer, forever the spoiled child of American politics, made particularly pitiful cries.

The times were reflected strongly in the arguments, pro and con, which were served up during the campaign on the referendum.

27

"The project will ruin the state financially," shouted the opponents of the project. "Unless we build this project, hundreds, nay, thousands of acres of productive land will go back to desert," countered friends of the Act. "Unless these lands are kept in production, they will leave the assessment rolls—other taxpayers will have heavier burdens than ever."

"The project will furnish employment to more than 25,000 people for three years," bellowed the friends. "These jobs will support 100,000 people—without costing California a dime. This ties in with President Roosevelt's great recovery program."

"Foolishness," cried the foes. "It is very doubtful that the project will provide work for 25,000 men. And anyway, the people need jobs right now, not next year or the year after that."

The arguments have been summed up concisely by Mary Montgomery and Marion Clawson of the Bureau of Agricultural Economics.*

Against the Act:

The project would bankrupt the state as the citizens of California would have to pay for the bonds either in taxes or in assessments against their property. The bonds may run for 70 years at 5½ percent interest. Over that time, the interest alone would amount to $654,500,000. Every experiment with self-liquidating bonds in California has failed in whole or in part . . . . There is furthermore no guarantee whatsoever that power could help pay for the project because power cannot be sold at any price to private companies under 1933 conditions, and public agencies are not organized to take power.

What California needs is not more crops but less crops. At the present time (1933) there are more than 500,000 acres of land for which there is sufficient water for irrigation purposes now developed, which have not been brought under cultivation because crops could not be grown on them at a profit . . . . The Act would bring into production hundreds of thousands of acres of land which would make it even more difficult for the farmer to make a living out of crops he is now growing.

The project will interfere with private initiative. Competition from the proposed project will not be good for the stockholders and security holders

* *History of Legislation and Policy Formation of the Central Valley Project,* pp. 52, 53, 54.

of California electric and gas utilities which at the end of 1932 had 201,988 stockholders in California. Neither will it be good for the state. The picture of unfair governmental competition with existing industry is not conducive to investment of private capital in California. Furthermore, the project means a large increase in the number of state employes and the consequent enlargement of bureaucratic control.

The Federal government has indicated in no way whatever, directly or indirectly, that it intends to underwrite the Central Valley project.

Validity of the state estimates are open to question in light of the difference claimed by the state engineer as to the benefits from the project for navigation and flood control, and those found reasonable by the War Department.

The appointing power of the Governor under the bill creates the danger of a political bureaucracy. The legislation creating the project provides that it shall be governed entirely by the Authority, a board composed of the Attorney General, the State Controller, the State Treasurer, the Director of Finance and the Director of Public Works who shall serve as chairman. If any of these five offices is abolished the Governor may appoint any competent citizen to fill the vacancy. The Governor has to control only one of the three elective officials to control the entire group.

It is highly debatable that the project will provide work for the 15,000 to 25,000 men proponents of the project declare will be needed. In addition, the need for employment is immediate and it will take the greater part of a year to get the full quota of men on the job.

These arguments were countered by those in favor of the Act as follows:

Thousands of acres of developed farms and orchards in the San Joaquin Valley are going back to desert for lack of water. In the counties of Tulare, Kern and Fresno alone there are 200,000 acres of land formerly irrigated on which the water supply has practically ceased. Unless these highly-developed lands are kept in a state of production it will mean a loss of untold millions from our assessment rolls with the consequent additional burden on the remaining taxpayers.

Quick financing of the project is expected through Federal government contributions and Federal purchase of state revenue bonds. All costs of the entire program will be defrayed through Federal aid and a revenue bond system, or self-financing plan, which requires that the revenues of the project pay for it.

Closely linked with President Roosevelt's national recovery program, this Act provides for the construction of a great water project which will give immediate employment to more than 25,000 men for at least three years, thereby affording a livelihood for approximately 100,000 persons. This will be accomplished without a single dollar of cost or obligation to California taxpayers.

The "immediate initial" project proposed will not appreciably increase the area of agricultural lands in California. Its purpose is to assure sufficient water to present developed areas.

An adequate water supply will be made available for the manufacturing industries, agricultural areas, and domestic water users along the south shore of Suisun Bay. Millions of dollars are now invested in this area in manufacturing plants with large payrolls and products whose values run into millions. The region is in need of an adequate fresh water supply which the Central Valley Water Project will provide.

The navigability of the Sacramento and San Joaquin Rivers will be increased. The Project will restore the all-year navigability of the Sacramento River to Red Bluff. This will make possible savings in the transportation costs of goods in and out of the Sacramento Valley.

The San Joaquin-Sacramento Delta will tend to be freed of salt water. This involves the salvation of some of the richest agricultural land in the state. The irrigation water of the area is menaced by invasion of salt water from San Francisco Bay.

The generation of power at Kennett and Friant Dams will assure an adequate cheap power supply for the state and help insure its solvency. A main transmission line from Kennett to Antioch will make available cheap electric energy to farmers, houseowners and industrialists, as well as to cities and districts.

The project has been extensively studied by competent state engineers and is well planned. Four Federal agencies have approved and recommended it, namely, the California Joint Federal-State Water Resources Commission, the U.S. Senate Committee on Irrigation and Reclamation, the U. S. Bureau of Reclamation and the U.S. War Department.

Practically everyone who was anyone seemed to favor the Central Valley Project. Senator Hiram W. Johnson, William D. Stephens, C. C. Young, and George Pardee, former governors all, whooped for the project. Sunny Jim Rolph made himself hoarse with laudatory statements. The California State Federation of Labor (there was no CIO in 1933) through Paul Scharrenberg, its secretary, called upon one and all to "vote for their own interests and sound recovery under President Roosevelt's leadership." Farm leaders in the great valleys were practically beside themselves in their eagerness for a favorable vote—a fact indicated by their willingness to ask Labor to help them. Valley chambers of commerce backed the project but their brothers in the Los Angeles and San Francisco chambers fought on the side of the utilities in condemning the Act.

The *Sacramento Bee*, loudest voice of the McClatchy *Bee* papers (Sacramento, Modesto, Fresno) carried on the fight for approval of the Act in its traditional role of advocate of public ownership. In the files of the *Bees* are some of the more damning statements made against the P. G. & E. Thus, the *Sacramento Bee* on October 9, 1933, had State Senator J. M. Inman declaring: "We hope to force the power trust out into the open with its opposition. If power interests repeat their performance in the former water and power campaign, they will spend $500,000." And Inman reported in a later *Bee* that: "It is very gratifying that the power corporations have finally had the courage to come out into the open and drop all pretense."

And later:

There was really no doubt, at any time, as to the source of the opposition to this project, but it is well that the public should know—beyond any possibility of contradiction—that the power corporations are the real agencies seeking to defeat California's program of business recovery and unemployment relief. That the public does know now, inasmuch as the power companies, after repeated denials, have finally stopped fighting in the dark and stepped openly into the campaign.

We have the spectacle of power corporations using our own money— the money of California rate-payers—to fight a project essential to our economic recovery and which would provide relief for lack of work.

What brought about this blast, signed by Inman and State Senator Bradford S. Crittenden, was the fact that cards urging customers to vote "No" on the referendum were handed out at the Sacramento offices of the P. G. & E.

The *Sacramento Bee* also told its readers that the president of the P. G. & E. had written a letter to the company's stockholders urging them to rally around to defeat the Act at the special election.

He argued, according to the *Bee,* that the power and water project would add weight to the already great burden placed on taxpayers. He argued that there would be no market for the power produced and that their investment in the company would be jeopardized by the project because the state, in direct competition with the company, would take away its customers.

Many voices were raised. The project was hailed as a solution for almost all of the state's ills. But the biggest and best argument of all was "let's get something for nothing" an argument which always has had great appeal. California, in the depression, looked toward the project as a cure-all, a panacea, and a handout all in one. Thus former Governor Pardee summed up: "Uncle Sam offers California a Christmas present of $170,000,000. It would be an absurdity—and a cruel hardship to the people—to refuse it."

Said a San Francisco attorney, before the Commonwealth Club section on Water Resources and Irrigation:

In helping the recovery program we are also helping ourselves. The Federal government is advancing 30 per cent of the cost of constructing public works throughout the country. If we want to take advantage of these allotments we must be at the counter when the allotments are made. These Federal dispensations will not continue for long; they may end before the year is out; certainly they will end before the close of 1934.*

The Federal contribution will be an outright gift of $43,600,000 on a $170,000,000 project, and $6,000,000 more because of the interest of the Federal government in navigation and flood control. This would be a total contribution of $49,600,000 which would leave us $120,400,000. Then, in addition, if the government does with this project as it has with other public works projects, it will purchase the $120,000,000 in bonds. It is no easy job to sell $120,000,000 of bonds, but when the government of the United States is a willing investor, it is time to take advantage of that fact— now, while the opportunity is still here.

What possibly could be wrong with a project which would create jobs, cause prosperity to return, and still not cost very much?

There was a great worry in the minds of the pro-project campaigners, however. They looked toward southern California dole-

* How wrong can you guess?

fully. Los Angeles County, most populous in the state and hefty enough to determine the outcome of the referendum, was almost certain to vote heavily against the Act. There were two reasons for this. One was the fact that California has been divided traditionally —the south against the north—divided by political and competitive jealousies. In the north lie the most moving scenery, mineral wealth, the great natural harbor of San Francisco Bay, the historical traditions of the Mission fathers and the miners of '49. Southern California has the oil wells, the movies, the suave climate, the ambition. Then too, southern California had taken steps to solve its own water problem and did not want to be taxed—even though the risk seemed slight—to help the north solve its problem. The cleavage between the north and south was stronger in 1933 than it is today. But then, as now, any purely northern California project could count on an adverse vote south of the Tehachapi where most of the voters live.

Not a great deal was said publicly about this fear that selfish southerners might defeat the Act which promised so much for the north. Edward Hyatt, state engineer and one of the most important men in the development of the Central Valley Project, broached the matter, however, hopefully. Naturally Hyatt was a strong supporter of the project: it was his baby. "Los Angeles and San Francisco actually have more at stake—in trade dollars—than the area in the Sacramento and San Joaquin Valleys which will be directly benefited by the . . . . Project," said Hyatt, in trying to rally the metropolitan voters.

After all the shouting and lying, after all the emotional oratory, the voters marched to the polls on December 19, 1933, to give their opinions. The Central Valley Project Act was upheld. The vote was 459,712 to 426,109, a winning margin of 33,603 votes. True to expectation, Los Angeles County voted approximately two to one against the Act. But it could have been worse, much worse.

There is a political footnote to the election which is worth telling. It involves tuna fish, Slavonian fishermen who pursue them, the Cow of Catalina, a San Pedro barbecue, John McColl, Governor

Rolph, and the gray walls of San Quentin. It gives an idea of how elections are won and lost in California—and in many another state, too.

When the Senate passed and the Governor signed the Central Valley Project Act, John McColl was a happy man. In his pocket he had the dam Redding wanted. His happiness was short-lived. The referendum threatened his dam and it threatened McColl's political future—maybe, even, his popularity in Redding where he sold so many Cokes. McColl went to work. But the longer he worked, the more discouraged he became. For whenever he got out of the enthusiastic valleys, particularly when he went south of the Tehachapi, McColl saw that he would not have enough votes to plant the dam at Kennett. And then he ran into a situation made to order for politicking.

San Pedro is the dredged basin which serves as the Port of Los Angeles. Across twenty miles of water lies Santa Catalina Island, a garish pleasure dome complete with casino and hotel, dance bands, well-heeled tourists, sport fishermen, and glass-bottomed boats which bare the privacies of undersea life. For several years the powers of Catalina, who regarded tuna as a game fish and a lure for sportsmen, had been warring with the Slavonian fishermen of San Pedro who regarded tuna as something to be caught and put into cans. Catalina had forbidden commercial fishermen to fish its waters. Sportsmen were paying guests, Slavonian fishermen were not.

Naturally enough, the fishermen grumbled. According to their salty tradition, fishing is a business, not a game. Fish are where you find them. Marion Trutich, one of the fishermen, grumbled louder than most and decided to get revenge and have some fun at the same time. He sailed to Catalina, went ashore and shot a wild cow on the island's brush-covered hills. There was barbecued beef in the fishermen's colony that night, wine and dancing and singing. "If we can't have Catalina fish, we at least have Catalina beef," roared Trutich.

A few days later the affair took a more serious turn. The lords of Catalina had Trutich arrested. "So what," shrugged Trutich. "The lousy cow is worth maybe $15. I'll plead guilty." Then he learned the sad news. In California the theft of a bovine animal is a felony. Trutich pleaded guilty anyway and asked for probation. Then the joke fizzled completely. The judge told Trutich that California law does not allow probation in cases where a felony is committed by an armed man. Trutich was sentenced to San Quentin, the state penitentiary, for from one to fourteen years. An appeal was denied. Trutich was surely headed for prison. Then the San Pedro Slavonians appealed to John Miscovich of Fresno, leader of the Slavonian dairymen, vineyardists, and fishermen of California.

The Central Valley Project and the Case of the Catalina Cow came together a few days later in the office of Stanley Mitchell, a San Francisco newspaperman. John McColl was there, discussing the sure defeat of his Act if the southern California vote went too strongly against it. Miscovich was there seeking advice on how to save Trutich. Mitchell saw the solution. Miscovich, as leader of the Slavonians, controlled about 30,000 votes. McColl needed those votes to save his project. The needs of the Central Valley Project Act seemed to dovetail with the needs of Miscovich. The story was taken to Governor Rolph who agreed to commute Trutich's sentence. The secretary of the Fishermen's Association heard the good news from the Governor. As he stepped from the Governor's office, he was reminded that the 30,000 Slavonian votes were required for the Act at the special election. "Central Valley?" he asked. "That's easy. The fishermen don't even know where Central Valley is but they'll vote right, now that Trutich is out."

Came election; the fishermen voted right. They voted for the Central Valley Project Act, a northern California measure. Without the Catalina cow and their man Trutich on the way to San Quentin it is as certain as anything can be in politics that they would have voted against the project. Their 30,000 votes, cast wrong, would have defeated the Act. In this particular measurement, the fishermen's votes swung the day for the Central Valley Project, for Redding's dam and John McColl.

IV. Yes, Said the State

THE CENTRAL VALLEY PROJECT is a Federal project being developed by the Federal government in accordance with authorizations enacted by the Congress. It is not being constructed and developed pursuant to the Central Valley Project Act of California although in many respects the Federal project is being developed along the lines contemplated for a State project authorized by the State Act."

The preceding paragraph was submitted to the Congress in 1945 as an explanation of its position by the Bureau of Reclamation. Something drastic, obviously, had happened between 1933 and 1945. The Legislature and the people had voted for a state project and had hoped for federal financial assistance. Now, in 1945, it was apparent the state had little to do with the Central Valley Project. How had such a thing come about?

There never was any doubt as to the need for federal assistance for the project. Hopes, in 1933, were based on a Public Works Administration grant. Even before the referendum election, Governor Rolph had applied for federal money from the Emergency Administration for Public Works, forerunner of the PWA. In January 1934, following the special election, the State Water Project Authority sent a second application to the EAPW and a month later shot off a third. The Public Works Administration looked into the possibilities of making a grant-in-aid but no action was taken. For obvious reasons, no effort was made to borrow from the Reconstruction Finance Corporation. A RFC loan simply was not in the books, because the state could not have paid RFC interest rates. An economically sound Central Valley Project was possible only with a federal grant, as large as possible, and provision for federally loaned, interest-free money.

36

From the start, state officials and the California Congressional delegation, avid for federal financing, seemed to forget that the project was a state undertaking. No effort, for instance, was made to sell the $170,000,000 of revenue bonds. Although there is nothing in the record to substantiate such a thought, it is not improbable that state officials had begun to realize just how golden a flood of cash was beginning to roll out of Washington. Nothing could have been more natural than their desire (if such there was) to let Uncle Sam foot the bills for the project. Once again, it must be remembered that this was in the depression of the 'thirties. Times were bad. Money was tight. And the word was out: get that federal dough. The boys really went to work to get it. If they surrendered the state's interest—*if* they did—they at least were aware of doing so.

State Engineer Ed Hyatt was sent to Washington to see what could be done to get money. He was dispatched with the authority of a special emergency act of the Legislature which granted $50,000 to hurry things along. Hyatt appeared before the House Committee on Flood Control early in 1935. At one point he was asked by a Michigan Congressman:

"Do you prefer that this matter (CVP) be taken over and put under state control rather than have it under federal control?"

"That is a secondary matter," replied Hyatt. "The state wants this project before the country dries up and blows away. My personal view is that it would be handled better under a state authority than it would under a federal authority."

A Louisiana Congressman asked Hyatt: "Is it your view that this project should be undertaken as a federal project with the state assistance or as a state project with the assistance of the federal government?"

Hyatt answered: "That is a matter of secondary interest in California. California wants the project constructed and if the federal government desires to take charge of it, I am sure the people of California will say well and good. They are desperate. Our view is that it should be done by the state and we have filed this application with the Public Works Administration and are pro-

ceeding under the State Water Authority. It is now believed that
this is the preferable way to handle it. However, the great desire
is to get the project constructed and to safeguard this country; and
the government's desires in this matter will come first."

Some Eastern Congressmen seemed puzzled by California's attitude. Representative James M. Fitzpatrick of humid New York
was one. He asked Representative Englebright of California: "Did
I understand you to say that when the state gave up this project,
they gave up the proposition of trying to irrigate the land?"

"No," said Englebright, "they simply had an act of the Legislature which would give them the authority to, had they been able to
finance it."

"Why would they not do it?" asked Fitzpatrick.

"Because of bad financial conditions in the country, the state
was not able to finance the project," replied Englebright. "It was
brought here under the Emergency Relief Act . . . ."

The embarrassing Mr. Fitzpatrick also wanted to know about
California and the RFC. "Did the state try to borrow money from
the Reconstruction Finance Corporation?"

"No, sir. From the PWA," answered Hyatt.

"You wanted a grant?" asked Fitzpatrick.

"Yes," answered Englebright.

"Why didn't you try to borrow money from the RFC?" chimed
in another representative.

"We did not try, sir," said Hyatt.

"Aha, you mean you were too smart to borrow from the RFC.
You wanted to get the grant."

While Hyatt and the Congressional delegation were arguing
vainly for PWA money, two federal agencies—the Bureau of Reclamation (Department of Interior) and the Army Engineers (War
Department) were moving into the Central Valley picture. Actually they'd been on the scene all along. Both had long experience in California water affairs. The Engineers, for many years,
had been engaged in constructing extensive flood control works in
the Sacramento Valley and had plans and requests for many more.

And, too, following the completion of the Army's *308 Reports* which outlined possible developments on all the rivers of the United States, the Engineers had recommended, in 1931, multiple-purpose dams at Kennett and Friant.

The Bureau went into California in 1905, only three years after it had been set up as the Reclamation Service, to study a proposed reclamation project for the entire Sacramento Valley. That project was dropped, but in 1907 the Bureau had undertaken the Orland project in the Sacramento Valley. The Bureau had made studies (so had the Engineers) of the Iron Canyon and Table Mountain dam sites on the Sacramento River south of Redding. The Bureau also had reported on the water resources of the great valleys of California in 1931 and studies had been made for a salt-water barrier to keep the salt of San Francisco Bay from the rich Delta lowlands.

In the Rivers and Harbors Act of August 30, 1935, upon recommendation of the Army Engineers, Congress authorized a federal contribution of $12,000,000 toward the cost of the Central Valley Project. This amount was to compensate, in part at least, for the flood control and navigation features of the project. The money, however, was never appropriated. In the spring of that year an appeal had been made to President Roosevelt, through administration supporters, for $20,000,000 from the Emergency Relief Appropriation which he administered. The money was to be the initial amount to start the Central Valley Project as a reclamation development. The application received favorable action and on September 10, 1935, President Roosevelt approved $20,000,000 for start of the work. The final date of approval was December 2, 1935, which is regarded as the official start of the project. Later the $20,000,000 was reduced to $4,200,000. In authorizing the appropriation President Roosevelt indicated that the money should be returnable under provisions of reclamation law.

The Bureau at first planned merely to take over the state's plan for development of the project. Later, the plan was changed considerably. Hyatt did most of the work on drafting the feasibility report which Secretary Ickes submitted before the money could actually be awarded. The report contained this statement:

I find that the project is feasible from engineering, agricultural and financial standpoints, that it is adaptable for settlement and farm homes, that the estimated construction cost is adequate and that the anticipated revenues will be sufficient to return the cost to the United States . . . . I therefore recommend the approval of the Central Valley development as a Federal reclamation project.

The $4,200,000 was enough to get a start on the necessary field studies which began late in 1935. There seemed no doubt in the mind of anyone that the project had been transformed from a state to a federal undertaking; no doubt and no regret. The battle was immediately joined to keep the federal funds flowing. Allocation of federal funds by a jealous Congress is a long-term, piecemeal affair. Following the award of the first $4,200,000, the Bureau, aided by state officials and members of the delegation, began the long period of nagging for funds. That battle still goes on—Congress has appropriated more than $200,000,000 to date.

In 1936, the Congress approved $6,900,000 to continue the work and once again placed the project under the limitations and advantages of reclamation law. Of this sum $6,000,000 was earmarked for Friant Dam. First project construction began at Friant —a warehouse for the construction camp—on February 19, 1937, amid much heady Democratic speechmaking. Senator William Gibbs McAdoo pointed out that such great engineering works as the Central Valley Project were the result of the great vision of the warm-hearted party of Jackson and the later Roosevelt. You don't, he told the assembled faithful at Friant, get dams and canals and other good things by voting the Republican ticket (cheers). On October 19, 1937, construction started on the first unit of the Contra Costa Canal and on September 12, the Reclamation Commissioner, in appropriate ceremonies at Kennett, had officially named the dam-to-be "Shasta Dam."

The year 1937 was marked by far more than speechmaking and ground breaking and name giving. In that year the entire project was reauthorized by Congress in the Rivers and Harbors Act passed on August 26. The Bureau of Reclamation was handed the job; the Army Engineers were left out in the cold. The section dealing with this reauthorization is frequently quoted by all partisans of the Central Valley plan, particularly opponents of the Bureau's power policies, so pertinent parts are given here:

That the $12,000,000 recommended for expenditure for a part of the Central Valley project, California, in accordance with plans set forth in the Rivers and Harbors Committee document Numbered 35, Seventy-Third Congress, and adopted and authorized by the provisions of Section 1 of the Act of August 30, 1935, entitled "An Act authorizing the construction, repair and preservation of certain public works on rivers, harbors, and for other purposes," shall, when appropriated, be available for expenditure *in accordance with the said plans by the Secretary of the Interior instead of the Secretary of War*; provided that the transfer of authority from the Secretary of War to the Secretary of the Interior shall not render the expenditure of this fund reimbursable under the Reclamation law; Provided further, That the entire Central Valley project, California, heretofore authorized and established under the provisions of the Emergency Relief Act of 1935 and the First Deficiency Appropriation Act, fiscal year of 1935, is hereby reauthorized and declared to be for the purpose of improving navigation, regulating the flow of the San Joaquin River and the Sacramento River, controlling floods, providing for storage and for the delivery of the stored waters thereof, for construction *under the provisions of the Federal Reclamation laws* of such distribution systems as the Secretary of the Interior deems necessary in connection with the lands for which said stored waters are to be delivered, for the reclamation of arid and semiarid lands and the lands of Indian reservations and other beneficial uses, and for *the generation and sale of electric energy as a means of financially aiding and assisting such undertakings* and in order to permit full utilization of the works constructed to accomplish the aforesaid purposes; provided further, that, except as herein specifically provided, *the provisions of the reclamation law as amended shall govern the repayment of expenditures and the construction, operation and maintenance of the dams, canals, power plants, transmission lines and incidental works deemed necessary to said entire project,* and the Secretary of Interior may enter into repayment contracts and other necessary contracts with State agencies, authorities, associations, persons, and corporations, either public or private, including all agencies with which contracts are authorized under the reclamation law, and may acquire by proceedings in eminent domain, or otherwise, all lands, rights-of-way, water rights, and other property necessary for said purposes;

And, provided further, *That the said dams and reservoirs shall be used, first, for river regulations, improvement of navigation and flood control; second, for irrigation and domestic uses; and, third for power.*

This language did not frighten anyone at the time it was written. The California Congressional delegation was anxious to have the bill passed and no great objection was raised. The bill was passed and control of the Bureau of Reclamation was complete; the project was to be built and administered by the Bureau under reclamation law. The project which had started as a state plan had become officially a federal undertaking. As Ed Hyatt noted, the people said well and good.

"Reclamation law" perhaps should be looked into briefly here. Reclamation law provides, first of all, extremely easy financing terms. Money advanced for construction of irrigation facilities is interest-free. The law allows forty years or more for repayment—in actual practice, this forty-year period has been extended and other aids to the farmer have been set up. In addition, certain moneys advanced by the federal government, money allocated to navigation and flood control (and possibly to salt-water repulsion) do not have to be repaid at all, being traditionally the responsibility of the federal government.

But reclamation law also limits the number of acres which can receive reclamation-project water. The 160-acre limitation provision forbids the delivery of water from projects built with interest-free money to more than 160 acres in any single ownership, or 320 acres in case of joint ownership (in California). Reclamation law also has provisions (to be discussed later) designed to prevent land speculation and excessive price increases as a result of improvements based on government investment. The basic law was passed in 1902 during a Republican administration, and has not been changed materially—except for certain amendments which had strengthened the original intent—since then. It is unlikely that it will be changed drastically.

There can be no doubt that the Central Valley Project is subject to the land-limitation features of reclamation law; at the same time, the project benefits by the advantages of liberal repayment terms. Since acceptance of the Central Valley Project as a reclamation work, certain other reclamation projects have been exempted from the acreage limitations. It is possible that some exemption will be worked out for the Central Valley. This will be discussed later.

The point is this: when California was seeking federal money for the job, when the project was accepted as a reclamation project, there was no voice raised in warning or opposition. The opposition developed later and in recent years has become more and more violent.

The rank and file of California farmers probably did not know the implications of a project to be built and administered under reclamation law, but their leaders did and accepted those implications.

In 1937, Representative Frank Buck of California declared before a House committee hearing: "The state, as I understand it, has no authority whatsoever to enter into this picture. It is intended to be, in my opinion, and I think I speak for all of my colleagues in Congress, that it is intended to be a Federal Project, reimbursable under the reclamation law."

And Hyatt echoed: "Absolutely. That is the position. There is no question about that at all."

The lack of opposition is understandable. California relied from the beginning on federal assistance; without federal aid the project could not have been constructed. In the scramble to get federal money, the people and the officials did not look too closely into just what conditions were imposed. It must be remembered, too, that the entire emphasis on the need and aim of the project was different in those early days of the project. The state act was passed when the country was in business depression. It was passed at a peculiar moment of history—the first year of the Roosevelt administration—when the major problems were make-work projects, unemployment, and farm relief. It was logical, then, that advocates of the plan placed the major emphasis on the "rescue" aspects of the irrigation and power plan. They repeated over and over again the fact that the project would not bring "new" acreage into production. In 1933 and the years following, up until the outbreak of war, the big idea was to curtail agricultural production.

A California Congressman said: "I desire to point out that the project is in keeping with the administration's policy in that it is not designed to bring any new agricultural territory into production."

Said Hyatt:

It will save one-half million irrigated acres from returning to desert and prevent extinction of a high type of American civilization on this vast area. It will restore another half-million acres to a self-sustaining basis, and prevent an ultimate capital loss of $100,000,000 and present annual loss of 20 millions to agriculture alone. It will save 50,000 American citizens from abandoning their homes and loss of livelihood, and save the National and State relief rolls by that number of persons.

It is not a new land project, but a rescue project or relief enterprise for large areas now settled and developed . . . .

It is true, too, that during the Roosevelt regime, the states began to look more and more toward Washington for the final solutions— as well as for the ever-welcome money which Washington dispensed. The idea was to get the money for the Central Valley—get the dams and canals and powerhouses—and argue later if necessary.

There has been some speculation as to why the Public Works Administration did not advance money for the Central Valley when the state applied. Other states apparently found it easy to get PWA money. Ickes said simply that the project was not considered feasible with money at 4 percent. An answer possibly lies in the basic outlook and policies shared by Roosevelt and Ickes. Both men were strong advocates of conservation of the national resources. By 1935, it was clear that Roosevelt was committed to a program of federal development of the hydroelectric potential of the country. Ickes shared his views. It is well to remember also that Ickes was the Public Works Administrator, just as he was Secretary of the

Interior and boss of the Bureau of Reclamation. It is undoubtedly true that the PWA grant was rejected because Roosevelt and Ickes believed that the best way to achieve federal aims as far as the Central Valley was concerned was to make the project a job for the Bureau. Ickes rejected the PWA grant but Ickes set up the project as a reclamation undertaking.

Harold Ickes was Roosevelt's loyal instrument—they saw things the same way. When Roosevelt appointed Ickes, the relatively little-known Chicago reform politician, the old progressive, he declared: "Mr. Ickes, you and I have been speaking the same language for the past twenty years and we have the same outlook. I want a man who can stand on his own feet. I particularly want a Western man. Above all things I want a man who is honest and I have come to the conclusion that the man I want is Harold L. Ickes of Chicago."*

So the final determination of the place Central Valley was to have in the national scheme was decided, not by the legislators or the people of California, but by Roosevelt and Ickes in the promising early years of the New Deal. There is nothing sinister about this and there was no objection from Californians. There is every indication that it was a wise move; it is probable that the project would not be as far along as it now is—indeed, the project might never have been started—without their decision.

* Chicago, of course, was West to old Groton-boy Roosevelt. The quotation is from Ickes' book, *The Autobiography of a Curmudgeon.*

V. The Army and the Bureau

AFTER YEARS of dreams, after years of careful study and planning, California's great project was to become real. It was hard to believe. A thing of steel and concrete, a pattern of great monolithic dams and canals stretching to the horizon, carrying the cool, green water to the land.

The magic of four million dollars (with the promise of more millions to come) did its work. The Bureau of Reclamation opened an office in Sacramento. Along came the engineers in their scuffed shoes and puttees. The slide-rule boys, the surveyors, and the chainmen went into the hills, sweat whitening their khaki trousers and dust caking in the ribbons of their shapeless hats. They passed and repassed the Marysville Buttes, saw Chico turn into a golden city when frost nipped the leaves of the towering black walnut trees. They watched the great valleys turn green after the first rains, learned the smell of alfalfa on a hot day. They breathed the red dust on the banks of the Sacramento. They heard the soft tones of the valley doves and the rustle of quail in the thick foothill underbrush. They scouted the dusty mountains and searched the river bottoms. They worked under trees stunted by fumes of departed smelters. Their diamond drills bit through the topsoil, ground through the hardpan down to the solid rock, brought up core after core to show the composition of the earth at the dam sites. They gauged the water and tested the soil. Times off, they downed a beer in Clovis or lounged around the pot-bellied stove in the Diamond Saloon in mouldering Kennett.

(Jobless migrants squatted around Friant and Redding waiting for the work to begin—smoke from poison oak burning in their camps gave Redding an itching epidemic.)

In the Sacramento and Denver offices of the Bureau, draughtsmen carefully plotted their curves and ruled their lines on the crisp tracing paper. The dams and canals were taking shape on the drawing boards. The deskmen worked over the specifications, the amount of cement, the kind of steel. Others negotiated, talked of water rights and rights-of-way and juggled the money.

California got an efficient package in the Bureau of Reclamation. The package included policy-makers, administrators, rate-makers, engineers, photographers, draughtsmen, inspectors, negotiators, laboratory technicians, and publicity men. The Bureau, then thirty-three years old (child of Theodore Roosevelt), had spent its lifetime solving the problems of building dams and distributing water in the arid West. The Bureau knew its business. For most of its life it had been a constructing agency; by the time it came into California to build the Central Valley Project it had been changed by the Congress into a contracting agency. The Bureau draws the plans. Construction is done under contract by private firms with the Bureau on hand to see that it is done right. It is up to the Bureau to see that the water and power get to the people—and to see that the government gets its money back. The Bureau works to a solid set of principles, in part set up by the original Reclamation Act, in part stemming from interpretations of law and local conditions.

Those principles, in direct relation to the Central Valley Project, were set forth by a Bureau official in 1945 as follows:

Every structure should be built to achieve the maximum benefits for the people that can be derived from the expenditure of public money—not only flood control and navigation, but also such uses of water as irrigation, domestic and industrial use, power development, conservation of fish and wild life, salinity control and recreation.

Every structure should be planned, built and operated in coordination with other structures in a given basin. In Central Valley, no dam or other works should be built unless it fits into the larger picture of basin-wide development, its functions articulated with other structures in the basin. Haphazard development and operation cannot be tolerated in a region where water is that region's life blood.

The cost of these works should be equitably distributed among the beneficiaries in accordance with the mandates of Congress. Water and power users must pay their share; the government its share. Experience shows the advisability of providing as far as possible before construction for repayment to the government of reimbursable costs.

The dams and other works should be planned, constructed and operated in recognition of state laws and all vested water rights acquired under state laws should be protected.

All reclamation works should be planned, built and administered with the closest possible consultation and cooperation with the State and local interests.

Hydro-electric energy should be developed wherever feasible and preference in the sale of electric energy should be given to municipalities, cooperatives and other public agencies. Power should be developed concurrently with irrigation for these reasons:

1. To assist irrigators by making low-cost power available for pumping works needed to transfer the water from one area to another.
2. To assist in defraying the costs of the project by producing revenue and thereby reducing the cost of water to the irrigator.
3. To encourage rapid industrial growth and appurtenant commercial activities which stimulate agricultural markets and assist the irrigator in selling his produce, and
4. To make power available to consumers at the lowest possible cost.

Water users under these federal projects must be protected from the evils of land monopoly and speculation, and the principle of the family-sized farm encouraged.

It is upon these principles that the Bureau of Reclamation firmly stands. Regardless of what agency builds these conservation works, the Bureau must and will oppose any deviation from these principles.

A similar listing of principles, briefer and somewhat different in emphasis, was presented before the California Water Conference late in 1945 by Richard L. Boke, soon after he was appointed regional director of the Bureau. He listed six points. Five of them are controversial.

1. "Maximum development of the water resources of California and the spreading of benefits of this development to all the people." Nobody can argue sensibly against such a statement, but it gives some people an opportunity to shout against the long-haired bureaucrats who are trying to take over the water resources of the

state. These people intimate that the Bureau sneaked into California after dark to seize the state's water.

2. "The comprehensive, integrated, and articulated construction and operation of the works necessary to carry out this development on a basin-wide scale." This, it is said, is a plot by the Bureau to grab off all the construction work to the detriment of the Army Engineers; it is further a scheme to control the water of the state for all time to come.

3. "Low-cost water and low-cost power, the main objectives of the program." Low-cost water is all right but low-cost power is not, in some camps. These partisans want the power to be sold at as high a price as possible: high-cost power will make lower-cost water, they declare. Their main argument is that the project is first and foremost a water project; that power is included only to help pay for the water.

4. "Repayment to the Government of costs attributable to irrigation, domestic use and power, such repayment from the farmers on water to be on reasonable terms based on the water users' ability to pay." There is no argument on this one. Even the unblushing farmer realizes he's getting the best of the deal here.

5. "The encouragement of family-sized farms and the discouragement of land monopoly and speculation." We'll kick this one around in a later chapter. Briefly, according to opponents of the Bureau, this principle is New Dealish, un-American, unreasonable, and possibly treasonable.

6. "Cooperation with the State and local interests in all matters pertaining to the development and administration of the project." Just a blind, the foes of bureaucracy chant, to cover up the fact that affairs of the Central Valley really are being run by some fellow three thousand miles away in Washington.

Now that the war is over, the Bureau, serene in its principles, is going ahead with its work. That work falls into three phases, all with the same goal—beneficial use of every drop of California's water. The first job, of course, is to complete the "initial features" of the Central Valley Project.

The second job is a fifteen-year (1945–60) building program. This program, says Boke, is "for immediate construction in expanding the project to meet the needs of our expanding population. This program will bring under irrigation about one million acres which will provide for the normal expansion of irrigated farm lands." Boke is aware that a "normal" expansion probably will not be enough but, he says, "the least we should do is to prepare for our normal growth . . . . this does not provide for an abnormal growth of population that seems certain to occur."

The third job is the long-range development of California's water resources—"a fully completed, wholly integrated, comprehensive, basin-wide Central Valley Project."

Admittedly the ultimate development of the Central Valley is a long way away. And the Bureau is having troubles enough with the initial phase. The trouble does not stem from engineering problems; rather it is a difficulty with people. So far, the Bureau has made little progress in efforts to sell its water to the irrigators. Only one permanent contract has been signed—with the Southern San Joaquin Municipal Utility District—although others are near the signing stage, awaiting only the necessary approval of the voters of the districts. Only one public-agency contract has been signed for purchase of power generated at Shasta powerhouse—and the Bureau has so far failed to deliver the power.

The Bureau has a constantly recurring chore of going to Congress for funds. Getting the money will remain the biggest problem; compared with the financing, the engineering is relatively simple.

Harry W. Bashore, former commissioner of the Bureau of Reclamation, summed it up in an off-the-cuff speech before Governor Warren's 1945 Water Conference:

Of course, you have engineers that can build [the project]. You have the Army Engineers who build big works and they are competent to do so. Your Reclamation Bureau people are not Boy Scouts either—we can do good work; we have done it in the past and will do it in the future. But financing these things in the future will be the difficult thing.

The money problem is complicated by competition. Naturally, other Western reclamation projects compete in Congress—and to an extent within the Bureau—for the available money. But there is another competition—between the Bureau and the Army Engineers—for authorizations and funds to build the dams. Everyone denies that such competition exists. Officially, harmony between the Bureau and Engineers is closer than a barbershop quartette. Actually, the two federal agencies are very much competing for construction of California dams—outspoken Harry Bashore to the contrary:

> I wanted to comment on another statement that has been made in this meeting [California Water Conference] that this problem between the Bureau of Reclamation and the Army is bad, that it is just liable to disturb this whole program—this competition. Now, the Bureau of Reclamation is not competing with the Army and I don't think the Army is competing with the Bureau of Reclamation to come down here in California and spend Federal funds.
>
> Now, we *are* competing with each other to develop good engineering plans; they are watching us and we are watching them and, in my opinion, that's the way it should be. I wouldn't give a whoop for a government outfit or a State outfit that was not competitive in this respect; when they are not they are a dead-end oufit.

All right. Let's take the official word: There is no competition between the Army and the Bureau. But unofficially there is bad feeling. The Engineers regard the Bureau as a radical upstart. Off the record, Army Engineers will tell you that the Bureau is interested only in political power; that it wants to control the future destiny of California by having a firm grasp on the state's water— its life-or-death resource. The Bureau on the other hand, aggressively pursuing its principles, regards the Engineers as the tool of the Bureau's foes—the Pacific Gas & Electric Co., anti-Bureau farmers. The Bureau sees in the Army's plans a design to wreck the Bureau's hope of operating, some day, a co-ordinated, basin-wide water and power system.

Army men are hurt when they are accused of battling the Bureau. They insist that they carry no chip on their shoulders. They feel they simply have a job to do; they intend to go ahead and do it, following the directives of the Congress. An Army spokesman put it briefly: "The only policy the Engineers have is to follow orders and to do a conscientious job of it . . . . We are not ag'in anybody. All we want to do is to harness a little water."

Bear in mind that the Bureau already has the initial features of the Central Valley Plan under its arm. The system of dams, powerhouses, transmission lines, and waterways now under construction, however, was only part of the State Water Plan developed by Ed Hyatt and his Division of Water Resources, and it is only a part of the great Central Valley Project that Boke talks about. Both the Army and the Bureau have compiled comprehensive reports on the development of the Central Valley basin. These comprehensive reports, the ultimate plans, are the fodder for battle.

The Corps of Engineers operates under various River and Harbor Acts and various Flood Control Acts. The Bureau operates under the Reclamation Acts of 1902 and 1939. The Flood Control Act of 1944, however, made an attempt to co-ordinate the work of the Bureau and the Engineers. This Act, in a sense, broadens the scope of the Engineers and sets up machinery so that, God willing, the two agencies could work more closely together. The Act clearly delineated the responsibilities of both agencies. The Act reaffirmed some basic principles:

1. Existing uses of water and state water laws must be respected.

2. Costs of reservoirs attributable to navigation and flood control will be borne by the federal government.

3. Cost of irrigation facilities will be repaid by local water users.

4. West of the 98th meridian [which cuts through North and South Dakota, Nebraska, Kansas, Oklahoma, and Texas] the use of water for navigation will be subordinated to consumptive purposes.

The Act further set forth:

1. All electric energy produced by federal plants, whether

constructed by the Bureau or by the Engineers, will be turned over to the Secretary of the Interior for disposal. (But, the net power revenues from Army-built dams goes to the federal treasury as "miscellaneous receipts"; while power profits from Bureau dams remain with the project to help subsidize irrigation and other features.)

2. The Secretary of Interior will have jurisdiction over all irrigation water impounded in federal reservoirs; "new" water impounded will be distributed in accordance with reclamation law, including the acreage limitation and anti-speculation provisions.

3. The Secretary of War will have jurisdiction over operation of federal reservoirs as far as water used for flood control and navigation is concerned.

4. Both the Engineers and the Bureau are required to cooperate and confer with each other and with the state affected by their projects. Before being submitted to the Congress, all proposals must first be submitted to interested federal departments, such as the Fish and Wildlife Service, the Department of Agriculture, the Forest Service, and to the governors of the states affected.

5. All beneficial uses of available water supplies must be considered in planning new facilities—a provision for multiple-purpose structures.

6. Proposals for conservation projects will also consider the benefits or damages to fish and wild life and recreation.

It would seem, then, that Congress had solved the problem; never again will there be any conflict. Except . . . .

Certain differences in powers cause jealousies. The Bureau of Reclamation may undertake investigations of any project on its own initiative; the Secretary of Interior may authorize any project without submitting it to Congress unless there is opposition to it. When there is opposition, Congress must authorize. The Engineers have no power to initiate or authorize. They must wait for Congressional authorization which must be requested by local interests. To get funds, the Bureau must convince the Congress that reimbursable costs will be repaid under reclamation law; the Engineers must show that local interests will co-operate with federal flood-control regulations.

As noted, officially there is no competition or conflict between the agencies and we have accepted that stand. The conflict is absent in public statements and documents. An interesting document has come to hand, however, which is an official "voice" of the Engineers. It is one of those "spokesman who refused to be quoted" or "it was learned from a high and unimpeachable source" sort of thing, confidential and all that. It sets forth clearly the basic differences between the Bureau of Reclamation and the Corps of Engineers. According to this document:

Basically, both departments conscientiously attempt to comply with the intent of Congress as enunciated in various directives. Their viewpoints and approach to various water problems under consideration, however, often differ materially.

One major difference results from the fact that the need and desire for flood control, by the time it gets to the investigational stage, is real and immediate, whereas, in many cases, the need for additional water supply for irrigation and other consumptive uses is in the distant future. Pursuant to their primary responsibility, the Corps of Engineers accordingly take into consideration the advisability of constructing projects in steps, so as to give immediate flood protection and still make possible their future enlargement to provide additional irrigation storage . . . .

The Bureau of Reclamation, on the other hand, not only plans their improvements for ultimate requirements but also objects to step construction and, in lieu thereof, desires construction of the various facilities to their final desired capacity in one step . . . .

The Bureau's objection to step construction is brought about by the unjustified fear that after an initial unit is completed and in operation, engineering and legislative problems will make it difficult in the future to increase reservoir capacities, and also by the knowledge that if the theory of step development is adopted, most of the projects under consideration will be constructed by the Corps of Engineers under a flood control authorization.

The foregoing difference in departmental policies, combined with natural competition between two agencies, is the main reason that the Bureau is so strongly opposed to the present authorized projects of the Corps of Engineers.

There is one other major difference in the policy of the two departments which results in certain local groups backing the one organization and opposing the other. The Corps of Engineers have rigidly *adhered to and complied with* the policies established by Congress in regard to federal irrigation and power developments while the Bureau of Reclamation has not only *adhered to and complied with such policies but has aggressively fought those who officially and personally differed with such policies.**

The Bureau has strongly indorsed the policy of applying the existing land limitation provisions of the Federal Reclamation Act to the lands in the Sacramento–San Joaquin Basins, and has, accordingly, strongly clashed with certain local interests who are attempting to obtain a revision of such law. The Corps of Engineers has no direct interest in and has never officially taken a stand on this matter, and accordingly has not become involved in the resultant controversy.

A similar situation exists in regard to the policy pertaining to public ownership and operation of power facilities. Such public ownership has not only been strongly indorsed by the Bureau but has been actively promoted by that agency. The Corps of Engineers meanwhile has never taken an official stand on this matter, other than to comply with the dictates of Congress, as they feel it is outside their jurisdiction.

The foregoing differences in policy of the two departments results in the projects and the plans of the Corps of Engineers being strongly indorsed by certain local groups who desire immediate flood protection, by organizations working toward a modification of the land limitation features of the Reclamation Act, organized irrigation districts and communities who have their own power developments, and by other interests and organizations who are opposed to and mistrustful of the Bureau's social-economic theories, policies and intentions.

The Bureau on the other hand has the strong support of various groups, organizations and newspapers whose policies indorse public ownership of power facilities, the breaking up of large private land holdings into family size farm units, and the general extension of Federal activity and control into the local economy . . . .

That, I know, is a fair statement of the Engineers' position. It is also a pretty fair sample of slanted writing. But it is true that the Bureau of Reclamation does aggressively fight for the policies established by Congress. And if the unofficial spokesman of the Engineers has been able to make this sound like something bad,

* The emphasis is mine.

there is no help for that. The fact remains that it is not bad. Congress has laid down the policies of acreage limitation and low-cost power, and the Bureau has fought for those policies. Perhaps those policies, with only meek compliance and adherance, would not have survived as the policy of the people's representatives. The Army Engineers interpret their duties, I believe, in the narrow sense of "Halt" or "Shoulder Arms" rather than in the broader sense of accepting orders with trained and disciplined initiative.

VI. We Ain't Mad at Nobody....

ONE OF THE best examples of this Army-Bureau beef—the conflictless conflict—is the Donnybrook over the proposed dam to be built either at Table Mountain or Iron Canyon on the Sacramento River south of Redding. Inherent in the dispute is the Army policy of "step construction."

The Bureau of Reclamation proposed originally to construct a high-level dam at Table Mountain. This dam, according to the Bureau's plan, however, would not be built for many years—one of the last units of the comprehensive program. Now, however, the Bureau is studying an alternative plan to dam the tributaries of the Sacramento—a more expensive plan—which would provide flood control and other benefits while eliminating the need for a dam at Table Mountain.

The Corps of Engineers, meanwhile, received Congressional authorization to build a low-level dam at Table Mountain. This proposal aroused a great clamor from the people of Redding and Shasta County generally. With this clamor in its ears, the Corps of Engineers, although its authorization was for Table Mountain, decided to move downstream and build a dam at Iron Canyon. Studies for this dam are under way now. The same unofficial spokesman for the Engineers quoted earlier has this to say about the Table Mountain–Iron Canyon project:

. . . . Iron Canyon reservoir and power plant on the upper Sacramento River . . . . is an alternate development to the authorized Table Mountain reservoir on the same stream. The Corps of Engineers originally recommended a large capacity reservoir at the Table Mountain site, to be constructed in two steps so as to fit into the Bureau's ultimate plan which contemplates a future high dam development on this site. Organized opposition to such development by the City of Redding, sport and commercial

57

fishermen and the Bureau of Reclamation resulted in Congress limiting the
authorization for that structure to a low-level dam. Primarily so as not to
interfere with the Bureau's ultimate plans for the Table Mountain site, the
Corps of Engineers proposes to transfer the authorized storage to the downstream Iron Canyon site. The Bureau of Reclamation, however, is still fear-
ful that if the authorized low dam project is constructed it will detrimentally
affect their program for the high dam at Table Mountain by deferring the
need therefor. As a result of that fear, the Bureau is now investigating the
feasibility of providing flood control storage on the tributaries of the upper
Sacramento River in lieu of constructing such authorized storage at the
Iron Canyon site.

This analysis of the Bureau's motives is, of course, the Army's.

The Army attaches much importance to the Iron Canyon plan.
Said Lieutenant General R. A. Wheeler, chief of engineers, in a
letter to Governor Warren, December 3, 1945:

Flood control for Butte Basin and Sacramento River is urgently needed
and the Iron Canyon Project should be built immediately rather than postponed for many years as proposed by the Bureau of Reclamation. It is not
agreed that it is economically justified to build reservoirs on tributaries
above the Iron Canyon site as a substitute for a dam on the main river.

Local interests are rabidly against a low-level dam at Table
Mountain or a low-level dam at Iron Canyon. As for a high-level
dam at Table Mountain, a Shasta County spokesman says simply:
". . . . a high-level dam at Table Mountain, which was originally
proposed by the Army Engineers . . . . would destroy the economic life of Shasta County."

A low-level dam at Table Mountain would flood land worth, he
said, two million dollars; reduce the tax income of the county
$16,630 annually; adversely affect the towns of Cottonwood and
Anderson by destruction of part of their trading area; disrupt the
county road system; jeopardize the finances of the Anderson-Cotton-
wood Irrigation District and cause loss of $1,633,750 in annual
revenue from the lands to be flooded.

The spokesman continued:

It is noted, however, that Colonel Lester F. Rhodes has suggested that
the discussion of the people of Shasta County relating to a dam at Table

Mountain is out of place, for the reason that the Army now proposes to construct its dam at Iron Canyon. As a matter of fact it is quite doubtful from a legal point of view whether or not the Army has authority . . . . to construct a dam at Iron Canyon . . . .

As a matter of fact any one who is at all familiar with the water history of California knows that many years ago the site at Iron Canyon was condemned for dam purposes by reason of its inadequate foundation . . . . We have not seen any signed report by the Army Engineers to the effect that it considers the site at Iron Canyon presently satisfactory . . . .

We deem it quite inappropriate for the Army Engineers to now suggest that the only matter at issue is a dam at Iron Canyon. The Army Engineers have not, so far as we know, committed themselves to a dam at Iron Canyon . . . . When the Engineers formally and unequivocally abandon the Table Mountain site as a proposed dam, we will be pleased to discuss with them the matter of a proposed dam at Iron Canyon . . . .

The people of Shasta County have suggested on many occasions that the flood control desired could be accomplished by damming the tributary streams to the Sacramento River in its upper reaches and which enter the river above the proposed dams at Iron Canyon and Table Mountain. The Army Engineers have rejected such suggestions and, in fact, ridiculed them. The U.S. Bureau of Reclamation has accepted the good faith of the people of Shasta County and has instigated investigations concerning the feasibility of damming several of the larger tributary streams in order to accomplish the flood control desired to be contained by damming at either Table Mountain or Iron Canyon. The Army Engineers contend that the result desired could not be obtained by such dams. However, the Bureau of Reclamation, as a result of a more comprehensive study, state that complete flood control, insofar as the upper reaches of the Sacramento River are concerned can be accomplished by the employment of tributary dams on the major streams involved . . . . the investigation of the Bureau of Reclamation revealed that more satisfactory flood control will result if the tributary dams are constructed.

The same Shasta County spokesman cited the legislative action which set up a program of state co-operation with the Engineers at either Table Mountain or Iron Canyon. The language of the Legislature was as follows:

It is the intention of the Legislature that, if a feasible plan can be found which will provide adequate flood control in the upper Sacramento Valley without the necessity of constructing a dam across the Sacramento River at the Table Mountain site, or any other site in the same general vicinity and thereby prevent the necessity of flooding valuable agricultural land and at the same time prevent damage to the fishing resources of the Sacramento River, such alternate plan should be adopted.

The voice of Shasta County had one final slap for the Engineers:

Such procedure [consultation with local interests] has not been followed with reference to the Table Mountain–Iron Canyon proposed dams; and, in fact, every principle of fair hearing and the due process of law has been violated in connection with the program to construct a dam at the mentioned sites, regardless of the legitimate aims and desires of the local people.

While the people above the site are against the dam, the people below the site ardently want the dam constructed. The California Central Valleys Flood Control Association, presented an excellent statement before the Water Conference (1945).

Unless something is done to increase our flood protection, some day we are going to get wet and we may get wet right here in Sacramento—or at any other given locality in the valley, depending upon who gets the combined fury of the peak runoff.

Currently many people seem to be losing sight of the fact that flood control is our main water problem in the Sacramento Valley. Currently, many people apparently think that questions of political philosophy and sociological doctrine are much more important to this valley . . . .

Reduced to simple statement, the principal disagreement between this association, which favors construction of the Iron Canyon project, and the interests which oppose it is that the latter believe a substitute project may be found which ultimately will prove of benefit to a greater number of interests and that construction should be delayed until plans for the substitute project are perfected.

We believe that sufficient investigation has already been made a number of years ago showing the substitute plan to be economically unjustified and that exhaustive studies already made prove the Iron Canyon project to be the only feasible method of insuring the reclamation of the huge Butte Basin area, with increased flood control insurance for the whole Sacramento Valley.

To delay may be disastrous—will be, if we get the flood in the next few years which all engineers conceded to be a possibility.

The downstream ranchers agreed:

We are asking that a plan be adopted for flood control that will correct the conditions in this area [the Colusa Flood Control Basin] and that it be done within a reasonable time—from two to four years. We believe as previously stated that a dam at Iron Canyon, a dam at Black Butte with a system of levees in the basin, will solve our problems. . . . .

We are very much in favor of Table Mountain or Iron Canyon dams.

Colonel Lester F. Rhodes, district engineer, present at the meeting as an advisor, made this contribution to the proceedings:

In the first place the remark was just made that the Corps of Engineers was sponsoring the Iron Canyon Project. The Corps of Engineers is not sponsoring any project. It is immaterial to the Corps of Engineers whether Table Mountain or Iron Canyon is built. If local interests want flood control, and Congress has seen fit to authorize us to proceed with plans, we, of course, are glad to go ahead with these projects. Iron Canyon is a key project in the control of floods in the Sacramento Valley. Without that key project—Iron Canyon or Table Mountain—it may be necessary to revert to the old plan previously referred to in this discussion, of channel and levee treatment on the Sacramento. If we go to that old plan, it will not be as effective as the reservoir plan . . . .

Just one final point. The authority is already there for Iron Canyon. The appropriations to construct have not yet been made . . . . It is again a question whether the State of California wants to build the Iron Canyon dam or whether we pass it up and revert to the old levee plan and consequent loss of multiple benefits.

There the matter stands: the Army is continuing its planning for the Iron Canyon project despite its questioned right to use an authorization for the Table Mountain site for the current plan. The Bureau of Reclamation is about halfway in its studies to determine the economic justification of the plan to dam the Sacramento tributaries—which would result in elimination, possibly for all time, certainly for many, many years of a high-level dam at Table Mountain. The upstream population is angrily against any dam at Table Mountain or Iron Canyon; the downstream people, fearing floods, are prayerfully for the project. Commercial and sports fishermen are also against dams at these sites. Their plight and plea will be considered later.

There is another large disagreement in the Fresno district regarding the respective roles of the Bureau of Reclamation and the Corps of Engineers. Principal point of disagreement is the Pine Flat Dam on the Kings River. The Army has authorization for the structure and a $2,750,000 appropriation. But the Bureau regards the Kings River development as an integral part of the Central Valley Project, and has instituted studies of the Pine Flat works, as part of the project, complete with a power unit.

This state of affairs, which has gone on for several years, is maddening to many irrigators in the Kings River Water Association. The consulting Engineer of the Kings River Water Association sums up the situation:

Now speaking of the projects in the San Joaquin Valley, with particular reference to the Kings River area and the Kern River area, which serve about a million and a quarter acres between them, the surveys by the Army were invited by us back in 1937. The waters of those two streams are wholly utilized and wholly in the ownership of the canals and districts which they now serve. There is no public land in either area, and the service areas are not contemplating the use of Central Valley water. They have their water supplies; all they need is some regulation, which they propose to receive and pay for through the medium of the excess storage capacity which will be created by the reservoirs. But there is now, and has been for years past, a very serious flood situation. Millions of dollars of damage have occurred, and the average annual damage runs into millions.

In 1937, with the initiation of the investigation by the Army Engineers, we began to assist them collecting the necessary information to prepare a comprehensive, stable and sound plan, in which we propose to participate to whatever extent it is found under the law is necessary for us to participate because of incidental irrigation benefits . . . . Before those reports were done the Bureau of Reclamation came into the area and initiated two investigations, one in the Kings and one on the Kern. I think I stated a moment ago there is no excess water today that the Bureau of Reclamation, under the law, can claim for the use of a new project. There has been no invitation to them to undertake the works planned by the Army.

He contended that the Bureau sought to delay the Army construction program in Washington.

The next opposition we received at Washington in the hearings before the congressional committee was that these projects were part of the Central Valley project and, as such, should be taken over by the Bureau of Reclamation. Of course, they were not a part of the Central Valley project. They were never included in it. There is no necessity for their being so considered because they have owned their own water and owned their lands for about seventy-five years. They have developed an area there the like of which, as an irrigating enterprise, is not to be found elsewhere in California.

It doesn't appear to us that there was any need for social reforms. We have a social condition down there with which we are well satisfied—of which, in fact, we are inclined to be proud.

After we had disposed of that, the next contention was that it was necessary that the provisions of the Reclamation Law having to do with limiting the size of farms to family size should be imposed. There was no such provision in the arrangements made with the Army; therefore, it should be turned over to the Bureau of Reclamation. Well, we simply don't believe that. I cannot see (I am speaking personally now, but I think it is the general opinion of all those down there who are concerned with that project) that our social set-up . . . . needs to have its control exercised from over 3000 miles away . . . .

Charles Kaupke, engineer and watermaster for the Kings River Water Association, is wholly set against the Bureau of Reclamation's intention to get into the Pine Flat picture, primarily because he fears federal control of the Kings River. He frequently quotes a letter prepared by John Page, former Commissioner of Reclamation and approved by Harold Ickes, then Secretary of the Interior:

It is not contemplated by the Bureau that any surplus water remains above the needs of the Kings River area with proper operation of the reservoir. A full and complete allocation of all the flow of the Kings River should be made primarily for use by the irrigators' representatives who will designate the releases of water from Pine Flat reservoir. For this purpose, it is important that local interests prepare and adopt schedules covering as fully as practicable the entire flow of the stream.

It is likely that the stream will at times exceed the maximum of such schedules and thus leave water to fill unallocated storage capacity in the reservoir. The surplus water so impounded will be available for later disposition by the organization representing the irrigators. In any event, the arrangement should contemplate that all such water will remain in the Kings River unless it is mutually agreed that it could be diverted.

This being so, argues Kaupke, why should the Kings River and the Pine Flat Reservoir be considered a part of the Central Valley Project? The Pine Flat Reservoir, he says, will benefit no area other than the Kings because all the water, "every drop of it," is used for irrigation now. Kaupke, afraid of federal control of his stream, is also afraid that the Bureau might be tempted to divert Kings water into the Friant-Kern Canal. The canal will cross the Kings River and Kaupke is afraid the temptation to dip into his water would be too much for the Bureau.

And yet, Kaupke told the California Water Conference, despite the Page-Ickes statement that no surplus was available in the Kings River:

I went to Washington and appeared before the Commerce committee of the United States Senate, which was considering the Flood Control bill. Representatives of the Department of the Interior, including the secretary, the commissioner of reclamation and others appeared there and outlined their plans for the Central Valley project. They said something like this: "There is a lot of surplus water in the Kings River. Down there in Kern County and Tulare County there is a large area where the ground water supply has been depleted and we propose to take this surplus from Kings River, both surface and underground, take it down there to replenish that area. Why should we be required to go to the Sacramento River when there is a supply closer at hand?"

Now if there is any surplus water in the Kings River we will let anybody use it who can, but we don't want some organization coming on our stream and making a diversion and telling us what is surplus and what is not surplus . . . .

Now we are not taking any dog-in-the-manger attitude here at all. Our water rights have been developed over a period of seventy-five years. I defy anyone to show an area anywhere in the United States that shows a higher development than we have. We have operated these projects for seventy-five years; now the Bureau finds the water rights on the Kings River are complex and involved; therefore the dumb clucks living in this area can't operate them and they should be taken to Washington and administered from there. Do you wonder that we are up on our ears?

Kaupke, backing the Army plan to build the Pine Flat Dam without immediate installation of a power plant, argues that there is no sense at all in developing power on the Kings. "If they wanted power so badly," he asks, "why didn't they build a powerhouse at Friant?" Even though he asks the question, Kaupke knows that power facilities were not contemplated for Friant, where water is diverted into the canals high on the dam surface. He stubbornly contends that there is enough head on the canals to generate power —a conclusion not held by anyone but Kaupke, as far as I can find.

Although power aspects of the Central Valley Project will be considered at some length later, the generation of power is one of the sub-controversies in the conflict between the Bureau and the Engineers—just as the 160-acre limitation enters the fight. Kaupke and his followers (they are many) argue that the Kings River Dam at Pine Flat is purely a flood-control project and take alarm because the Bureau would make it a multiple-purpose installation. They feel the project should be constructed by the Army for flood control alone, overlooking, for the moment, the Army's ultimate, multiple-purpose design.

While Kaupke stands firm in his belief that power generation at Pine Flat is unnecessary and unsound (he means power generation as contemplated by the Bureau, and is silent on the Army's ultimate plans for power generation), others in his own and neighboring districts do not share his views. The Grange, particularly, is backing the Bureau in the Pine Flat controversy. A representative of the Fresno County Pomona Grange, made this statement before the California Water Conference:

The Dinuba area is served by the Alta Irrigation District. "Served" maybe isn't the right word, for after about the middle of July the Alta goes dry like most all the canals that get water from the Kings River. Right when the irrigation requirements are the heaviest, we have to start pumping and that is expensive business under the rate schedules cooked up by the private utility boys.

If the rates were lower, I'd use a lot more electricity on my place and a host of neighbors would do the same thing. But we can't do it now and we won't be able to do it if the Army builds Pine Flat. For, mark my word, if they do, they will turn the power plant over to the Kings River Water Users Association; and if that happens we're sunk as far as cheap power is concerned. The reason I say that, is that the association officials will in all probability sell the power, at the plant, to the P.G.&E. Then we will be no better off than we are now. Maybe the association officials haven't said out in public they would do that, but we're not deaf. We get pretty accurate reports on some of their private goings on and we think we know what they have in mind.

To a lot of us in my section it looks like our only real hope to get all there is to get out of the Kings River development is to have the job done by the Reclamation Bureau. They stand up and fight for lower power rates and that's what we need. Beyond that, they believe tying together the power and water developments of the whole Central Valley into a unified system makes good sense. The Kings River needs to be tied into that system, not only because it will bring low-cost power to our area, but it will make for a better system of water distribution, too. We might run into two or three dry years on the Kings River watershed; and, in that case, it might mean the difference between a profit and loss to us if we could draw on the Friant-Kern Canal. It could work the other way round, too. By that I mean that in some years water from the Kings might be fed into the Friant-Kern Canal without hurting us. This kind of operation could be done if the Bureau also handled the situation on the Kaweah, Tule and Kern Rivers. It is pure folly to build a fence around the Kings River. It seems to me that I will gain the most, and that other farmers and local businessmen, too, throughout the Central Valley will gain the most from the unified development of our remaining water resources. The Bureau of Reclamation has a plan to accomplish this, and what is more important, they have definite and understandable policies under which they propose to do the job. The Army Engineers have stated proudly that they have no policy.

. . . . in the Kings River area, we have gone out with petitions, we have asked the people, the irrigationists, to tell us by whom they wish to have the Kings dam built, and I believe it was close to 95 percent of the farmers wanted it under the Reclamation Bureau, for the reason that it would be cheaper power. I am under the impression that our elected representatives are not representing us, but our watermaster [Kaupke].

And a representative of the state Grange:

Many years ago the Kings River Water Association came before the Fresno County Grange and asked us to assist them in getting the Army Engineers' survey in the area. We did. At the same time they made talks before the Grange all over the county on the number of millions of kilowatt hours that could be developed.

Power at Pine Flat was never intended as primary power, but under that Reclamation Bureau's first survey, the intention was, and the line in the report shows it, to run a power line from Pine Flat to Antioch, to connect with the power from Shasta Dam, so as to make delivery of power to all the people in the valley, including the Kings River watershed.

You have heard repeatedly of the Kings River Watershed Irrigation District completing the setup. We have only half enough water to go around. Today, as the land is further developed and the water becomes thinner, we have much less water, so we need that power to assist us—not with the idea of delivering water to somebody else. No Reclamation Bureau or any other organization has so far made the statement that they will take our water away.

The power bill is the great bugaboo of the irrigator. The streams of the San Joaquin dry up sometime during the summer and when the surface water is gone, the farmer must start his pumps to water his land. After labor costs, the power bill usually is the biggest expense of the irrigator.

"My pumping bill is four times as much as my irrigation district bill," one farmer declared.

Despite the language of the 1944 Flood Control Act, there was continuing friction throughout 1945 and into 1948. In December 1945, Lieutenant General R. A. Wheeler, chief of engineers, in a letter to Governor Warren, speaking about flood-control dams in the San Joaquin Valley, said:

Since these reservoirs will not be operated for the benefit of water users until satisfactory provision has been made for payment to the United States for conservation storage, it is important that local interests proceed immediately with the formation of appropriate organizations and arrangements necessary to insure such payment.

The actual agreements for such repayment will be between local interests and the War Department. It is not mandatory under the law that these agreements comply with the provisions of the Reclamation Acts.

Within a few hours this statement was countered by Commissioner Bashore:

Another statement was made—I believe it was in General Wheeler's letter to Governor Warren—that excess land laws did not apply to water sold by the Secretary to irrigation users. I am not a lawyer and I am not going to argue the point, but I will say this: that I don't think the project is going to be worked out that way. It is inconceivable to me that two Federal agencies, working in a State, could either one of them give a group of people a more satisfactory deal in the disposition of irrigation water than the other. So don't get the idea of playing the Army against the Bureau, or the Bureau against the Army, with the idea of getting a better deal out of one than the other, because in my opinion, you won't get it. These things are going to be worked out in a coordinated way, and Federal funds, if they are expended, will be returned under the same provisions.

An uneasy sort of compromise was ordered by President Truman—a compromise which satisfied no one. The President, in approving funds for Army construction of the Pine Flat Dam, attached this statement:

The War Department Civil Functions Appropriation Bill, 1947, which I approved May 2d, 1946 makes appropriations for a number of thoroughly worth-while projects which will further the development of the water resources of the Nation. I am also glad to note that the Congress, by the addition of certain provisos to the item for the Kings River Project, California, has afforded an opportunity for assuring that the Federal reclamation policy, including repayment and the wide distribution of benefits, will apply to that project. This is in accordance with the view that I have heretofore expressed and the position repeatedly taken by the late President Roosevelt. It is consistent with the policies laid down by the Congress in the Flood Control Act of 1944.

Consistently with the action taken by the Congress on the Kings River Project, I propose in the near future to send to the Congress my recommendations regarding an over-all plan for the development of the water resources of the Central Valley area in California. I am withholding action in that regard pending receipt of comments from the Governor of California. The over-all plan for the Central Valley area of California will include means for achieving comprehensive development and utilization of its water resources for all beneficial purposes, including irrigation and power, and it will provide adequately for flood protection. It will have regard for the need for integrated operation of reservoirs which is essential for the complete utilization of the land and water resources of the area. It will provide for application in the Central Valley area of the Federal reclamation policy —including the repayment of costs and the wide distribution of benefits. I hope that the Congress will, by the adoption of the plan, act to put an end to a situation which, in California and in Washington, has been productive of administrative confusion as well as confusion to the general public.

In the meantime, in view of the legislative history of the provisos in the Kings River item, and in view of the disadvantageous position on which the government would be placed if repayment arrangements were unduly postponed, I am asking the Director of the Budget to impound the funds appropriated for construction of the project, pending determination of the allocation of costs and the making of the necessary repayment arrangements.

The President's statement clearly follows the intent of the Congress as voiced in the Flood Control Act of 1944. Although the consulting engineer of Porterville could say in 1945: "The advantage of operating under flood control projects is that the respective owners of water rights on the stream will control and operate their rights in a normal, usual manner without interference or further contracts which might place additional obligations and restrictions on their rights and lands," it was apparent by 1946 that this claimed advantage might be fading.

Thus, in the case of the Pine Flat project, the water users of the Kings River wanted the Army to construct the dam, primarily as a flood-control structure. They proposed to pay $10,000,000 for whatever incidental irrigation benefits they would receive. Under the Flood Control Act of 1944, however, even though the Army builds the dam, the irrigation water would be administered under reclamation law.

Kaupke returned from an Omaha conference with Interior Department officials in mid-October of 1946 to report a changed interpretation of the Bureau's role in administering the water. Said Kaupke:

When I was in Washington last Spring, it was agreed that the excess land law would apply only to areas where there was new water on new land. A definition was lacking for new water and new land, however.

Now they tell us—and it came from Commissioner of Reclamation Michael W. Straus himself—that the excess land provision applies to all lands receiving water from the reservoir even if the water is retained only temporarily.

That means that districts which have perfected water rights and which have been operating for fifty years or more will have to come under the 160-acre limitation.

We told Straus that, in that case, it was no soap for the dam. We simply don't want a dam under those conditions.

We are willing to pay for the irrigation benefits—we've offered to pay $10,000,000—but we won't do it under the terms they lay down now.

Kaupke was quoted to that effect in the December 5, 1946, issue of the *Reedley Exponent*:

"It would be better never to build the Pine Flat Dam than to have it built under the regulations proposed by the Bureau of Reclamation," Charles Kaupke, Kings River Water Association watermaster, told the Lions Club Tuesday noon.

"If and when the dam is built, its benefits to irrigation will be not nearly as great as some people now imagine," Mr. Kaupke said. Waters impounded by the dam would add only 6 per cent to the present irrigation water of the Kings River basin, he declared.

"It would be folly to jeopardize our rights to 94 per cent to gain the extra 6 per cent," he said . . . .

The speaker said he believes there is little possibility that the Pine Flat Dam will be built until there is a change in administration in Washington. He pointed out that funds of the Army Engineers have been impounded by President Truman until the project can be built under Bureau of Reclamation rules . . . .

Straus said he had been informed by San Joaquin Valley leaders that they planned "to go back to the original law" for clarification of the Kings River controversy. He said he believes that means opponents of the Bureau would seek amendment of the Flood Control Act of 1944 to exempt the Pine Flat project from the provision which co-ordinated the authority of the Army Engineers and the Bureau.

Since the Kings River project was requested as an Army flood-control project there has been a shift of emphasis, to a degree, from flood control to conservation. Thus, the *Shafter Press* was able to comment in September of 1946:

At a meeting of some Kern, Kings, Tulare and Fresno county citizens in Hanford Tuesday night, Congressman Alfred Elliott of the Tenth District charged that President Truman is holding up the construction of flood control dams by the U.S. Army Engineers on the rivers south of the San Joaquin which flow into the valley.

Congress, Elliott declared, appropriated funds early this year for the construction of these dams, but the president, at the insistence of the Department of Interior, has impounded the funds and stopped the projects.

These dams, which include the Kern and Kings River projects and the control of several smaller streams, will serve the dual purposes of flood control and water conservation.

The president's decision to hold up these projects springs, no doubt, from a controversy which has been raging for several years as to whether the U.S. Army Engineers or the Bureau of Reclamation of the Department of Interior should build the dams.

The feud is partly ideological and partly plain cussedness, of which neither side is entirely free.

But the urgent and appalling fact is that the Southern San Joaquin Valley, one of the most fertile land areas in the whole world, is rapidly running out of water and, unless all available water sources in this valley are quickly conserved and made available to valley lands, the consequences to our valley economy will be tragic . . . .

The loss from flood damage during one flood year on any one of these streams is almost sufficient to pay the cost of construction of the dams and the dams can quickly justify their expense as flood control projects.

But of greater immediate importance is the fact that these dams are needed right now for water conservation . . . .

Early in 1947, President Truman released to the Army $1,000,-000 for Pine Flat which he had impounded earlier. His order cleared the way for construction to start. The Engineers said the $1,000,000 would be enough to complete excavations for the left abutment of the dam and they immediately began this work. The President's action was called "a great victory for the people of the San Joaquin Valley" by one colonel of Engineers. The Bureau of Reclamation was correspondingly glum. The glumness stemmed from the fact that the Bureau men believe that if the Army completes the Pine Flat Dam as a flood-control project, it will be difficult, if not impossible, to integrate the Kings River into the Central Valley system.

Theoretically, of course, as we have seen, any irrigation benefits stemming from the project will be administered under reclamation law by the Secretary of the Interior. So Congress has said. Whether such a thing actually will occur remains to be seen.

"We are opposed to all further grants of lands to the railroads or to other corporations. The public domain should be held sacred to actual settlers."—Democratic National Platform, 1872.

"We are opposed to further grants of the public lands to corporations and monopolies, and demand that the national domain be set apart for free homes for the people."—Republican National Platform, 1872.

VII. The 160-Acre Limitation

DURING THE coming years, heavy attacks will be made against reclamation projects in general and specifically against the so-called 160-acre limitation as it applies to the Central Valley Project. Opponents of the limitation are sure to raise the issue of communism. They will say that the 160-acre limitation is a Communist-inspired work. This is ridiculous. The Grange and the CIO support the limitation. So does the Catholic Rural Life Conference. So does the Communist party. But that support does not make the limitation a "Grange" or a "CIO" or a "Communist" or a "Catholic" measure.

Bills have been introduced in both the House and the Senate aimed at repeal of the limitation. A similar attempt was made in 1944. Naturally, no one can foresee what Congress will do. Since 1902, however, when the limitation first was written into law, Congress has refused to change it. The original Reclamation Act was hailed as a great Republican triumph and since that time, during both Republican and Democratic administrations, the law has been strengthened rather than weakened.

The law is difficult to understand and opponents of limitation purposely have beclouded the issue. The ranchers of the great valley, many of them at least, are thoroughly confused. They have been told that under the law they can own no more than 160 acres if they want to get water from the Central Valley Project. They have been told that the Secretary of the Interior can regulate the size of their farms. They have been told that the Secretary can force them to sell their land in excess of 160 acres. None of these things is true.

Land limitation is a basic policy of the United States. It is one of the foundation stones of the Republic. When Europeans first reached America, they found a land without the rigid systems of land ownership of the old country. Crown grants were made, giving great parcels of land to individuals. But among the first actions of the United States were steps to guarantee that great land-holding feudal dynasties would not be built up in the new republic. The early statesmen saw clearly that equality of individuals could best be promoted and protected by assuring every man an opportunity to get enough land to provide for himself and his family. Thus the young republic declined to accept the European system of entailed estates and primogeniture. Thomas Jefferson in 1776 brought before the Virginia Legislature a bill to abolish entailed estates, a bill designed to eliminate and forestall establishment of landed families which could become rulers of people as well as exploiters of the land. Said Daniel Webster, many years later:

Our New England ancestors . . . . left behind them the whole feudal policy of the other continent . . . . They came to a new country. There were as yet no lands yielding rent, and no tenants rendering service. They were themselves either from their original condition or from the necessity of their common interest, nearly on a level in respect to property. Their situation demanded a parceling out and division of the land, and it may fairly be said that this necessary act *fixed the future frame and form of their government.* The character of their political institutions was determined by the fundamental laws respecting property . . . . The consequence of all these causes has been a great subdivision of the soil and a great equality of condition; the true basis, most certainly, of popular government.

Possession of land by free men, and the opportunity for free men to possess land, marked America as the land of freedom. Land was the gift of a grateful government in many cases. Soldiers of the Civil War, of the War of 1812, and of the Spanish-American War received the thanks of their country in land scrip—land on which to make their homes. The veterans of the first and second World Wars are given preference in competition for the remaining public domain. In these grants of government land to the soldier and the settler, 160 acres came to be the measure of the proper size of farm which would provide (diligence and hard work were necessary) a proper living for a family. It was considered more than a minimum; 160 acres could provide prosperity and comfort and even luxury on the American land. The traditional land policy of the United States was reflected in the Constitution of California which declares:

The Legislature shall protect, by law, from forced sale, a certain portion of the homestead and other property of all heads of families.

The holding of large tracts of land, uncultivated and unimproved, by individuals or corporations, is against the public interest, and should be discouraged by all means not inconsistent with the rights of private property.

Lands belonging to this state, which are suitable for cultivation, shall be granted only to actual settlers, and in quantities not exceeding three hundred and twenty acres to each settler, under such conditions as shall be prescribed by law.

The limitation in reclamation law needs clarification. First of all, it is important to remember that the limitation written into the law in 1902 and broadened and strengthened in various ways in 1911, 1914, and 1926, is a limitation not on land but on *water*. It limits the amount of water a rancher can receive from a public reclamation project built with public money provided without interest. The 1902 law provided for delivery of water both to public lands (which were to be opened to homesteaders) and to private lands. This is important in the light of statements being made today by opponents of the limitation. The provisions of the 1902 reclamation law affecting public land may be ignored here. This, however, is what the original law said about the relation of private lands to reclamation projects:

No right to the use of water for land in private ownership shall be sold for a tract exceeding 160 acres to any one landowner, and no such sale shall be made to any landowner unless he is an actual bonafide resident on such land, or occupant thereof residing in the neighborhood of said land, and no such right shall permanently attach until all payments therefor are made.

In 1911, this basic law was amended by the Warren Act which provided that water from reclamation projects (project needs had to be met first) could be sold to lands in private ownership which needed supplemental irrigation water. The Act limited the water which could be sold to any single owner to that amount necessary to irrigate a maximum of 160 acres.

By 1924, it was apparent to students of irrigation that certain improvements could be made. A group of investigators submitted a study called the *Fact Finders Report* (1924) which said, in part:

When the reclamation act was passed it was believed that it would apply mainly, if not wholly, to the public domain. It was at first a question whether its provisions could be applied legally to land in private ownership. When, however, the locations for projects came under consideration, the advantages of those where the land was in private ownership were vigorously pressed, and it was found in some instances that a project where the land was in private ownership afforded greater opportunities for development and better settlement conditions than could be found in the public domain. As a result, some of the projects included only privately owned land, and on nearly all of the projects a considerable percentage of land was privately owned. Although the Reclamation Service attempted to compel the subdivision of these privately owned lands into units fixed by law, yet the legal enforcement was found difficult; and what was still worse, in many cases the owners of the land capitalized the Government expenditures and the liberality of its terms of repayment by selling the lands to settlers at much higher prices than could otherwise have been obtained. The benefits of the reclamation act, therefore, went in such case almost entirely to these speculative owners, and an obligation of paying interest on inflated land prices was imposed on the settler in addition to his other burdens . . . .

And in another section:

One of the first questions before the Reclamation Service was whether [private] lands should be allowed the benefits of the reclamation act. It was answered affirmatively, not only because private and public lands in the arid region had become inextricably mingled, but also because the real purpose of the reclamation law, that of home making and of reclaiming arid lands, could be accomplished by furnishing water to privately owned lands. Of the 1,293,906 acres of lands now under water-right contract with the Government, approximately two-thirds were in private, the remainder in public ownership at the time the projects were constructed.

The *Fact Finders Report* was reflected to an extent in the Omnibus Adjustment Act of 1926. This Act said:

No water shall be delivered upon the completion of any new project or new division of a project until a contract or contracts in form approved by the Secretary of Interior shall have been made with an irrigation district or irrigation districts organized under State law providing for payment by the district or districts of the cost of constructing, operating, and maintaining the works during the time they are in control of the United States, such cost of constructing to be repaid within such term of years as the Secretary may find to be necessary, in any event not more than 40 years from the date of public notice hereinafter referred to, and the execution of said contract or contracts shall have been confirmed by a decree of a court of competent jurisdiction.

Prior to or in connection with the settlement and development of each of these projects, the Secretary of the Interior is authorized in his discretion to enter into agreement with the proper authorities of the State or States wherein said projects of divisions are located where by such State or States shall cooperate with the United States in promoting the settlement of the projects or divisions after completion and in the securing and selecting of settlers.

Such contract or contracts with irrigation districts hereinbefore referred to shall further provide that all irrigable land held in private ownership by one owner in excess of one hundred and sixty irrigable acres shall be appraised in a manner to be prescribed by the Secretary of the Interior and the sale prices thereof fixed by the Secretary on the basis of its actual bonafide value at the date of appraisal without reference to the proposed construction of the irrigation works; and that no such excess lands so held shall receive water from any project or division if the owners thereof refuse to execute valid recordable contracts for the sale of such lands under terms and conditions satisfactory to the Secretary of the Interior and at prices not to exceed those fixed by the Secretary of the Interior; and that until one-half the construction charges against said lands shall have been fully paid no sale of such lands shall carry the right to receive water unless and until the purchase price involved in such sale is approved by the Secretary of the Interior and that upon proof of fraudulent representation as to the true consideration involved in such sales, the Secretary of the Interior is authorized to cancel that water right attaching to the land involved in such fraudulent sales . . . .

In brief, those are the laws relating to the 160-acre limitation as they apply to the Central Valley Project. The mere recital of law does not complete the case, however. As Commissioner Bashore said in 1945:

I will admit that the reclamation laws are a little difficult to understand because they have been developed over a period of 43 years; and it is a little difficult at times to really find out what has been changed or amended. In order to do that you must look at the decisions of the Department of Interior which have been made, say, since 1914 as they relate to the public lands and lands in reclamation projects. You cannot just pick up the Reclamation Manual and say, "This is the law" unless you look up the departmental interpretation of it. And the departmental interpretation of the law is the law until the courts say otherwise; whether it makes the right interpretation or not, that is the law.

With Bashore's admonition in mind, here is a late statement of the law and the Bureau of Reclamation's interpretation of it:

Two misconceptions of the acreage provisions of the Reclamation Law seem current in the Central Valley. The first is that a man must sell all his excess acres in order to obtain any water for his land. The second is that the Secretary of Interior is empowered by law to set the acreage for a farm in the Central Valley at any figure he desires. The law makes neither of these provisions.

By the terms of the Reclamation Law and the contract between the Bureau of Reclamation and the Southern San Joaquin Municipal Utility District (which may be considered as a pattern for contract for any water district in the Central Valley) a land owner may retain undisputed ownership of his entire acreage and yet receive water for 160 self-designated acres of the holding—or for 320 acres if owned by husband and wife. A "recordable contract" agreeing to sale of the excess lands enters only as a condition for obtaining water for the excess acres.

This means that a landowner may obtain water from the Central Valley project for 160, or 320, of his acres and continue to own and operate his remaining acreage exactly as he has done in the past. If, however, he desires water on his excess acres, he must sign a recordable contract to the effect that, within ten years, he will sell his excess land at a price set by an impartial board. This board, by the terms of the aforementioned contract, is composed of three men: one representing the Secretary of the Interior; one representing the water district; and one chosen mutually by these two.

After the fair price has been set, the owner may retain his land for ten years without selling, or may sell at any time. If, at the end of this period, he has not disposed of his excess acres, then the Secretary of the Interior is authorized to offer the land for sale, at the fairly evaluated price.

The only compulsion is with regard to the amount of *water* a single owner may obtain. Water in the Central Valley is scarce, and it can only be regarded as just that any one man should receive a stipulated amount of it from a public project. The limit has been set to the amount requisite for irrigating 160 acres. If the owner desires more water than that, then ownership of the land must eventually pass to another, because no man is entitled to a "lion's share" of the public wealth.

It will be appreciated from this account of the operation of the statutes, that whereas everybody in the Central Valley will benefit from the Reclamation Law, nobody is going to be any worse off. A large owner will receive his fair share of the available irrigation water, and will be able to continue to operate the rest of his acreage exactly as he has done in the past. If, in addition, he desires project water for his excess acres, he may have it for ten years, but he must then be prepared to sell his excess lands.

The powers of the Secretary to establish the acreage for which a single owner may receive water in the Central Valley are non-existent. That limit is set by law—the Reclamation Law as amended in 1926. It is true that the Secretary was granted such powers in the Reclamation Law of 1914; but in the 1926 amendment the limit of such acreage was fixed at 160 acres for single ownership.

The only powers held by the Secretary in this regard are to ensure observance of the law. This observance is recognized in the contract between the Bureau and the Southern San Joaquin Municipal Utility District. Section 27 of the contract confirms the 160 acres in a single ownership, and 320 acres in the ownership of husband and wife, as the limit for which water may be obtained without a recordable contract for sale. Section 28 defines the powers of the Secretary of the Interior to take necessary steps to enforce the terms of the contract. Nowhere is the Secretary empowered to change the terms of the law.

The Reclamation Law does empower the Secretary of the Interior to set the acreage for *Public* lands which are opened for sale. There are no irrigable public lands in the Central Valley, except for some lands now held by the military. In setting limits for individual ownership of these public lands, the Secretary is to be guided by consideration of potential land-use. A case *outside* the Central Valley where the Secretary may establish a feasible acreage lower than 160 or 320 acres is in the Columbia River Project. This is a result of special legislation, initiated by the delegation to Congress from the State of Washington. This State desired, apparently, to settle as many new farmers on the land as possible, so into the law was written a special clause, setting 160 acres as the maximum and 10 acres as the minimum which one man may own. This special legislation has no application to the Central Valley of California.

A good summation is: In practice it is not a limit on land but a limit on water . . . . on the fair amount of water one man may receive from a public project.

It will be noted that departmental interpretation has modified the original intent of Congress by raising from 160 to 320 the number of acres which can receive project water, with the provision that the 320 acres must be held by husband and wife. This interpretation is based on the fact that California is a community-property state, a fact which gave department interpreters a chance to make the water limitation somewhat more palatable to Californians. The more liberal interpretation, however, has led opponents of limitation to declare that the action of the Department indicates that the whole idea of limitation is unsound. Said the *Los Angeles Times*:

. . . . the Reclamation Bureau itself is proposing to suspend it [the limitation] by ruling that because of California's community-property law a man and his wife shall each be entitled to hold 160 acres of irrigated land. Bureau officials have even suggested that an additional 160 acres be allowed water service for each child in the family . . . . a situation which amounts to an admission that the limitation does not properly apply to Central California conditions . . . .

The law on the statute books and the law as interpreted by the Department of Interior and its Bureau of Reclamation, however, are the direct outgrowth of the United States' historical policy against land monopoly, absentee ownership, and land speculation. These basic ideas were reflected in the thinking of the men, Western men, who were responsible for passage of the Reclamation Law. The law was a Western idea, tailored to Western specifications to meet a Western need. Its aim was to make the desert produce for the benefit of the small farmer and the country, not for the land monopolists, the absentee owner, and the land speculator.

"The object of the Reclamation Act is not so much to irrigate the land as it is to make homes," declared F. H. Newell, first chief of the Reclamation Service. "It is not to irrigate the land which now belongs to large corporations, or even small ones; it is not to make these men wealthy; but it is to bring about a condition where-

by that land shall be put into the hands of the small owner, whereby
a man with a family can get enough land to support that family, to
become a good citizen and to have all the comforts and necessities
which rightfully belong to an American citizen." This statement
was made in 1905.

In praise of the Reclamation Act, aptly named Senator Francis
G. Newlands of Nevada, a pioneer in irrigation and conservation,
said:

> We have provided that only those can obtain title who live upon the
> [public] land for five years and reclaim the land . . . . residence for five
> years—honest work for five years—is required as the condition of this title.
> Thus, this work is dedicated forever to the homebuilders . . . .

> The existing landowner, also, is not neglected. The sentiment which at
> first prevailed that this Act should be applied only to government lands was
> overcome, and we have a provision, ample and comprehensive in its charac-
> ter, which permits the Interior Department to grant water rights as to the
> land in private ownership.

> But even there it secures the country against the evils of concentration
> of land in single ownership and of land monopoly; for instead of selling
> the large landowner a water right covering his entire tract, the Act provides
> that the right can be granted for 160 acres only. But whilst the large land-
> owner can secure a water right for only 160 acres, he can divide his tract
> into 160-acre farms, and each grantee can buy from the government a water
> right . . . . and thus large tracts of land in private ownership today
> [1903], lacking the water sufficient to give them value, and for that reason
> lacking a market, will be brought to market. The owners will be able to
> dispose of them by subdivision into 160-acre farms.

Briefly we have seen what the 160-acre limitation is and how it
came to be part of the reclamation law; how it was an outgrowth of
a fundamental principle of American political life; how it was designed specifically to apply to privately owned lands; how it so far
has withstood change; how it was designed to provide fair sharing
of the water resources of the West developed by interest-free public
money; how it was aimed directly at absentee landlords, land
speculators, and land monopolies.

Opponents of the limitation have been spreading their arguments as widely as possible since 1944. They are hopeful the

Congress will see things their way and repeal the limitation in the Central Valley. The arguments against limitation fall into certain broad lines.

The most common argument is that the Central Valley Project is not a reclamation project at all. Rather it is a "rescue" or a "conservation" project designed to bring supplemental water to acres already developed for irrigation and in private hands. Further, says this argument, there is not a single acre of public land in the Central Valley, except for a few military reservations which can be overlooked. Thus, it is incorrect to apply a limitation designed to be operative on public lands reclaimed by federal funds.

We have seen that the reclamation law was drawn in such a way as to provide for private lands as well as public. On land owned by the government, the 160-acre limitation was unnecessary: the government could set any kind of a limit it thought proper in distributing its own land—the limitation was written into the law specifically to apply to *private* land. The further argument that the limitation should not apply to supplemental water runs smack into the Warren Act which set up conditions under which supplemental water could be distributed; the 160-acre limitation was written into that Act to assure fair distribution.

Governor Warren of California used this argument when he declared for repeal of the limitation early in 1947. Governor Warren said he favored repeal of the limitation in reclamation projects which brought no new lands under cultivation but agreed with the limitation principle in the case of new land brought under irrigation and sold by the government. He was quoted as saying: "Farmers who have cultivated their land before a reclamation project is started should not be discriminated against by the limitation." Governor Warren added that he was in favor of small farms and said, "if there was a way to do it, there should be some limitation on the use made of these great holdings."

Following Warren's declaration, the *San Francisco Chronicle* argued editorially:

Governor Warren's lucid statement in Washington on the 160-acre limitation issue in the Central Valley project should help clear away a mass of misunderstanding and misrepresentation of the question.

People have been confused by the fact that the Central Valley project is being carried out under the Reclamation Act. Yet the Central Valley is not a reclamation project. Not one foot of Government land is involved in it. There is no land in it to be distributed to veterans or anyone else. All the land has been privately owned and farmed for generations. The Central Valley project merely supplements the existing water supply, and this additional water from storage in the mountains is to be sold to the farmers at prices intended eventually to reimburse the Government for the cost of the irrigation part of the undertaking.

A true reclamation project, like the Klamath, is a case where irrigation water is developed for arid Government lands, which then became available to settlers. In such a project the limitation by which water is supplied to no more than 160 acres in one ownership is a proper one. Its intent is to prevent gobbling up these lands in large single ownerships. We hear no objection to this limitation in connection with the Klamath or any other reclamation project where public lands are to be made available for distribution to settlers.

But the importation of this 160-acre limitation into the Central Valley project where it has no justification, is an anomaly. It would mean rank discrimination between the people who now own the land, saying to a farmer who owns 160 acres or less, "You can buy water" and to one who inherited 200 from his grandfather, "You can't buy." And this in a project for which the farmers have to pay on the installment plan!

This limitation has been eliminated from the similar Big Thompson Project in Colorado and Washoe and Humboldt rivers projects in Nevada. It should be eliminated from the Central Valley and every other irrigation project where the land is already in private ownership and use.

Another argument is that the limitation is evidence of the federal government's plan to take over state functions: in this case, that "some man 3,000 miles away in Washington is trying to tell us how to run the valley." This argument overlooks the fact that federal aid, under reclamation law, was eagerly sought by state officials; that the federal government came into the project at the request of the state; that some measure of federal control is inherent in the federal investment.

Another argument: 160 acres is too little land for a family

farm. (This overlooks the fact that in California a family farm has been stretched to 320 acres.) Obviously the type of land and the kind of crops it will yield determines the worth and return on 160 acres. An orange grove of 160 acres is usually a very large, very profitable farm but 160 acres of grazing land could be an unprofitable unit. The Fresno Chamber of Commerce (incidentally, opponents of limitation are most vocal in the Fresno area) has published a two-color brochure designed to attract settlers. This brochure lists the "economic units" for several crops grown in that section of the valley, "economic units" being the size necessary to support a home and family from a single crop. These are the "economic units" listed: for figs, 60 to 80 acres; peaches, 20 to 30 acres; oranges, 20 to 30 acres; cotton, 120 to 160 acres; alfalfa, 80 to 120 acres; grapes and raisins, 30 to 60 acres; grain and flax, 320 acres.

Still another argument against the limitation in the Central Valley points out that on three reclamation projects the limitation has been waived. With this as a precedent, it is claimed that there is no reason why the limitation should not be repealed as it applies to the Central Valley. The limitation was removed from the Colorado–Big Thompson project by Congress in 1938, on the plea that very few landholdings in the project exceeded 160 acres, that enforcement of the limitation in the project would be difficult and, in relation to its benefits, not worth the trouble. Two years later, the limitation was removed from two Nevada projects. In these latter cases, the plea was made that, because of the high altitude and the short growing season, 160 acres was not productive enough—that larger farms were necessary for family living. The special conditions which led to the removal of the limitation in these instances —few farms over 160 acres and short growing season—do not apply to the Central Valley where there are many holdings over 160 acres and where the growing season is as long as any place in the world.

There is a special condition in the Central Valley, however, which Senator Downey made the basis of his opposition to the limitation. In the San Joaquin Valley the major part of the irrigation water is raised by pumps from underground stores. Dropping water tables which made pumping too expensive or impossible, dramatically showed the need for the Central Valley Project in the 'thirties. A major function of the project is to replenish underground water, to raise the water table. Under the riparian principle, in California law, a landowner has the right to use the ground water under his land. The flow of ground water is difficult, perhaps impossible, to control. Downey contends that to apply the limitation under these conditions would permit the large landowner to continue to pump ground water which would be augmented by seepage from the project. In the end, he contends, this would penalize the small landowner for the benefit of the large landowner who could continue to pump project water from a replenished water table without having to pay for it. In short, his argument boils down to the contention that the 160-acre limitation could not be enforced; that large landowners would get the benefits of the project without being bound either by the limitation or by the necessity of helping to pay for the project. This comment on this special situation was made by Mary Montgomery and Marion Clawson in *History of Legislation and Policy Formation of the Central Valley Project:*

Confusion exists regarding the powers of irrigation districts, with respect to groundwater. An irrigation district can levy an assessment upon all land within it to pay costs incurred in obtaining additional water. These charges are levied upon all land, irrespective of size of landholding and irrespective of water use. The irrigation district cannot deny a landowner his right to pump his share of the groundwater available prior to the importation of additional water. It has been contended by some that, unless rights to groundwater are adjudicated, the district cannot restrict a landowner to previously available water but must permit his use of imported water as well. According to this view, the only way in which a district could conform to the present reclamation law would be to secure a court adjudication of groundwater rights; otherwise, it would be in the impossible position of having contracted with the Federal Government not to supply water to holdings in excess of 160 irrigable acres, while lacking power to refuse delivery of water to such lands. A contrasting viewpoint is that the district does have the authority to control the use of water obtained by it, and thus could restrict use of this water. A difficult situation thus exists in the Central Valley, which is not found where irrigation water is wholly surface.

The cure Downey suggests, repeal of the 160-acre limitation, is the same prescription offered by the large landowners themselves. It is fair to ask why the large landowners who would benefit so greatly under the limitation, according to Downey, are the ones who are agitating for repeal of that limitation. Certainly the smaller farmer, the man who farms fewer than 160 or 320 acres, can have no great interest in repeal of a limitation which does not affect him. It would seem evident that the large landholders who are so active in the fight for repeal have something else in mind. And that something can only be a desire to get project water for all their acres, without restriction, and thus take a proportionately larger share of the water to be delivered from a project built with interest-free government money.

Dr. Paul S. Taylor of the University of California, an advocate of acreage limitation, recently said:

The reclamation law is generous, and I find no one in the Central Valley who wants to repeal its generosity. The taxpayers of the Nation from Minnesota to Florida have shown repeatedly that they are willing to put their hands down in their pockets, to ask no interest on their investment, and to allow Western water users more than a generation in which to repay capital. Reclamation law extends the benefit of a strong Federal credit, allows the use of public power to raise project water to thirsty lands at rock bottom rates, and foregoes any direct return upon the public investment for irrigation. What the people of the East and South do want and expect in return is that we shall use these Federal resources to build the West in the traditional American way, distributing the benefits widely among citizens. But that much they expect . . . .

Just how generous to private landowners is this reclamation law? The Bureau of Reclamation has prepared figures. Let us look, for example, at Class I irrigation water to be supplied from Friant-Kern canal to the Southern San Joaquin Valley.

The water rate which it is proposed that users shall pay is $3.50 per acre foot. What would that rate have to be if the landowners were not given the special benefits and subsidies of the Reclamation law, but were charged for water on commercial terms? The answer is: *they would be obliged to pay $14 per acre foot*, or $10.50 more per acre foot than the proposed rate of $3.50 . . . . Without public assistance such as reclamation law provides, the lands of the Southern San Joaquin Valley would go without the water which they need . . . .

I want . . . . to present a couple of computations made from the Bureau figures, which show how much the public assistance extended through reclamation law means to landowners in the Southern San Joaquin Valley. For convenience, I round to an even $10, the differential between the $3.50 proposed rate and the $14 rate which would be necessary if . . . . special benefits and subsidies were removed.

First example: What this means to the holder of 160 acres.

(*A*) If he needs only supplementary water in order to eke out what he already has, say he needs one acre foot per annum, then the measure of this public assistance to him is $10 × 160 or $1,600 per annum. Not $1,600 once, but $1,600 per annum beyond what he is asked to pay.

(*B*) If he uses a full water supply from the project, say 2½ acre-feet per annum, then the measure of these benefits, beyond what he is asked to pay for them, is $25 × 160 or $4,000 per annum.

(*C*) If 320 acres is allowed for man and wife, as present interpretation permits, then these figures must be doubled, to $3,200 if supplementary water only is taken, and to $8,000 per annum if a full supply is used.

Some land holders are not satisfied with this amount of assistance, ranging in value from $1,600 to $8,000 per annum, i.e., year after year. They want us to repeal the limitation that holds them down to such a minimum, which to another citizen might look like the pot of gold at the end of the rainbow.

If repeal should win, the only limitation to the amount of the assistance that landowners can get, beyond what they pay for, will be the amount of land which they hold and to which they can persuade Congress to bring water. Let us see what that would mean to some people. In Tulare and Kern counties and the Tulare Lake Basin, some twenty landowners own about 360,000 acres of irrigable land. Assuming supplemental water only, and assuming they take water for their entire acreage, to repeal the acreage limitation would secure to these landowners public assistance valued at $3,600,000 per annum. Assuming full water supply, the value of the assistance which repeal would confer upon them would be $8,000,000 per annum; $8,000,000 year after year.

The demand for repeal is, in effect, a demand for a legal right to receive assistance on this scale from the public . . . .

In almost every discussion of the 160-acre limitation someone brings up the statement that such a limitation is un-American; that is, un-American to limit the amount of land a man or a family can possess; that to limit the land is to place a ceiling on industry and ingenuity. This argument overlooks several facts, notably that no limit is placed on the number of acres a man may own. The limitation is on the amount of water he can get from a public project. It overlooks the fact that the limitation is on single ownerships; it is not a limitation on operation. It is possible under the law for an operator to lease the entire floor of the San Joaquin Valley and work it as a single ranch and still get project water through the ownerships he leases.

More clearly than at any other point does the philosophy of the Bureau of Reclamation—the philosophy handed down by Congress—emerge in a discussion of the acreage limitation. The Bureau believes in the principle of the family-sized, family-operated farm. "The object of the Reclamation Act is not so much to irrigate the land as it is to make homes." The theory of the family-sized, family-operated farm naturally is opposed to and by bigness. And California agriculture is big. One rancher of the west side of the San Joaquin Valley told a Congressional committee: "I, together with my wife and four children, operate a family-sized farm of 42,000 acres." The land of the Central Valley is free of rocks; it is level; much of it is treeless. It is fertile. It is ideally suited for mechanized farming, for large-scale operation. "In the East and South, farming may be a way of life," one farmer said, "but in California it is a business and it is run like a business."

The Bureau of Reclamation and advocates of acreage limitation are fond of referring to a study comparing two California towns: Arvin, which lies in Kern County, the center, such as it is, of an area devoted to large-scale farming, and Dinuba, in Tulare County, the center of a small-scale farming area.

In the comparison made by Walter R. Goldschmidt of the Bureau of Agricultural Economics, Dinuba comes off far the better. Goldschmidt found, for instance, that Dinuba proportionately had three times as many independent farmers as Arvin; twice as many business and professional men. Dinuba's retail stores did 61 percent more business than Arvin's. Arvin has almost twice as many farm laborers as Dinuba. Dinuba had streets, sidewalks, sewers, parks, churches—all accessories which are generally considered as assets. Arvin, on the other hand, while it had a sewer, seemed to have little else to recommend it. Its people felt they were not a permanent part of the community and did not build for permanence. The two communities, however, were comparable in size and the value of the agricultural products each produced was roughly the same. Goldschmidt concluded: "Size of farming operations is the basic cause of the impoverished social conditions in Arvin as contrasted to Dinuba."

Bigness has its advocates, too. Professor B. H. Crocheron, director of the University of California's Agricultural Extension Service, was quoted in the *Los Angeles Times* as fearing "that the real danger in California is not that farms will be too large, but that they will be too small for economical operation."

"Large ranches usually produce a better product and greater supply than the same acreage in smaller holdings," said an irrigation district adviser. "Large operators support the stores and professions of the larger towns and cities which may or may not be less useful to society than the same support to local towns. There is nothing in the picture of small farms that offers any promise of social security, unemployment insurance, decent housing and wages to the agricultural worker."

Although California is the home of the large, corporate ranch, the overwhelming number of the holdings are small. A 1940 study by the Bureau of Agricultural Economics, found that in the valley-floor areas of Madera, Tulare, and Kern counties, 9,814 farmers owned fewer than 80 acres and 11,434 owned 160 acres or fewer—this out of a total of 12,941 owners. There were 12,305 farmers who owned farms of fewer than 320 acres. These 12,305 owners own 47 percent of the irrigable land of these counties. On the other hand, the remaining 636 owners hold 53 percent of the irrigable land. The study shows that the 18 owners holding ranches larger than 5,120 acres own as much irrigable land as the 11,434 owners farming units of 160 acres or fewer—21 percent.

A more recent study made by the Bureau of Reclamation surveyed 774,156 acres in the Central Valley Project area. It revealed that 33.1 percent of this acreage was excess, i.e., over 160 acres per unit. This excess acreage, 33.1 percent, was held by 469 owners, 4.9 percent of all ownerships.

Relatively few landowners are affected by the acreage limitation. In fact, those farming less than 160 or 320 acres would be injured by repeal of the limitation. Without the limitation, there is little chance for them to enlarge their holdings through breakup of the large ranches.

VIII. The Battle of the Contract

NOTHING much was said about the 160-acre limitation in California until 1944. Then, somehow, word got to the farmers about it. In most cases, the word was distorted. Regardless of distortion, however, for many ranchers of the San Joaquin Valley it was the first they had heard of the reclamation law and its limitation on the amount of water any one farmer could receive. The reaction was one of puzzlement, hurt, and then anger. Nobody, especially nobody back in Washington, it was frequently said, is going to tell me how to run my ranch. The 1944 farmer was a different man than he had been back in 1935 when the Central Valley Project first was taken over as a federal undertaking. Then he had been a hat-in-hand boy, eager to let Washington tell him how to run his farm, eager for the Agricultural Adjustment Act checks the man in Washington sent out. But in 1944, he was in the middle of a war boom. He was prosperous. And when he heard the word that the size of his farm would be regulated by someone in Washington, he was mad. He did not have to inquire whether the facts were correct. He was mad. Many San Joaquin Valley ranchers have stayed mad.

What was the reason for the long silence about the limitation provision of reclamation law? Why the mystery? Mary Montgomery and Marion Clawson, writing of the 1935–43 period which they call "the period of drift," when little was said about the acreage limitation, suggest that the various groups interested in the project were united on the necessity for continuing appropriations and that controversial issues were not brought up for fear they might have split the supporting groups.

The questions of acreage limitation, repayment and related problems were not actively raised during this period perhaps because they might

91

have divided the project support. To the extent that landowners and irrigation groups could get the Federal Government committed to the project by the expenditure of large sums of money prior to the completion of repayment contracts, the stronger was their position in bargaining with the government. Once the canals were completed, the Bureau of Reclamation would be in a poor position to deny their use to landowners because contracts were not signed, even though they had legal authority to deny them water. This strategy may not have been in the minds of many supporters of the Central Valley project but certainly there is nothing in the record to indicate that it was not. [They admit, however:] Of course, if the Bureau of Reclamation had submitted repayment contracts for signature in the years immediately following 1935, this situation would not have arisen.

The Bureau of Reclamation certainly can be criticized for its long silence as to the meaning of reclamation law. Worse than that, irrigationists and ranchers say, the "Bureau boys" went into the Valley and, in effect, told ranchers: "Don't worry about the reclamation laws. Let's get the dams and the canals built. Then we can argue about the law."

This statement was made to a Congressional subcommittee: "I personally discussed this matter with Walker Young, at the time supervising engineer of the Central Valley Project . . . . I said, 'How about the provisions of the 160-acre limitation, and the rest of them, that go on?' 'Well,' they said, 'the project won't work with those limitations on, and don't worry about it, they will have to come out . . . .' "

The Bureau loudly denies that its men made such statements but the denial somehow is less than robust. "There is no public record of any instance where the officials of the Bureau of Reclamation declared that reclamation laws would not apply to the Central Valley Project," the Bureau says. "To the contrary, the contracts entered into between the Bureau and the State for cooperative investigations clearly state that the agreement was made pursuant to reclamation laws. We have no authoritative information of any informal promises made by any Bureau official that reclamation laws would not apply."

It is certain that a majority of the ranchers knew nothing about the reclamation law. Those irrigation district officers and state officials who did know about it apparently hoped that the limitation would be ignored or repealed. They apparently did not foresee that the Bureau would attempt to enforce the law.

The whole matter of the federal government's role in the Central Valley Project was confused and confusing to the uninformed public. It is hard to go back into people's minds, but it is easy to recall that the great majority of Californians had no real idea that the federal government had taken over the project. When the state voted on the Central Valley Project referendum in 1933, the strongest argument for a favorable vote was that federal assistance would make the project possible. The people voted for a state project, a project which was to be built with federal financial assistance. For years no one told them that the Central Valley Project had become something quite different. No wonder they were shocked. Even a man so well informed on water affairs as State Senator Bradford S. Crittenden was confused. "The original law which the people of the State of California voted for this great project did not have any such limitation or thought in it . . . . I am saying that we should follow the law, and no more, under which we acted when we put through the Central Valley Water Project, and that had the farthest from its conception any limitation on the ownership of property," he said in arguing for repeal of the limitation in 1944. When Commissioner Page declared at Friant Dam in November of 1939: "I want to emphasize that the Central Valley Project now stands as a 100 percent federal reclamation undertaking," it is probable that few of his listeners knew what he was talking about, although he enlarged his theme as follows:

In the light of its multiple purposes, several of which are of major national interest, it is entirely logical that the project should be and remain such . . . . Under the existing plan, the Bureau of Reclamation . . . . is to build the Central Valley project and to operate its major features. No new administrative machinery is required to complete and operate these features.

Now, although the general run of Californians did not understand what had happened, no excuse can be offered for state officials. They knew what was going on. So did members of the state Legislature. So did members of the California Congressional delegations during the years when appropriations were sought. Time and time again, California Congressmen referred to the project as "reimbursable under reclamation law" and they knew what the phrase meant. They knew that it mean compliance with the acreage limitation. Vocal in Washington, they were strangely silent when they were with the folks at home.

Nevertheless, when it became generally known that reclamation law limited the amount of water which would be delivered to a single owner of land, the opposition went to work. In 1944, the so-called Elliott amendment which would have repealed the 160-acre limitation was attached as a rider to the Rivers and Harbors Bill of 1944. The amendment was passed by the House, rejected by the Senate, put back into the bill in conference, finally rejected by the Senate, and the entire bill died when no further conference was held. Senator Downey in arguing before the Senate for passage of the Elliott amendment declared:

. . . . out of the 500 most intelligent and experienced people who know about this matter, there is not one person who does not know that the limitation can not be enforced. Every representative from the State of California in the House of Representatives who comes from the area including the Central Valley project is firm in the opinion that the limitation can not be enforced. Our Legislature by almost unanimous vote of both the Senate and the Assembly resolved in favor of the Elliott amendment.

I should like to state briefly . . . . why the 160-acre limitation can not be enforced.

In the first place, Mr. President, there are 2,000,000 acres of land in this project. It is the most complicated, most variegated project in the whole world. Four hundred thousand acres of those two million lie in the delta of the Sacramento and the San Joaquin Rivers, and are subject to inundation almost every month of the year except where islands have been created by building dikes right out into the delta. Those islands generally consist of 1,000 or 1,500 acres. They are below sea level. They are mosquito-infested. They are so hot that no one will live there. How any Senator can be so unrealistic as to believe that the area should be cut up into small farms when no one could or would live there is beyond my comprehension. Not only that, Mr. President, but it would be utterly impossible to farm that under those conditions unless we were to go into collective farming . . . .

Let me now in a few words state why the acreage limitation can not be applied to underground waters. It is because if you allow a man with 160 acres to have the water you can not prevent the owner adjacent thereto from using it on a parcel of 640 acres. Gentlemen might not like that; they might desire to break up and disturb all these farms of over 160 acres developed over a hundred years, and apparently that is what they want to do; but they simply can not do it by this acreage limitation, because they can not repeal the law of hydraulics.

But I speak very firmly when I say to the Senate that after long investigation and consideration, after 20 years of living with the Central Valley project, I can assure the Senate that ultimately we can do nothing if we are ever going to utilize this water, except pass the Elliott amendment.

As an indication of how Senators from nonarid states felt about the Elliott amendment, here is a brief word from Senator Robert M. LaFollette of Wisconsin in answer to Downey:

Mr. President, there are many aspects of the situation in California which the Senator from California has not discussed, but if we are to consider it in conjunction with a conference report, which can not be amended and must be adopted or rejected in its entirety, I want the Senate and the country to know some of the other aspects of this problem, and some of the far-reaching consequences which I think would flow from the adoption of the Elliott rider . . . . because, Mr. President, the people in the Central Valley Project and those who are interested in it can not secure this blanket meat-ax exemption from the traditional policy of reclamation . . . . without establishing a precedent which will justify those who see advantage in obtaining money from the Treasury of the United States for the development of land not now useful, and for their own enrichment, without carrying out any national policy with regard to the land of the United States.

So much for most of the pros and cons. Californians, who may have been misled, still find themselves in a delicate moral position in regard to reclamation law. Recall that in 1933, California voted for the Central Valley Project with the proviso that federal financing was necessary. The project was designed as and called a "rescue project." It was designed to deliver supplemental water to parched acres of the San Joaquin Valley—acres which may go out of production without the supplemental water. Greatly in need of rescue, the state called loudly for help. Help was forthcoming from the federal government, and the state, happy to be rescued, accepted the terms of the rescuer: in this case, accepted federal financial aid with the clearly stated and many-times-repeated condition that the Central Valley Project was to be a reclamation project. The leaders knew what the terms meant. They accepted them eagerly. Now, more than ten years after the thrilling rescue, the once-helpless state wants to go back on its agreement. Whether the agreement should ever have been made is beside the point except as a measure of the state's leaders.

In any event, the Bureau of Reclamation is charged with enforcing reclamation law. The Central Valley Project is more than half finished. Work is under way on the great canals. Its goods are on the shelf. Now the Bureau must go out and do a job it should have done beginning in 1935: now it must get irrigation districts to sign contracts for delivery of project water—and these contracts must comply with reclamation law; they must include provisions for the enforcement of the 160-acre limitation. The Bureau uses the depression as the excuse for its failure to negotiate repayment contracts. During the depression, it says, the main idea was to put men to work regardless of whether contracts were signed or not. Which is not a very good excuse. So far the contract job has been a difficult one. The Bureau, in 1947, had signed only one long-term contract. Three additional contracts were near the signing stage; but only one was actually signed and delivered. That is the contract between the Bureau and the Southern San Joaquin Municipal Utility District. It is a model contract; future contracts will be similar. It contains a provision for enforcement of the 160-acre limitation. The sections of the contract relating to excess lands are quoted:

25. No water shall be delivered to any excess lands as defined in Article 27 hereof unless the owners thereof shall have executed valid recordable contracts in form satisfactory to the Secretary, agreeing to the

provisions of this contract between the United States and the District; agreeing to the appraisal provided for in Article 26 hereof and that such appraisal shall be made on the basis of actual bona fide value of such lands at the date of the appraisal without reference to the construction of the project, all as hereinafter provided; and agreeing to the sale of such lands under terms and conditions satisfactory to the Secretary and at prices not to exceed those fixed by the Secretary, as hereinafter provided. No sale of any such lands shall carry the right to receive water made available hereunder unless and until the purchase price involved in such sale is approved by the Secretary and upon proof of fraudulent representation as to the true consideration involved in such sales the Secretary may instruct the District by written notice to refuse to deliver any water subject to this contract to the land involved in such fraudulent sales and the District thereafter shall not deliver said water to such lands.

Valuation and Sale of Excess Lands

26. (a) The value of the irrigable lands within the district, held in private ownership of large landowners as defined in the next succeeding article hereof, for the purposes of this contract, shall be determined, subject to the approval thereof by the Secretary, by three appraisers. One of said appraisers shall be designated by the Secretary and one shall be designated by the District and the two appraisers so appointed shall name the third. If the appraisers so designated by the Secretary and the District are unable to agree upon the appointment of the third, they shall so advise the Secretary and the District and the designation of the third appraiser shall then be made by the Secretary.

(b) The following principles shall govern the appraisal:

(i) No value shall be given such lands on account of the existing or prospective possibility of securing water from the project.

(ii) The value of improvements on the land at the time of said appraisal shall be included therein but shall also be set forth separately in such appraisal.

(c) The cost of the appraisal shall be paid by the United States.

(d) Any improvements made or placed on the appraised land after the appraisal hereinabove provided for prior to sale of the land by a large landowner may be appraised in like manner, and the same shall be subject to approval by the Secretary or his authorized representative.

(e) Future sales of irrigable lands of large landowners under the project shall not carry the right to receive water made available hereunder for such land and the District agrees to refuse to deliver water to land so sold until, in addition to compliance with the other provisions hereof:

(i) A verified statement showing the sale price upon any such sale shall have been filed with the District; and

(ii) There shall have been complied with by the landowner such reasonable rules and regulations as may now or hereafter be promulgated by the Secretary for the better administration and enforcement of the Reclamation Law and of the provisions hereof, which may include, among others, the requirement that prior to the delivery of water of any District lands acquired from a large land owner, the owner thereof shall furnish the District with an affidavit describing in detail the affiant's purchase of such lands made prior thereto.

(*f*) The District agrees, by all reasonable means, including the quarterly examination of county records or procurement of necessary title abstract service and otherwise, to ascertain the occurrence and conditions of all sales of irrigable land of large landowners in the District and to inform the Secretary or his authorized representative in charge of the project concerning the same . . . .

Excess Lands

27. (*a*) As used herein the term "excess land" means that part of the irrigable land within the District in excess of 160 acres held in the beneficial ownership of any single person; or in excess of 320 acres held in the beneficial ownership of husband and wife jointly, as tenants in common or by the entirety, or as community property; the term "large landowner" means an owner of excess lands and the term "non-excess land" means all irrigable land under the project which is not excess land as defined herein.

(*b*) Each large landowner as a further condition precedent to the right to receive water for any of his excess lands shall:

(i) Before the initial delivery date or before the expiration of six months from the announcement thereof, whichever occurs first, execute a valid recordable contract in form satisfactory to the Secretary, agreeing to the provisions herein contained and agreeing to dispose of his excess lands in accordance therewith to persons who can take title thereto as non-excess land as herein provided and at a price not to exceed the approved, appraised value of such excess lands and within a period of ten years after the date of the execution of said recordable contract and agreeing further that if said land is not so disposed of within said period of ten years the Secretary shall have the power to dispose of said land subject to the same conditions on behalf of such large landowner subject to conditions all as herein provided, and the District agrees that it will refuse to deliver water to any large landowner other than for his non-excess lands until such owner meets the conditions precedent herein stated.

(ii) Within thirty days after the date of notice from the United States requesting such large landowner to designate his irrigable lands under the project which he desires to designate as non-excess lands, file in the office of the District, in duplicate, one copy thereof to be furnished by the District to the Bureau of Reclamation, his written designation and description of lands so selected to be non-excess lands and upon failure to do so the District shall make such designation and mail a notice thereof to such large landowner, and in the event the District fails to act within such period of time as the contracting officer considers reasonable, such designation will be made by the contracting officer who will mail a notice thereof to the District and the large landowner. The large landowner shall become bound by any such action on the part of the District or the contracting officer and the District will deliver water only to the land so designated to be non-excess land.

This contract has been bitterly attacked. At the 1945 meeting of the executive committee of the Irrigation Districts Association of California, a resolution was passed: "Resolved, that it is the recommendation of the executive committee that no contracts be entered into between any district and the Bureau of Reclamation until the precise language of such contracts has been analyzed and found by the Irrigation Districts Association to be legally practicable and to protect the interests of the landowners and the irrigation districts of California."

On the other hand, the Southern San Joaquin Municipal Utility District seems reasonably content with the model contract. Its representative told the California Water Conference:

This is one organization . . . . which isn't too much worried over controversial issues . . . . We know that any water we get we are pumping

150 to 300 feet, and some of our farmers are going to be ruined inside of a very short time unless we get water in the northern part of Kern County . . . . We in the northern part of the county need water and need it badly. We are given certain laws under which we are supposed to operate. One is the Reclamation Law. From an engineering point of view, we think we could improve on that. But we haven't sat down and said, "We won't play with you." But we have gotten busy the last two years, the directors of our district have worked diligently and come up with the best answer they could get for their district. That answer was the signing of the first, and so far the only, long-term contract signed by the Bureau of Reclamation for project water in the State of California.

We have many other problems that other districts have. We have a 160-acre limitation, and we have one director that has 640 acres. He doesn't particularly like the law; he didn't make it, but he has to work under it. We were told we couldn't sign a contract; we did it. Maybe we didn't have any business to sign it, but we hired an attorney and the attorney said to sign it, and there it is . . . . You can get what you want in a lawyer: if you want a "can" lawyer or a "can't" lawyer—you can get either one. I think we have a "can" lawyer. Anyhow we signed the contract and that is not the only contract we are going to sign. Now we are going to ask for a contract for a distribution system. We are going to get a closed conduit system in our district for the entire area, designed, built by the Bureau of Reclamation, and paid for over a term of 40 years, without interest. That beats bonding your district all to pieces. I have worked for irrigation districts that have gone broke—where they bonded the district and broke the district. During hard times 75 percent or more of the districts in California went broke because they were bonded. I have been through all that. We don't propose to do it again . . . .

We also hope to have a contract for power. I am not a power man or power engineer—I just hope we will get power at considerably less than we are paying at present . . . .

After conferences with California irrigationists and officials of the Bureau of Reclamation, Senator Downey announced that he would introduce a resolution in the Senate asking that the model contract be investigated. He said the contract was "designed to place the Federal Government in perpetual ownership and control of all water from the Central Valley project." Senator Downey said the contract, "far from dealing with the excess lands problem in a practical way, would permit the large landowners to continue pumping from underground sources . . . . while their supply would be augmented by seepage from the smaller landowners who buy surface water under the contract." He said it is highly doubtful under federal and California laws that an irrigation district could compel the large landowner to contribute anything toward the district's contract for water service and that as a result "a crushing obligation might be imposed on the small farmers."

"I have told the irrigation districts' representatives," he said, "that I think it would be ill-advised for any district to enter into a contract with the Bureau of Reclamation on the terms so far offered . . . ."

So it is that the 160-acre limitation and the contract to deliver water under its terms are both under fire. And the Bureau of Reclamation is under fire, too, for attempting to enforce the limitation, through attempting to get signatures on the model contract. So far, as Paul Taylor observed, no one has tried to repeal the generosity of the Reclamation Act; what they want to get rid of are the Reclamation Act's restrictions which gall them so. They, in short, are willing to accept interest-free money, flood-control and navigation subsidies, power revenues, and the significant engineering ability of the Bureau of Reclamation while trying to escape the terms of a bargain made by their state and local leaders some ten years ago.

Michael Straus, then Assistant Secretary of the Interior, gave a significant summation of Reclamation aims and progress in an address before the National Reclamation Association in Denver in 1945. In part:

> For those who are willing to look, it is not hard to find the perspective on our program. It is reflected clearly in the Reclamation Laws of this Nation . . . . Several recent chapters have been written. All of them to date have the objective of cheap water. Though they appear to touch on many items, including mining, Indians, fishermen, stockmen, acreage restriction, power generation, recreation, monopoly and a myriad of other interests, those laws uniformly seek out, as an end objective, low-cost water for the West . . . .

> Right at the start, when the West outgrew the early days of private and

simple local water projects, such as a summertime turning of a creek onto adjoining lowland, and irrigation assumed a stature that caused your fathers to demand that it be made a Federal function, the Senators of that day, such as Newlands of Nevada, Dubois of Idaho and Smoot of Utah, wrote down the principle that the way to get cheap water was to pay for it. Now to a lot of people of that day, this seemed a paradoxical principle and not very smart. Why, those who were shortsighted asked, would it not be better, if you wanted cheap water, to get free water from the Federal Government. But the men of vision from the West explained patiently that the Federal Congress was a large body of men and that, even if the plump delegations of the East were persuaded by the sparse delegations from the West to vote free water once out of national funds, those from the humid East could not be expected to vote again and again for free money for water for the arid West, and so Federal Reclamation would die before it really started. Their wisdom prevailed and the principle was laid down in the basic and original law that we would get low-cost water at a price that the farmer could afford to pay, but the Federal funds advanced must be repaid—without interest. That principle has been protected and the Nation—all of the Nation, including the humid East as well as the arid West—has been voting Federal funds for reclamation for nearly half a century. We all accept that principle now even if some doubted it when the first chapter of the book was written. Although all Federal reclamation projects have not met all obligations, how well we have accepted it and how well you have kept the trust is shown by the Federal reclamation repayment record of 97.3 percent of all construction charges due to date. And how well this principle has served the cause of low-cost water is shown by the fact that to date annual Federal investments in western reclamation have increased 400-fold from a quarter of a million dollars a year 42 years ago to upward of $100,000,000 today. I think it is the best investment Uncle Sam is making.

But there is another basic corollary in the original law which blazed the way to low-cost water that was written at the same time as the repayment principle with the same wisdom and for the same broad purpose of winning Federal financial support from the whole Congress for low-cost water. That is the restriction on the acreage in individual ownerships to which Federal reclamation may deliver water. It is designed to spread the benefits of Federal irrigation to the greatest numbers. Some of you have recently lost perspective on that item. I could talk all day on the community, the county, the state and national, the social, human and economic benefits of the family-sized farm principle which is a companion piece to the repayment principle, but that is not necessary. Leaders of your own choice who wrote the family-sized farm principle into the law considered those items, but they also knew that through that principle lay the only route to low-cost water. The Congress of the Nation, as a whole, would vote and has voted reclamation money to the West because the Congress, as a whole, had assurance, written into the law, that that money would go to provide individuals—including settlers from the East—with the low-cost water that would make it possible for them to establish, with an American standard of living, family-sized farms in arid areas. Your reclamation giants of yesteryear asked the Congress to provide no-interest national funds for family-sized farms and not for closed corporation farm enterprises because they knew that Congress would not grant that kind of money. That is just as true today as it was 42 years ago. I counsel you to support your reclamation giants of today, such as Senators Hatch, Hayden, O'Mahoney and others, in the same position that Newlands took 43 years ago. Do not ask them to justify funds except for the assured benefit of family-sized farms. And, also, don't expect your Department of Interior officials, who must lead in justifying reclamation appropriations, to go before Congressmen from the Bronx, Boston or Cleveland and win from those communities appropriations for western reclamation devoid of any promise that the irrigated areas will be devoted to family-sized farms where a settler or veterans from an Eastern city can establish himself. We may think we are good, but we know we are not that good. Let no local controversy cloud your vision. Abandonment of the family-sized farm principle, which is implicit on repeal of all acreage limitation, is not the path to low-cost water—it is the road to hamstringing Federal irrigation; it is the highway to high-cost water . . . .

IX. Power Politics

RECENTLY a Bureau of Reclamation official said: "The agitation over the 160-acre limitation is a red herring dragged across the floor of the Valley. If it were not for competition between public power and private power no one would be worrying about it." His contention was that the interests fighting for repeal of the limitation are the same interests fighting to see that hydroelectric power generated at the project powerhouses is controlled and marketed not by the Bureau of Reclamation but by the Pacific Gas & Electric Co.

The fight over the Central Valley power is fairly simple. It is a continuation of the fight between public ownership of utilities and private ownership. When you say public ownership in northern California you mean a few small communities which own their own electrical distributing systems—and the considerably larger and tougher Bureau of Reclamation. When you say private ownership, you mean the Pacific Gas & Electric Co., a giant utility formed from 449 water and power companies which has a monopoly on northern California territory 200 miles wide and 500 miles long. So far in the battle between the Bureau and the P. G. & E., the latter has a slight edge.

The Bureau, according to the Central Valley plan, already has built a powerhouse at Shasta Dam and a powerhouse at Keswick Dam. It proposes to build a powerhouse—a steam plant to generate electricity—at or near Tracy. It further proposes to build transmission lines to connect the hydroelectric plants at Shasta and Keswick with the Tracy steam plant and the project's pumping stations. It proposes to construct lighter-voltage lines down the middle of the Sacramento Valley so that customers for surplus power can tap the lines, and it envisions other lower-capacity lines out of Tracy to serve the Contra Costa Canal pumping stations and customers in the San Francisco Bay area.

To all of these works—with the exception of the Keswick and Shasta powerhouses—the Pacific Gas & Electric Co. is opposed. The P. G. & E. has been successful in convincing Congress that funds for major transmission lines and for the steam plant are unnecessary, although the Bureau has won some funds.

War stopped construction of the water-giving canals of the project when only the Madera and Contra Costa canals were near completion. Before the war interfered, however, two generators had been installed in Shasta powerhouse and since June 26, 1944, these generators have been whirling out energy. Thus, power—by statute, an incidental and by-product of the project—became the first major product.

When Shasta's first two generators started, the Bureau was in an unhappy spot. It had power but no way to move it. Congress, under the adroit prodding of the P. G. & E., had refused money for construction of the necessary transmission lines. Then, as a wartime measure, Congress ordered Secretary of the Interior Ickes to sign a contract selling the entire Shasta output to the P. G. & E. This contract will remain in effect not beyond December 31, 1949.

The Pacific Gas & Electric Co. devoutly hopes that this temporary contract will be the precedent for a permanent contract which will guarantee that Shasta and Keswick power will continue to flow through company transmission lines to company customers. It will continue its fight against the Bureau's requests for funds for transmission lines and the steam plant. For without transmission lines and a steam plant to "firm" the fluctuating output of hydropower, the Bureau will be unable to sell its power to anyone but the P. G. & E. This already has happened. The Bureau has signed a contract to wholesale power to the city of Roseville for its municipal system. So far, lacking transmission lines, it has been unable to furnish the power. The P. G. & E. has refused to let the Bureau use its transmission lines to fulfill the Roseville contract. Other cities which operate municipal distribution systems have refused to sign

Bureau contracts on the ground that the Bureau cannot deliver. Publication of the Bureau's interim rate schedule for power, however, forced the P. G. & E. to reduce its wholesale rates to these municipalities.

In opposing transmission lines and a steam plant for the Central Valley Project, the P. G. & E. proposes that it buy all the power generated at Shasta and Keswick at the powerhouses. This power would be co-ordinated with the company's own sources of supply. It proposes that power needed for project pumping be supplied by the company on an exchange basis. Thus, it argues, the government will save the cost of "unnecessary" transmission lines and the steam plant, and would still have power plus a greater revenue than would be possible if the transmission lines and steam plant were constructed.

The rub is this: the Bureau is not in the power business to make big money. It is bound by law to sell power at a rate which will pay off the costs of power installations, plus 3 percent interest. Above that amount, any money it collects for power goes to pay off the irrigation features of the project. The Bureau is bound by law to "transmit and dispose of . . . . power and energy in such a manner as to encourage the most widespread use at the lowest possible rates to consumers consistent with sound business principles." It does not believe that sale of its electrical output to the P. G. & E. in any way complies with this directive. But its opponents argue that the Bureau should sell its power at the highest possible price (i.e., to the P. G. & E.) so that increased power revenues would lighten the load of the irrigator. They contend that the project is, first and foremost, a water project, a project to provide irrigation water and to improve navigation and control floods. Only incidentally, they declare, is it a power project. They point to the law.

In 1937, in the Rivers and Harbors Act, the Central Valley Project was reauthorized. In the language of Congress, provision was made for "the generation and sale of electric energy as a means of financially aiding and assisting such undertakings" (construction of dams, canals, and reservoirs), and further: "That said dams and reservoirs shall be used first, for river regulation, improvement of navigation and flood control; second, for irrigation and domestic uses; and, third, for power."

In 1940, the project once again was reauthorized and Congress restated the purposes and aims of the reclamation work:

Provided further, That the entire Central Valley project, California, heretofore authorized and established . . . . is hereby reauthorized and declared to be for the purposes of improving navigation, regulating the flow of the San Joaquin River and the Sacramento River, controlling floods, providing for the storage and for the delivery of the stored waters thereof, for construction, under the provisions of the Federal reclamation laws, of such distribution systems as the Secretary of the Interior deems necessary in connection with lands for which said stored waters are to be delivered, for the reclamation of arid and semi-arid lands and the lands of Indian reservations, and other beneficial uses, and for the generation and sale of electrical energy as a means of financially aiding and assisting such undertakings, and in order to permit full utilization of the works constructed to accomplish the aforesaid purposes.

Actually, the Congressional authorizations contain some gobble-dook language. In the words of Congress, flood control and navigation are given precedence over irrigation: "that said dams and reservoirs shall be used, first, for river regulation, improvement of navigation and flood control; second, for irrigation and domestic uses; and third, for power." But no one would contend that the project is primarily a flood control and navigation work. Navigation and flood control are, at best, secondary considerations. The project, of course, is a multiple-purpose program. It was designed as a water-exchange which would provide irrigation water for the San Joaquin Valley. Such an exchange is impossible without the power generated at Shasta and Keswick. Incidentally, it will help to control floods and may even improve navigation on the Sacramento River, a minor consideration. Incidentally, also, it will provide other benefits: repulsion of salt water in the Delta, recreational areas, and may even promote fish and wild life although there is dispute about that. One water-wise engineer summed it up: "Navigation and flood control have to be put in there. That is like naming a baby after the rich uncle. When navigation and flood control are mentioned it means that the Federal Government is going to put up some money which it doesn't expect to get back."

The project is large and complex. It cannot function as an irrigation system without the power it generates. It is an integrated plan whereby water stored in Shasta reservoir is released to flow down the Sacramento River for transfer to the San Joaquin Valley. To transfer the water to the San Joaquin it is necessary to pump it vertically over 200 feet. The power for this great lift will come from the Shasta and Keswick power plants. Without that power the project is unworkable. In other words: no power—no water.

The Pacific Gas & Electric Co. has a monopoly in northern California. Its natural gas does the cooking and heating and its electricity does the lighting, some of the cooking and heating in almost every northern California home. The energy generated in its 58 mountain hydro plants and its 15 steam plants runs the factory wheels of the territory. It has long been against the Central Valley Project. The first scuffle came in 1922 when the P. G. & E. and other utilities went to bat against the Water and Power Act which authorized the important features of the Marshall Plan—including the basic features of the Central Valley water exchange and the generation of electrical power. The P. G. & E. and other utilities spent $501,000 to defeat the measure and considered the money well spent. The money was not spent directly by the utilities. Rather it was spent by a number of dummy campaign organizations which pulled the chestnuts out of the fire, notably "The Greater California League."

Again in 1924 and 1926, the utilities were able to defeat proposals to establish the Water and Power Act. When the Central Valley Project Act was passed by the 1933 Legislature, it was the P. G. & E. which forced it to a referendum vote. It should be noted that the P. G. & E. did not oppose the Central Valley Project bill until the Legislature amended the original draft to incorporate plans to construct transmission lines. Up to then the company correctly assumed that any power generated by the state project would have to be sold for resale, there being no other outlet for power in northern California. The company's referendum against the Central Valley Project Act failed, however, and the state was committed to a project including power plants and transmission lines. The state was further committed to the preferential sale of its surplus power "to State agencies or other organizations not organized or doing business for profit but primarily for the purpose of supplying water or electric energy to their own citizens or members." The Act also included a recapture clause whereby the state could cancel contracts with private agencies for water or electricity whenever a state or nonprofit agency applied for it. That would have seemed to have cut out the P. G. & E. No wonder the company fought the Act and, thus, the Central Valley Project as a whole.

The shift from state to federal control of the project following the 1933 special election made no change in the procedure for disposing of project power. Indeed, the state's policy had been written into the Central Valley Project Act to meet federal requirements to insure federal aid for the project. Reclamation Law in 1906 provided that public bodies should have preference in the purchase of power generated on reclamation projects and this principle has been restated in many acts of Congress since then. The Reclamation Project Act of 1939 says that in sales of electric power or leases of power privileges "preference shall be given to municipalities and other public corporations and agencies; and also to cooperative and other nonprofit organizations financed in whole or part by the Rural Electrification Administration."

In general, the Bureau of Reclamation took over the state plan for the Central Valley Project but many changes were made. The Bureau enlarged on the state design. At the end of 1947, the Bureau had constructed powerhouses at Shasta Dam and Keswick but these installations were far from complete. Ultimately, Shasta powerhouse will have five generators with a rated capacity of 375,000 kilowatts. Keswick's plant will have three generators with a capacity of 25,000 kilowatts each. Total capacity of the two plants will be 450,000 kilowatts. The Bureau also has constructed a 97-mile transmission line from Shasta to Oroville where the line ties into the P. G. & E. system. Funds have been authorized for an Oroville-Sacramento extension of this transmission line and $200,000 has been appropriated for engineering studies for the steam plant.

Shasta, Keswick, and the steam plant will produce approximately 2,150,000 kilowatt-hours of firm power and 234,000,000 kilowatt-hours of secondary energy in an average water year. Of this tremendous block of power, the Bureau estimates approximately one-third will be used for project pumping—on the Contra Costa Canal, and to lift Sacramento River water into the Delta-Mendota Canal. Another third, it is estimated, will be used by auxiliary pumping—by irrigation districts and in pumping works to lift water from canal levels to high benchlands. This leaves a third as surplus power which is to be sold at low cost and on a preference basis to governmental agencies and co-operatives.

Now, had Congress handed the Bureau all the funds it needed for the project at once, the Bureau simply would have gone out and built the works as soon as possible. Congress, however, appropriates funds from year to year; it does not write big blank checks. Faced with the Bureau power program, the P. G. & E. decided it could best forestall such plans by doing its best to see that Congress did not approve funds for the steam plant and the transmission lines. The transmission lines were the obvious bottleneck. Without them, the Bureau could not transport its power, and would be forced to sell to the P. G. & E. The campaign to force sale of project power to the utility has been under way, with little change, for several years. The P. G. & E. presents a persuasive case and it sends its best men into the fight—usually James B. Black, its president, or P. M. Downing, its general manager.

On December 10, 1942, the P. G. & E. presented a full statement of its position to the Legislature's joint committee on water problems. After reviewing the beginnings of the Central Valley Project and recalling that falling water tables in the San Joaquin Valley showed the necessity for the plan, the statement says:

This history is recited for the purpose of showing that the whole problem is a *water* problem—namely, securing an adequate water supply for the Central Valley and the Delta. There is no power supply problem because, as the demand for power increased in central and northern California, new facilities were provided, interconnections were made and the numerous hydro and steam plants operated as an integrated system, so that today the supply of electric energy is ample for present needs and adequate provision is being made for estimated future demands.

The power feature of the project was conceived as a revenue-producing measure and not to supply any need for power. The responsibility of providing an adequate supply of power rests with the Pacific Gas and Electric Co. . . . . The company has always met that responsibility. . . . . There is no power shortage in this territory.

It is clear that up to this time the Central Valley project is a Federal reclamation enterprise financed and controlled by Federal authority. All these millions of Federal money have been invested in the project for water conservation, flood and salinity control, reclamation and navigation. The generation of power is entirely incidental and only for the purpose of helping to meet the cost of the project. As Edward Hyatt, State Engineer, told the Committee on Flood Control of the House of Representatives (1935) . . . . "Having built a great dam for irrigation and navigation and flood control, it would be a waste of money not to build a power house . . . . It would be an economic waste. There is a valuable reserve there. Why not develop it?"

For a long time prior to the inception of the project the Pacific Gas and Electric Company (or its predecessor companies) has supplied under effective regulation about 95 per cent of the electricity delivered to ultimate consumers in Central Valley territory. The other five per cent is distributed by several small private or municipal enterprises which purchase from the company all or much of their power at wholesale. The company has a network covering the territory and supplied by fifty-one hydro-electric and twelve steam electric plants and various other sources from outside the area served by the company. The only outlet for project power is through the company's facilities, unless (*a*) the project can find new industries to whom it can sell all its power at less than rates charged by the company, or (*b*) the project deems that it can afford the delay and cost of trying to build up a market by taking away the company's customers. That could be done only by selling project power for less than its market value and that would mean a financial loss instead of gain to the project and to the farmers hoping for power revenue that will cut down water rates . . . .

Besides, a huge deficit would accumulate during the years when project power was trying to find a market in a competitive field. The ultimate net income from power would be less than the return through the company facilities.

Mr. Ready [Lester S. Ready, consulting engineer for the State] when he testified before the Flood Control Committee of the House of Representatives, stated that disposal of power through the company's system would give the "State relatively the largest price it could get immediately as against what it could get if it went into the retailing of power." He said further on this occasion:

"It is well to keep in mind, when discussing revenue that the need of this project is to supply water for irrigation. It would not be of much value to these farmers to have 25 or 30 cents taken from a lighting bill if they had no water for irrigation.

"As has been said many times the basic need of this area is water. If they [the farmers] have water they can pay their domestic bills. If they do not have water, low domestic rates mean little. Revenue for this project is more important than lower domestic or commercial rates. This is basically a water supply project; power is a by-product."

Then, after outlining the Company's policies in regard to expansion, the statement goes on:

Foreseeing the day when power from Shasta and Keswick would seek an outlet in territory already completely served, the Pacific Gas and Electric Company long ago planned its new sources with an eye to keeping open a place for Central Valley hydro-electric power.

It is as much to the interest of the Company as to that of the public that the project's hydro-electric power should find a profitable outlet. Naturally, the company wishes to avoid competition with a power project financed by the Government. But the project should be quite as eager to avoid competition with the Company, for such competition would thwart the statutory intent that Shasta power shall be a means of financially aiding and assisting the primary water purposes of the project. If the Company were to have ignored Shasta and Keswick power in its plans it would now find itself confronting a government-financed project with a vast amount of power seeking a market. Such a policy on the part of the Company would have *forced* the project into competition, bad for itself and the public as well as for the Company. So, without claiming any higher motive than enlightened self-interest, the Company has planned a policy of *coordination*, by which Shasta power can be absorbed into the existing market with a financial result as favorable to the project as if the project, rather than the

Company held the existing market to the extent to which it could be supplied by Shasta power and *as if Shasta power were firmed by a steam plant and brought to consumers.*

Thus the Company has placed the project in a position where, without any investment in transmission lines or steam plant, and without the losses attendant on embarking in a new business under competitive conditions—losses which would take years to repair—the project, cooperating with the Company, can have all the benefits inherent in conducting an established business without competition.

The statement then outlines company offers to buy project power dating back to start of construction of the dams. Then, basing its figures on full production from Shasta and Keswick, it continued:

In money *the company's offer would mean a gross revenue to the Bureau, commencing January 1, 1945, estimated at $5,567,000 a year,* of which $5,147,000 was guaranteed. *When full use can be made of all available electrical energy the revenue will average $5,807,000 a year.* Revenue under the offer would be sufficient to meet all of the operating costs, including interest and amortization, of the Shasta and Keswick plants and the Keswick afterbay, *and leave a balance of over $3,500,000 a year to apply against the water features of the project* . . . .

In addition, the company offered to provide power for the project's pumping plants on an exchange basis so that the pumping plants would be assured of power at all times. The Company also offered to make "firm" any power which the Bureau may sell to public agencies for a cost no greater than if it were made firm by a project steam plant.

In response to an inquiry from the Bureau for an offer at Antioch in the event the Bureau were to build transmission lines to that point, the Company stated it would pay for the same power delivered at Antioch $6,092,000 annually, of which $5,678,000 would be guaranteed. With full use of all available energy possible in future years, the average revenue would increase to $6,339,000 a year. The Company also offered to submit to the California Railroad Commission and the Federal Power Commission the question whether the price offered is fair and represents the actual value of the project's hydro energy assuming it to be "firmed."

The Company's offer for the power at Shasta and Keswick would produce for the project a net return of $900,000 a year more than the offer for the power at Antioch. This represents the difference between the project's annual costs on an assumed investment of $23,000,000 in round figures in transmission lines and a terminal substation and the additional revenue which the project would receive for the power at Antioch . . . . [Antioch originally was to be the site of the steam plant now proposed to be located at Tracy.]

The arguments outlined in the statement quoted above have been repeated once or twice a year before Congressional committees considering appropriations for transmission lines and the steam plant. Here is an excerpt from testimony given by James B. Black before the House Committee on Appropriations on October 29, 1945. Black had appeared before the committee earlier. He has appeared often but the burden of his remarks have been consistently the same. Here's Mr. Black:

We again appear before this Committee in a spirit of cooperation.

It is now nearly five years since we offered to coordinate the operations of the Company's system with the Shasta and Keswick plants and to make our market available for Central Valley power. Our offers of cooperation have been repeated many times; the last time as late as October 11, 1945, when we wrote Commissioner Bashore that: "It has always been and is now, our earnest desire to cooperate with the Bureau in every way to the end that the Bureau's obligations and requirements are met. We have endeavored to make a market available for the Project's power output as fast as the various units come into operation, in order that the Bureau may receive the largest revenue possible from the output of its power plants. Our position has been stated many times."

The Company has offered and continues to offer to buy all of the Project's hydro-electric power at the Company's Shasta substation, 25 miles below Shasta Dam, at the price set by the Bureau for power now delivered into the Company's system under a war time contract. It has also offered to supply the Project's pumping plants on an exchange basis with power from the Company's transmission system, the Company to be paid in power delivered to it at its Shasta substation. The pumping plants would be assured of a power supply at all times, irrespective of the operation of the Project's power plants and at a cost no greater than if the power were transmitted from Shasta Dam over a tax-free, fully loaded, government-owned transmission system. We have further offered and continue to offer to make firm any power which the Bureau may sell to public agencies and to do this at a cost no greater than if such power were made firm by a Project steam plant. A steam plant and a transmission system are therefore not only unnecessary, but appropriations for their construction would be a waste of public funds . . . .

Company Cooperation Effective Under War Time Contract:

Our cooperation has been accepted in part; that is, for the power presently available from the Project, which is being marketed through the Company's system. Under a temporary war time contract we are paying what Secretary Ickes has publicly declared to be "a fair and equitable price," and from June 26, 1944, to September 30, 1945, have paid the Bureau for power $2,765,619.

Our payments for 1945 will exceed $3,000,000. After the Bureau has paid its operating costs for the year (approximately $400,000) it will have a net balance of about $2,600,000 to apply to the cost of the Project. This should be sufficient to meet all the annual charges, including interest and amortization at 3 per cent on the money expended to date on power facilities, and leave a balance of $1,400,000 to apply to irrigation features of the Project. More revenue is being produced for the government by this means than could be obtained in any other way. There is no market for the Project's power except the market now served by the Company. The Company's system offers the only outlet for the Project's power unless wasteful duplicating lines and other facilities are constructed in an endeavor to take away existing consumers or to compete with the Company for new consumers.

The appropriations now asked are not deficiency appropriations. On the contrary they are requests for new funds to engage in undertakings for which appropriations have been several times refused by Congress, the last time in the Interior Bill for 1946, approved July 3, 1945.

Despite the repeated denials by Congress the Bureau of Reclamation continues to repeat its requests. We are informed that in the present bill request is made for $6,065,000 for the initiation of construction of transmission loop from Shasta and Keswick Dams to Tracy, and for the construction of a transmission line with feeder lines and substations. This appropriation, as was the case with other appropriations already denied, is wholly unnecessary and a waste of public funds.

We are informed that the bill contains a further item of $1,600,000 for additional work at Shasta switchyard and to initiate work on switchyards at Keswick Dam, at Tracy, and at two switchyards north and south of Sacramento. That part of the appropriation which would apply to switchyards at Shasta and Keswick Dams would seem to be in order. The remainder is clearly unnecessary.

Requested Appropriations Not Necessary for Project Purposes:

When the last Interior Bill was debated on the Senate floor Senator Burton of Ohio (now Justice Burton) stated the issue very clearly. He said the question is "whether or not some $75,000,000 is to be spent by the government for transmission lines and steam plant, or whether the facilities of an existing utility are made use of to accomplish substantially the same result." It appeared to Senator Burton as it had to the House Committee that the "sensible, sound, sane and business-like way" to meet the situation would be to allow the local company which has the investment in the area to spend the $75,000,000 or whatever it is necessary to spend. Senator Burton said: "It [the company] is willing, able and ready to do so, and here is a case where the purposes of the Project will be carried out fully without the United States government putting in $75,000,000 to accomplish the result."

As Senator Burton stated it, and as we have stated before, there is no market for the Project's power except in the territory now served by the Company. The Company's system therefore is the natural outlet for the Project's hydro-electric energy.

Under the Company's offer and under its Policy of coordination, the Project is in a position to receive all of the benefits of an established and diversified system without making any investment in a transmission system or a steam plant, and without the financial losses attendant on embarking on a new business under competitive conditions.

Reclamation Primary Purpose, Electric Power Secondary:

The coordination and cooperation offered by the Company are in keeping with the intent and purpose of the Act of Congress of August 26, 1937, which establishes this Project as a reclamation and flood control project and provides "for the generation and sale of electric energy as a means of financially aiding and assisting" the water and reclamation features of the Project. There is nothing in the Act or in the Reclamation law itself to indicate that it is the purpose of the government to enter into the business of building steam plants or transmitting or distributing electricity as a separate or additional business.

The House Committee in its Report on the 1945 Interior Bill pointed out that "the reclaiming of arid lands by the construction of reclamation projects is and always has been the primary reason for the establishment of the Bureau of Reclamation and that the installation of hydro-electric power, important as it is, is a secondary consideration." A majority of the committee reporting as late as September 28 last, on an inspection trip that included the Central Valley Project, repeated this statement of principle and added: "Members urge that the Bureau keep this policy in mind in connection with the construction of Reclamation projects."

Company Prepared to Take Delivery of All Additional Power:

As we have often stated, we are prepared to take delivery at Shasta substation of all additional power developed at Shasta and Keswick Dams. We have agreed to pay therefore the rates set by the Bureau in the present contract.

When the complete installation is made at Shasta and Keswick Dams our offer, if accepted, will bring the Bureau an average annual revenue of $6,000,000. This revenue would be sufficient to meet all the operating costs on the Shasta and Keswick plants, including interest and amortization on the plants, the connecting transmission facilities, and the Keswick Dam, and leave a balance of over $3,500,000 a year to apply to the cost of the Shasta reservoir or other irrigation features of the Project.

When the Project pumping plants go into full operation they will require large amounts of power as well as additional releases of water from Shasta reservoir. Even then the Bureau under the Company's offer would receive an annual revenue of $4,000,000, and in addition the full power requirements of the Project pumping plants, estimated at 400 million kilowatt hours a year, would be supplied on an exchange basis.

The Company's offered price is possible because the Company, at relatively little cost, can absorb Central Valley power into its system and make it firm through use of the Company's numerous resources . . . . The Company's resources are adequate to support all of the assured capacity of the Shasta and Keswick plants and to provide all necessary standby. A Project steam plant never will be required if the hydro power is coordinated with the Company's system.

By accepting the Company's offer the Bureau obtains at once and without cost to the government, the benefit of the Company's various resources, its distribution network covering a territory 500 miles long and 200 miles wide and its established and diversified business. It also avoids going into unnecessary and destructive competition.

The Company will have transmission facilities ready whenever additional power is available. It has long owned a right-of-way for another transmission line between its Shasta substation and the Bay area. Soon after the end of the war in Europe materials and equipment were ordered for a double circuit steel tower transmission line to be constructed on this right-of-way and construction work is now actually in progress. The line with necessary substation equipment will cost $6,000,000 and when in operation late next year will be available to transmit additional Shasta power to the San Francisco metropolitan area.

Bureau Solicits Cities Long Served by Company:

Representatives of the Bureau have been promoting a program of competition and duplication in California for the last two years. Contracts have been and are being proposed to cities, towns and districts which we now supply. Efforts have been made to "sign-up" ten-year contracts with the cities of Redding, Gridley, Lodi, Biggs, Alameda, Palo Alto, Santa Clara, and Roseville, which operate their own municipal plants in the territory in which Shasta power must be used. With one or two exceptions, we have supplied all of these cities since they first established their municipal distribution systems. Redding, for example, has taken our service for over 25 years and Roseville for more than 30.

Of all these cities, Roseville alone "signed up" with the Bureau. The other cities not only refused to sign but made five-year contracts with us. To obtain these contracts it was necessary for the Company to anticipate an adjustment in its resale rates which it had expected to make next year, resulting in a reduction of these rates of from 7 to 14 per cent.

In commenting on the reasons which caused the cities to sign with the Company rather than with the Bureau, the Railroad Commission of California said, among other things:

"When [transmission] facilities are provided, if they be limited to single circuits, the Bureau's customers would not have the same assurance of continuity of service as that afforded by the Company, because of the latter's many sources of supply and alternate feeds over different circuits normally available. If customers of the Bureau purchase standby service from the Company this added cost would largely nullify the initial rate saving."

The Commission also said:

"Furthermore the Bureau's contract contains provisions requiring customers to apply certain rates and follow other procedures in the redistribution of electric energy. These considerations perhaps explain in part the ability of the Company to obtain contracts with all its existing resale customers, except one, at a rate materially higher than that offered by the Bureau."

Under the contracts offered by the Bureau these cities would be required to operate their municipal plants as separate departments with separate funds; they would be regulated by the Bureau as to what use would be made of surplus earnings and as to the amounts to be paid into the general funds of the city. They would be required to set up an accounting system prescribed by the Bureau; required to sell power at rates approved by the Secretary of the Interior and to submit yearly financial statements to the Secretary with the right on his part to examine the city's books and records periodically.

Bureau Would Sacrifice Revenue to Embark on Power Venture:

The contracts proposed by the Bureau offer what is described as a "low wholsale rate." On a 50 per cent load factor, which can be applied on the average to industries and municipalities, the rate is approximately 5 mills per kilowatt hour . . . .

Roseville may be cited as an example of what the Bureau proposes to do. It is a small city using about 1,300 kilowatts of capacity and 5,400,000 kilowatt hours of energy a year. It is 200 miles from Shasta Dam. On the basis of last year's usage, the Bureau proposes to serve Roseville for $26,680 a year. In the contract which has been signed the Bureau is to stand ready to supply up to 1,800 kilowatts. This same power delivered to the Company at its Shasta substation would bring $29,000. In other words, if the Bureau had the transmission line it asks for, it would deliver power to Roseville at a loss of over $2,000 a year. This does not take into consideration the annual charges on that part of the transmission and standby facilities required to bring the power to Roseville and assure adequate service. These charges would be in the order of $20,000 a year. When these charges are met the loss would be not $2,000 but $22,000 a year.

The Bureau has requested the Company to transmit power from Shasta substation to Roseville over the Company's system. It makes the request on the ground that the Reclamation law requires that preference be given public agencies and cooperatives in the lease or sale of government power. We have always recognized the preference is given public agencies, and our contract with the Bureau provides for withdrawals for this and other purposes, but as Secretary Ickes advised the Governor of California in a letter written on January 18, 1940:

"The preference is given in the right to buy and not in price schedules, since the Bureau of Reclamation must return to the United States the cost of its projects and therefore has a responsibility of obtaining a fair return in the sale of power."

It seems obvious that the Reclamation law does not require the Bureau to deliver power to preferred customers at a financial loss.

Heavy Financial Loss With Competing Power System:

If the Bureau sold all its available commercial power at its announced price of 5 mills per kilowatt hour, its gross revenue would be approximately $8,000,000 a year. In order to do so the Bureau proposes to invest over $68,000,000 of government funds in a steam plant and transmission system which otherwise would not be required. Under the Bureau's accounting methods the annual costs on this sum, including steam plant fuel, would be $6,300,000. This would leave a net of only $1,700,000 at our Shasta substation.

On the other hand acceptance of the Company's offer would produce $4,000,000 at Shasta substation and in addition provide for full delivery of power to the Project pumping plants on an exchange basis. The difference is $2,300,000 a year. This means that the Bureau would earn $2,300,000 more by selling its power at Shasta substation at the rates now in effect than by disposing of it at many points over its proposed transmission system, at its announced wholesale rates. The difference would be greater than $2,300,000 a year because the $68,000,000 would not be sufficient to accomplish the Bureau's purpose.

However, it will be many years before the Project will need large amounts of power for pumping. During these years the Company's offer would bring a revenue at Shasta substation not of $4,000,000 but of $6,000,000 a year. In this period the Bureau's plan would mean an annual loss to the government of over $3,000,000 even if the Bureau could obtain all the customers it needed.

No representative of the Bureau has ever denied that the Bureau would obtain more revenue by selling to the Company . . . .

There is of course no unserved market and the Bureau would have to obtain its customers in competition with the Company. During the years of competition, operating losses would be inevitable and would result in deficits of many millions of dollars. These large deficits would continue in greater or less degree, until the power was wholly disposed of and even then the Bureau would suffer a continuing loss of over $2,300,000 a year if it persisted in carrying out its competitive program.

The Project urgently needs the market now served by this Company. The only practical way of getting economic access to that market is through the coordination and cooperation which the Company offers, or by taking over its entire property. Piecemeal dismemberment or wasteful duplication of the Company's property, which would result from a competitive situation, would destroy the economics of diversified large scale operation and inevitably impose a burden on the water users, the Federal taxpayers or the consumers of electric energy in the territory served.

It is hardly necessary to repeat before this Committee that our offer to provide a market for Central Valley power is not a new policy. On the contrary it is in keeping with a policy of cooperation with cities, irrigation districts and other governmental agencies which the Company has practiced for many years. As we said before this cooperation has provided an assured market for power developed as an incident to the conservation and storage of water and has afforded the means of financing projects which otherwise would not have been feasible.

Company's Rates Low Under State Regulation:

This Company's rates are low and have followed a downward trend for years. Reports of the Railroad Commission of California frequently describe California utility rates as "among the lowest in the country, due to the Commission's policy of continuous investigation."

The Company's low rates should be a material factor in determining whether the Bureau should accept the Company's offer of coordination or seek a market in competition with the Company by endeavoring to attract consumers now served by the Company at these low rates.

Under the Commission's accounting rules any payments made by the Company to the Bureau of Reclamation for Project power would be entered as an operating expense item on the Company's books. It would be allowed in rate making procedure only to the extent that the Commission deemed the amounts paid to be reasonable.

The Company can make no profit from the power it purchases. All that it can earn is a fair return upon its investment in facilities for transmission and distribution of such power.

All demands for power in this area have been and are now adequately supplied. Full provision was made for all war time demands. Some of these demands have already commenced to recede. Irrespective of this reduction, however, we are prepared to take the output of any additional units that may be installed at Shasta and Keswick Dams, making a market therefore by further curtailing the output of our steam plants and the use of power that we purchase from others.

Estimates Grow Despite Need for Economy

As we stated before, requests for appropriations for this Project have already exceeded all expectations. When first submitted to Congress the cost was estimated at $170,000,000; now it is over $362,000,000. The estimates of the power features have risen from $31,000,000 to over $108,000,000, three and one-half times the original figure. Over $68,000,000 of the presently proposed expenditures for power features are unnecessary under the coordinated plan offered by the Company.

The House Committee on the last Interior Bill noted the increase in cost and said:

"Considering the need for economy, it would appear to be to the interest of the project to find ways and means of reducing rather than increasing estimates."

The same point was emphasized in the Senate when Senator Burton said:

"In these days, when the taxpayer is burdened with Federal taxes and the government is confronted by a huge national debt, if we have a chance to avoid payment from the Federal treasury of $75,000,000 we should take advantage of the opportunity and this is a good place to do that. The money asked for is not needed. The people will be supplied with this power and it will be supplied at fair rates under the regulation of the state utilities commission. Therefore I believe the House was entirely right when it concluded that this is a good place to start the economy program and not to spend $75,000,000 of public money to duplicate a private investment . . . ."

Company One of West's Largest Taxpayers, State and Federal:

The Company, which is an operating company, a California corporation, has over 125,000 stockholders, of which 80,000 reside in California . . . .

The Federal, State and local governments have a very real interest in the Company and its prosperity; for it is one of the largest taxpayers in the West. It pays taxes in 47 of the 58 counties of the State. In a number of counties it pays more than 50 per cent of the total collected for county purposes.

Since 1940, when the country began to prepare for war, to and including 1944, a period of five years, the Company's Federal taxes have amounted to over $91,000,000 and its State and local taxes to over $62,000,000. In 1944 alone our Federal taxes were $26,016,046 and our State and local taxes $12,737,916.

We conclude with a further quotation from Senator Burton's remarks in the Senate:

"There is no purpose in an irrigation project going into the power business if there is immediately available at its power dam a private distributing agency able to reach that entire area and willing and able to buy whatever is produced at the dam.

"We have that situation here. It is unique in that there is no claim made that anyone in the area will not be supplied with electric power in the absence of the Government line. The community is already supplied.

What will happen with the Government line is that it will proceed to take away customers from the private line already serving the public.

"There is no need for the Government to build this line for the sake of income. It is receiving that income. There is no need for it to build the line for the sake of supplying service, for the service is being supplied through the private company, and the private company agrees to transmit whatever power will be made available. Therefore I believe here is a case where the House is entirely correct."

There, at some length, is the Pacific Gas & Electric Co.'s case in the words of its officers. The effectiveness of that case is indicated by the attitude of Representative Jack Anderson of California. In a letter to the *San Jose Mercury Herald and News*, Anderson repeats, almost word for word, the Pacific Gas & Electric Co. line in justifying his stand on the Central Valley Project. A reproduction of the Anderson letter is circulated by the P. G. & E.:

I have before me a letter, dated Sept. 1 [1945] concerning my attitude on the Central Valley Project . . . . The letter questions my position on appropriations asked for transmission lines and a steam standby plant for the project and then proceeds to make some emotional arguments for cheap power. Of course, we are all for "cheap power" but let's take first things first.

The Central Valley project is essentially a water project. It was so presented to Congress by the State of California . . . . This view was accepted by Congress in 1937 when it declared the project to be for the purpose of improving navigation, controlling floods, for the storage and delivery of water, and for the reclamation of arid lands and lastly for the generation and sale of electric energy "as a means of financially aiding and assisting" the other features of the development.

Congress has consistently followed this purpose. Only a few months ago, the Senate Committee on Appropriations again directed attention to the 1937 legislation and to the purpose of power on the Central Valley Project, saying:

"It will be noted that the uses of the dam and reservoir are set up in a legislative order of priority, with power third, and that the use of power is to be as a means of financially aiding and assisting the accomplishment of the purposes."

Congress has appropriated money for the dams and canals and for electric generators. And as fast as power has been produced it has been sold as a means of financially aiding the project. This has been the policy of both the State and the Congress. I have gone along with it and was in accord with Secretary Ickes when he made a contract . . . . with the Pacific Gas and Electric Company for disposition of the power then available. Mr. Ickes made what he considered a very favorable contract with the P.G.& E. . . . .

To date, according to the records of the Bureau of Reclamation, the Government has received over $2,000,000 for its power. The Bureau estimates that it will receive well over $3,000,000 in the current fiscal year. This revenue has greatly strengthened the project in the eyes of eastern Congressmen who have been critical of its cost. It is a great help for the California delegation in the scramble for Federal funds to be able to show that some of the money put out by the Government is coming back into the treasury.

Some eastern Congressmen have already attacked the ever-increasing estimates for the project. They point to the fact that when the project was first submitted to Congress the cost was estimated by the State and by the Bureau of Reclamation at $170,000,000. Now the estimates exceed $362,000,000.

There is another practical side to the situation, which is often overlooked. That is: There is no market for the Central Valley power unless the power is put into the P.G.&E. system, or the P.G.&E. market is taken away from the Company. If the Government had gone out to fight for the market, instead of making the contract now in effect, it probably would have taken in little or no revenue to date. It certainly would not have collected $2,000,000. Even the enemies of the P.G.&E. would not expect the Company to buy Shasta power on the one hand and on the other give up its market in competition . . . .

There is another difficulty when it comes to advocating large appropriations for transmission lines and steam plants. No one rises up to show that electric rates are high in California and must be brought down by a Government yardstick or government competition. On the contrary, the testimony is usually the other way—that rates are low. Reports of the Railroad Commission are quoted to the effect that California utility rates "are among the lowest in the country" . . . .

I have gone along with this reasoning and with the purposes of the project as I understand them. I have supported every essential appropriation for the project and shall continue to do so. Power is being produced "as a means of financially aiding and assisting" the project. The more we keep this fact in mind and the more revenue we obtain from power now, the better we will stand with Congressmen from other states when we come to ask for the millions we must yet have to complete this great project, and the other flood control projects which Congress has already authorized for California.

Let's do first things first. Let's get the millions we need for the water features first, including those needed to complete the power plants at the Shasta Dam, and later decide what we want to do about transmission lines and steam plants. Meanwhile, I am willing to let Mr. Ickes or any other Secretary of the Interior negotiate for the sale of power in the existing market, confident that the best interests of the people will be protected.

X. Power Politics Compounded

AFTER LISTENING to Mr. Black, it is difficult to determine from his expensively tailored words just what the Pacific Gas & Electric Co. is up to. It must be remembered that the company is determined, as it has been since the beginning, that Central Valley power shall not be transmitted and distributed by public agencies. The company's attack on the project has been three-pronged: It wants to make sure that transmission lines and the steam plant (which would make the public system fully operative) are not built; it wants to make sure that no public distribution systems are set up, either by the state or by smaller utility districts; it has hurried to enlarge its own generating plant and transmission system so that it can continue to contend that there is no shortage of power and to decry public transmission and distribution systems as tax-wasting duplication of facilities.

After Black testified before the House committee, he was answered briefly by Harry Bashore, then commissioner of reclamation:

The few hours at our disposal do not permit a paragraph-by-paragraph analysis of the statement in which truths, half truths and errors are so skillfully blended.

Mr. Black seeks to convince the committee—as he has unsuccessfully sought to convince the Bureau—that this private power monopoly is, in effect, an eleemosynary institution seeking without profit to itself to pay the Government more money than the Government could otherwise obtain. This is incredible to me.

In my opinion, the Pacific Gas and Electric Company seeks to become the sole customer of the Shasta and Keswick power plants in order to reap for the company the power benefits produced by the Government's investment instead of passing the benefits on to the water users and ultimate power consumers, as is planned by the Bureau.

126

Here is an example of what Mr. Black would do to the water users, based upon his own figures. Mr. Black states that if this offer to purchase all of the project's power is accepted, the Bureau will receive an average annual revenue of $6,000,000 prior to the time when power is needed for irrigation pumping. After canal pumps are in operation he says the revenue would decrease to $4,000,000 a year. (We think it would be considerably less.) Since 400,000,000 kilowatt-hours are estimated to be used for this purpose (i.e., project pumping) it is quite evident that the $2,000,000 reduction in revenue admitted by Mr. Black represents a charge of 5 mills per kilowatt hour for the service rendered by the company in carrying this power from the Government's dams to the Government's pumps. No cost of energy to the irrigators nor our generating costs are included in the reduction previously stated.

The Bureau has proposed to charge only 2.5 mills per kilowatt-hour, or $1,000,000 annually, for energy delivered at the canal pumping plants. It is quite obvious that the charges to the water users for this irrigation pumping service can not be increased by more than $2,000,000 per year and still remain within their ability to pay.

I must admit that I am greatly surprised at Mr. Black's temerity in starting the construction of transmission lines and substations at a cost of $6,000,000 to transmit Shasta power to the company's own market in the San Francisco Bay area. Certainly the company has no present contractual rights which would warrant this large investment. Since this construction would duplicate part of the Bureau's proposed transmission lines, I cannot understand how such an expenditure can be justified to the company's stockholders, except as a desperate gamble.

With regard to the contracts offered by the Bureau to various municipalities, Mr. Black has apparently attempted to indicate that the Government is seeking control of city operations. This is not true. He gives only a small part of the story. The fact is that the Bureau is seeking only to provide that the ultimate consumer is charged a reasonable amount for the power used and that unlimited portions of the revenue are not diverted to uses having no relation to the costs of rendering electrical service.

Mr. Black states that the Bureau proposed to serve Roseville for $26,680, whereas he says the same power delivered to the company would bring $29,000. This is not true. The revenue which would be secured from the company for this same amount of power would be $23,300 per year.

Mr. Black's statement indicates that the Pacific Gas and Electric Company's rates are among the lowest in the country. He does not make this statement himself, but reports that the Railroad Commission of California has done so. Attached is a tabulation based on statistical data from the

Federal Power Commission. You will note that rates to customers in cities like Seattle, Tacoma, Portland, Kansas City, and even Washington, D.C., are very much below the Pacific Gas and Electric Company's charges.

In recent negotiations with the municipalities who have considered the purchase of Central Valley power, the company has reduced its rates from 7 to 14 per cent. It is quite significant that these reductions came only after the Bureau of Reclamation had made public its interim power rate schedule.

May I emphasize to the Committee that the Bureau proposes, for the benefit of the water users, to establish a charge of only 2.5 mills for project canal pumping and to charge other customers rates sufficient not only to repay the costs allocated to power, but also that part of the irrigation costs which is beyond the ability of the water users to repay. Thus he is aided in his operation and maintenance cost as well as in his capital cost.

To summarize, we do not agree that the project would be better off financially if the Pacific Gas and Electric Company became the sole purchaser of the project's power.

We feel certain that the irrigators would be adversely affected and the entire area would lose a material part of the benefits of the low-cost power that would otherwise be available.

In reading Black's statement with its declarations of friendship for the Central Valley Project, it is well to remember that the company has not always been so concerned with the success of the venture. In some instances, it could almost be supposed that the company was working against it.

Such an instance occurred in the spring of 1941. Then, P. M. Downing, vice-president and general manager of the P. G. & E., appeared before a House subcommittee on appropriations to oppose an appropriation for the Central Valley steam plant. He testified that there was no necessity for such a plant because the P. G. & E. was enlarging its own steam capacity.

This expansion program, he said, would take care of the needs of northern California until 1945, including stand-by steam service for project hydro power when that began to be produced. Thus, he reasoned, there was no need for expenditure of government funds for a steam plant. He said:

The Pacific Gas and Electric Company is not opposing the acceleration of the project, but does object to the suggestions that there is a threatened power shortage or that the steam plant is necessary in order to insure operation of the [project] pumping plants. No one is yet in a position to assert that a steam plant will enable this project to derive a better net income from its power . . . .

However, about the same time that Downing was telling the committee that there was no need for additional generating systems, Downing and another company crew were at work before the Federal Power Commission. There the story was very different. Pacific Gas & Electric Co. representatives testified before the F.P.C. that there was a prospective shortage of generating capacity. Said the Commission:

It is apparent that failure of the applicant [the P. G. & E.] to advise the Commission of its construction schedule and its decision to construct additional generating capacity was due to conflicting purposes which it desired to achieve. Applicant desired a license for construction of two large hydropower developments on the Feather River to give it further control over that important stream. At the same time it opposed construction by the United States of any steam generating capacity which might be used in competition with its own power system.

Because it desired a license from the Commission, applicant reported to the Commission that there would be a lack of generating capacity until after such license has been authorized. At the same time, applicant used its decision to construct 82,000 kilowatts of additional generating capacity as an argument against any appropriation by Congress for construction of the Antioch steam plant as part of the Central Valley project. The Antioch plant, it argued, would be uneconomic because the applicant's construction schedule demonstrated an excess of generating capacity in the area to be served by the Central Valley project.

Both witnesses, Downing and Dreyer, admitted that the Central Valley project would require standby steam capacity if operated as the sole source of power supply for an independent system. The opposition of applicant rather goes to its determination to see that the Central Valley power output is not distributed through a competitive public agency, but that it be distributed by and inure to the benefit of the Pacific Gas and Electric system.

In addition to these objectives, however, Mr. Downing admitted that if the Antioch steam plant is not built by the United States, his company would not be required to pay as much for any power which it might purchase from the Central Valley project as it would be required to pay with that plant in operation. Thus, it is evident that by making the Central Valley project dependent upon the Pacific Gas and Electric system for standby plants to firm up the Shasta power output, the applicant could cut off possible competition, utilize its own steam generating plants, and purchase power from the Shasta plant at a much lower figure than otherwise . . . .

. . . . the actions of the applicant have not been marked by candor or frankness.

The next year, Black appeared to argue again against funds for the steam plant. Again he was successful in persuading Congress that such funds were unnecessary. His testimony impelled Representative Jerry Voorhis of California to make a speech:

. . . . So long as the hydro power developed at Shasta and Keswick is not supported by Government-owned steam plants, this power can be absorbed only by a buyer which itself owns a steam plant.

The fluctuations in water supply are too drastic to allow the power to be marketed on a firm basis unless firmed up by steam. Either the seller must supply that steam plant, or the buyer must . . . . and if the Government, as seller, does not, then it can find only one buyer that can do so, and that is the power company.

The last thing in the world that the Pacific Gas and Electric Company wants to accomplish is the objective spelled out so clearly in the Reclamation Project Act of 1939, and the State's own Central Valley Project Act of 1933; namely, the distribution of this power through public agencies. The company wants no competition, and it is willing to pay for Shasta power for two purposes: first, for power; and second, for protection.

A year ago the company succeeded in staving off an appropriation for a steam plant on the plea that it could absorb all of the Shasta power . . . . In the same breath it was before the Federal Power Commission asking for permission to construct large projects on the Feather River, on the plea that it did not have power enough; and no sooner had it convinced Congress that a Government-owned steam plant was unnecessary, than it went before the Office of Production Management to convince that Office that priorities were justified to enable the company to build three large steam plants of its own . . . .

If the Government loses the opportunity to build the steam plant, the company's bargaining position will automatically improve. It will find that the power available at Shasta is less than it proposed because Congress has required mandatory releases for navigation, salinity control, et cetera, or it will find other reasons to modify its proposition . . . .

The P. G. & E. will continue its fight against the steam plant and the transmission lines. Despite its opposition, Congress has authorized construction of a line from Oroville to Sacramento. This line will connect with the line already constructed between Shasta and Oroville. This 97-mile line was erected on Ickes' order after Congress had refused funds for the work. Ickes had the line constructed—using wooden poles instead of war-short steel—out of unexpended balances in the Central Valley fund. Senator McCarran of Nevada, a man who votes against funds for transmission lines, reviewed the bidding in an Associated Press dispatch:

The requests of appropriations for transmission lines has been denied in the past. In the 1945 bill a request for $7,000,000 was refused. A request for $1,900,000 for a line from Shasta Dam to Oroville was denied in the 1944 bill, and Mr. Ickes, the Secretary of the Interior, defied Congress and built the line to Oroville out of "unexpended balances" . . . . In the last Interior Bill [1946] Congress denied $100,000 for plans and designs for transmission lines and $113,000 for studies for a steam plant. In the 1942 bill the Bureau asked $4,000,000 for a steam plant; in the 1943 bill, $5,000,000. Both were denied. The Bureau was given $200,000 in 1943 for engineering work [on the steam plant] only.

The P. G. & E. has been active in the California Legislature as well as in Congress. Efforts of the state to "unfreeze" the $170,-000,000 revenue-bond issue voted in 1933 to construct a public electrical distribution system were killed and the P. G. & E. lobby generally is credited with the execution. Again in 1940, then Governor Culbert L. Olson asked for unfreezing of $50,000,000 of these bonds for the same purpose:

The proposed amendment, in simple language, would free up to $50,-000,000 of the $170,000,000 of revenue bonds authorized in the present Act, to be used by the State in carrying out the purposes and objectives of the Act itself. It would place the State in a position to contract with the Federal Government for distribution of the electric power developed by the project, instead of leaving the Federal Government and the people to be served at the mercy of a private power distribution monopoly which would be the only purchaser.

Arthur D. Angel, in his thesis, "Political and Administrative Aspects of the Central Valley Project of California,"* quotes a letter from State Senator J. C. Garrison who introduced bills which would have freed the revenue bonds for use for distribution systems:

. . . . it is my opinion, based on knowledge gained from 20 years' experience, that at least 95 percent of the members of the Legislature who voted against my various revenue bond bills were influenced, whether they realized it or not, by some of the devious methods used by the power trust. There are very few genuine "conscientious objectors" to this type of legislation any more. But there is no question in anyone's mind, who is half awake to the issue, that the power trust, through campaign contributions, legal fees, social contacts, etc., did see to it that "the proper men" were gotten into the campaign and supported through to election.

Besides the "proper men" in the Legislature, the P. G. & E. also has the backing of the California State Chamber of Commerce, large landowners, the California Farm Bureau Federation, and indirectly, the Corps of Engineers. Many farmers have been won over to the side of the P. G. & E. by the argument that distribution of cheap power will mean higher water costs. They believe that by selling to the P. G. & E. at a relatively high price, the Bureau will be able to allocate more power revenue to pay off irrigation features of the project.

Against this array, the Bureau brings its guns and it, too, cites the law and its interpretation. Speaking before the National Reclamation Association in Denver, in 1945, Michael Straus, now Commissioner of Reclamation, declared:

. . . . without cheap power we can not hope to find the vast power markets that must develop to justify the multiple-purpose hydro projects. We cannot provide cheap power unless we protect and police those Federal kilowatts all the way down the line and see that they are delivered to the

---

* As quoted in *History of Legislation and Policy Formation of the Central Valley Project,* by Mary Montgomery and Marion Clawson, p. 188.

consumer without a lot of markups in price for private profit, just as you insist that we protect and police the Federal acre-feet to the irrigationist who frequently turns out to be one and the same person as the kilowatt consumer. And we can not deliver abundant low-cost power to the consumer unless we have transmission lines over which to send those kilowatts that are serving the cause of low-cost water.

New transmission lines are required to carry new reclamation power to new consumers—largely irrigationists. These lines must be dedicated to the purpose of delivering plentiful and low-cost power and not monopolized and operated for a dozen other recognized purposes having no relation to irrigation, including the return of handsome dividends to receptive absentee stockholders a few thousand miles away.

Therefore, to the end of low-cost water, it is written into the laws that steps shall be taken to insure abundant low-cost power, including the fact that the Bureau of Reclamation shall build and operate transmission lines and shall give preference in selling kilowatts to such non-profit bodies as water users' organizations, which are conceived for the benefit of their consuming communities and are not compelled to provide large profits to absentee stockholders.

Most of you recognize and support that thesis . . . .

A beautiful example of how all this works out is in the Central Valley of California, a Bureau of Reclamation project, as spectacular and essential to the fertile and water-hungry acres of California as any work of mankind. First of all, up to one third of the total power output of Shasta and Keswick Dams is required to operate the large project pumping plants. There some of the plentiful northern California water that Shasta holds and feeds into the Sacramento River can be lifted, by the power it itself generates, 209 feet up into the parched southern San Joaquin Valley. Furthermore, it is estimated that another third of the power will be taken by local irrigation districts and individual water users for irrigation pumping in their own districts. Thus, two-thirds of the power to be produced at Shasta Dam will go directly into irrigation service. Manifestly, power is not just a rich financial partner in the Central Valley of California; it is an essential working partner and the project never has been found feasible without it and never can be.

Therefore, publicly owned transmission lines were requested originally by the State of California, which planned the project, justified in the plan submitted by the Bureau of Reclamation to the Congress, and ratified by the Congress in approving the program. Every step was taken to insure cheap power and resultant low-cost water. But for the past two years certain minority California interests who are not serving the cause of low-cost water have sought to high pressure and bedazzle the Congress—so far in vain—to prevent the Government from building the needed transmission lines. All of the dust and confusion that can blind perspective have been scattered. And they are still at it today. Watch their performance. It's wonderful—well worth somebody else's money.

As indicated above, the battle between the Bureau of Reclamation and the Pacific Gas & Electric Co., is a late round in the fight between public and private power. In a sense, all the talk about dollars and cents and kilowatts and kilovolts can be disregarded. The battle involves them all but it is not primarily concerned with them. The battle is one for control of the Central Valley Project— a project, as has been pointed out, which involves an investment by the United States of at least $384,000,000. If the P. G. & E. is successful in forestalling erection of needed transmission lines and a steam plant, it will control the project as effectively as if it had made that investment itself. As a Bureau spokesman pointed out before the Commonwealth Club in San Francisco:

Surely, no one could logically contend that a part of the Central Valley project should be owned and operated by private interests; yet that is the logical result of the position taken by some that the Government should not build transmission facilities and serve its own interests, the interests of irrigators and the interests of the people who have a preference by law. No business, whether Federal, State or private could succeed under an arrangement whereby it could not control its business policy. The contention is made that we should not build transmission lines, and statements are also being made that direct sales to public agencies should not be permitted. If this were to be the situation, then the law giving preference to public agencies is meaningless . . . .

The obvious fact remains, however, that transmission lines are not now available for this potential generation, and such transmission facilities must be built. If built by the Government, they will be paid for and amortized over a period of years from power revenues. If they are built by private interests, the Government would pay rental for the use of those facilities indefinitely (without ownership), and the rental would include a profit to the utility company. No one, it would seem, could argue convincingly that a part ownership of this great project should be placed in the hands of any private interest; yet, if you prevent the construction of facilities to handle this power, that is exactly what would happen. The Government would surrender its right to operate a major feature of the project.

In a Bureau explanation of its program, this statement was made:

Transmission facilities, the construction of which has been retarded by the war, are required to provide an outlet for the generator installations. The existing line between Shasta and Oroville is only sufficient to take care of the output of the first two generators. The need for additional transmission lines is not disputed. The Pacific Gas & Electric Company in a statement to the War Production Board stated "the peak capacity of Shasta and Keswick plants is 450,000 kilowatts, so it will be necessary to provide three 230 kilovolt transmission circuits in order to deliver all of this power to the market." Their accompanying sketch showed two 230-kilovolt lines from Shasta to a substation at Contra Costa on the West side and one 230-kilovolt line from Shasta to their substation south of Sacramento, with additional lower voltage lines to strengthen their system. The need for these facilities was also confirmed at a conference held between officials of the Pacific Gas & Electric Company and representatives of the WPB and the Bureau of Reclamation for the purpose of conserving critical materials when it was concluded that at least three new transmission lines would be required to transmit the electrical energy from the Shasta and Keswick power plants to the San Francisco Bay region. This clearly points out that the issue here is not duplication of facilities but one of control.

As for market prospects, the Bureau observes:

Increasing population; industrial development; service to some areas now unserved; increased consumption due to low-cost power and irrigation pumping are the factors which make it essential that the power resources of the State be developed as rapidly as possible. The conservation of the exhaustible oil and gas resources of the State and Nation requires that in so far as possible the increase in demand for electricity be met by generation at hydro plants . . . .

Because of war restrictions, installation of generating capacity in the State of California has not kept pace with consumption. Between 1940 and 1944, electric power sales increased 65.2 per cent as against an increase in generating capacity of only 34.8 per cent, approximately 50 per cent of which was in steam capacity . . . . The normal annual growth in the Central Valley area is about six per cent. This means that over 75,000 kilowatts of new power installations, both in generating plants and transmission lines, must be added in the area annually to meet the growing demands. This figure does not take into consideration the accelerated consumption which would result from lower rates and from the pumping requirements of the project. The average energy consumption in the State of California in 1944 per residential customer approximated 1100 kilowatt hours. Increased consumption in the home and on the farm with the advent of low-cost power will double and triple this use within a few years. Technological development in the field of electrical house heating, as well as new uses for electricity on the farm, will be a major factor in increased usage of electricity in this region. The Central Valley plants and transmission lines fit into this plan to meet the additional needs of the water users and other people of the Valley . . . .

This statement explains that the Bureau has received inquiries regarding power service and applications for such service from five electrical associations, twenty-one irrigation districts, nineteen municipalities, eight municipal utility districts, and eight other public agencies.

The termination of the war has brought about a renewed and mounting interest in the power program of the Bureau for servicing public agencies in accordance with the expressed will of the Congress. This interest is only tempered by the fact that the Bureau is unable at this time to advise when power deliveries can be made due to lack of transmission facilities.

It can be conservatively stated that a market for all the power from Shasta and Keswick Dams not required for project pumping plants is available as soon as the power plants and necessary transmission facilities are complete.

The Bureau has been hampered in its negotiations with cities having their own distributing systems by the very real drawback of being unable to deliver power. This despite Senator Burton's statement to the Senate on behalf of the P. G. & E.: "The Pacific Gas & Electric Co. has offered to service any public agencies which might be entitled to public power." The P. G. & E. refused to allow use of its lines to transmit Bureau power to Roseville despite a clause in the temporary contract between the company and the Department of Interior which implied agreement on the point:

Preference to Public Agencies. During the term of this contract, and in order to meet the existing war emergency, the parties agree (without establishing a permanent policy in respect to the disposition of power of the United States) that they will endeavor to carry out the provisions of the Reclamation Law providing that preference be given public agencies and cooperatives in the lease or sale of Government power, by mutual agreements supplementary to this contract, if, as and when the occasion may require.

The occasion "required" after the Bureau signed a power contract with Roseville. But the P. G. & E. refused to service the city system over its transmission lines. "We had some reason to believe that the P. G. & E. would cooperate," Ickes rumbled at the time, ". . . . because of the testimony of its president in opposing the construction of Government transmission lines before the House and Senate appropriations subcommittees."

Roseville remains the only municipality to have signed a contract with the Bureau. The City could have canceled the contract on December 31, 1946, because power had not yet been delivered. The contract, however, was not canceled. The council reasoned that if Bureau power were delivered within five years, the savings under the Bureau contract would make up for larger payments being made presently to the P. G. & E.

Other communities in northern California, however, signed contracts with the company at reduced rates. The company insisted on five-year contracts and thus has control of the situation for at least that long in the following communities: Lodi, Palo Alto, Alameda, Biggs, Gridley, Healdsburg, Santa Clara, Ukiah, and Redding. Before the California Railroad Commission, a company spokesman said candidly: "The Company's proposal to give cities lower rates if they agreed to use Pacific Gas & Electric Co. power exclusively for five years is similar to a practice the company has used with industrial plants whenever threatened with competition from diesel electric plants."

Given the transmission lines, Bureau competition could be a serious thing in the municipal field. Here is a comparison compiled by the Railroad Commission which shows the differences between the company's P-6 schedule, in effect before the reductions in the P-31 schedule, and the Bureau rates:

BILLING COMPARISON

P. G. & E. SCHEDULES P-6, P-31, AND SHASTA-ROSEVILLE CONTRACT

	Roseville		Lodi	
Maximum Demand Kilowatts 1944.....	1,267		2,784	
Consumption Kilowatt hours 1944......	5,297,600		13,459,200	
Annual Load Factor, percent..........	48.0		55.2	
Billing on Schedule P-6...............	$44,628	100 %	$100,356	100 %
Billing on Schedule P-31.............	$41,636		$ 90,956	
Reduction P-6 to P-31................	$ 2,992	6.7%	$ 9,400	9.4%
Billing on Shasta Rate................	$26,399		$ 60,918	
Reduction P-6 to Shasta Contract......	$17,229*	38.6%	$ 39,438	39.3%
Average rate per KWH. Mills				
P-6 schedule	8.42		7.46	
P-31 schedule	7.86		6.76	
Shasta	4.98		4.53	

* This is the figure given in the decision. However, it is apparently a typographical error. It should be $18,229.

The Railroad Commission observed:

It was pointed out in the testimony presented by Pacific that the monetary differential . . . . does not reflect the whole measure of the difference between the rates in Schedule P-31 and those in the Shasta contract. In the first place, the Bureau of Reclamation is not in a position immediately to render service under any contract entered into because it does not have either transmission or distribution facilities. In the second place, even when facilities are provided, if they be limited to single circuits, the Bureau's customers would not have the same assurance of continuity of service as that afforded by Pacific because of the latter's many sources of supply and alternate feeds over different circuits normally available. If customers of the Bureau purchase standby service from Pacific, this added cost would largely nullify the initial rate saving. Furthermore, the Bureau's contract contains provisions requiring customers to apply certain rates and follow other procedures in the redistribution of electrical energy. These considerations perhaps explain . . . . the ability of Pacific to obtain contracts with all its existing resale customers, except one, at a rate materially higher than that offered by the Bureau, though lower than both the presently effective P-6 Schedule and resale contract rates . . . .

The battle continued. A Bureau spokesman said:

Marketing of power developed by the Federal Government in a manner most beneficial to the people, the community, and the State has involved serious clashes in philosophies. In considering our problem we can not afford to disregard the experience of other regions in developing and marketing power, even though the results are counter to the current philosophy of the private utility companies which operate in this region.

The philosophy of the Bureau of Reclamation as expressed in numerous Acts of Congress . . . . provides that surplus power and energy generated at reservoir projects shall be disposed of . . . . "in such a manner as to encourage the most widespread use at the lowest possible rates to consumers consistent with sound business principles."

The opposing philosophy of high price and low consumption is a threat to the development of the Central Valley project. Equally threatening is the argument that the marketing field has been preempted and none should trespass. The Bureau's right to sell CVP power has been determined by Congress . . . . Implication that any private utility company can not continue to buy and resell Federal power because the transmission lines are Government-owned, is not correct.

The extent of the inroads of public power on the domain of private utilities is not, as some would have you believe, due to Federal power policies. The extent in the past has depended and will in the future depend on the kind of job which utilities do. I have heard the president of a large utility company state that he could sell power as cheap as any public agency and still make a reasonable profit, and one wonders why he is missing the opportunity. When cities like Roseville, Redding and others exercised their right to operate their own utility business some 20 or 30 years ago, notwithstanding dire predictions of ruin, there was no Federal power plant and no Federal Government to blame. Today, the situation is no different, except that large Federal projects with power features have been or are being built which offer more opportunities to the people to demand better living conditions through the use of low-cost power . . . .

The issue of who shall distribute the power from these Federal dams will not be decided by laws enacted by Congress, for in the final analysis these laws only recognize the right of the people to decide for themselves.

To help the people decide the issue, both the Bureau and the P. G. & E., its friends and allies are doing all they can. Liberal opinion generally supports the Bureau in its announced aims of spreading the benefits of the project as widely as possible. Non-engineering Bureau men are attacked and ridiculed as "propa-gangineers" in some quarters. The P. G. & E. counters with its weapons: its employees, large landowners, community clubs and improvement associations subsidized by the company, and local bankers. The local manager of the P. G. & E. is invariably a power in his community; he is active on the service-club front, in the chamber of commerce, and on civic committees. The company can count on help from the bankers; company policy has made bankers friendly to the utility and, as a company spokesman said, "The bankers, as a rule, are economically minded about as we are, but, nevertheless, we came to the conclusion about fifteen years ago that as a practical incentive to get them to work with us, there is no substitute for deposits." Foes of the Bureau offer an alternative: the Corps of Engineers and its flood-control program. They favor the Engineers because the Engineers do not propose to build trans-mission lines and go into the power business. Engineers build facilities and turn them over to local management in most cases. If government does not build transmission lines, it can do only one thing with its power: sell it to the P. G. & E.

XI. Who Pays for What?

WHEN THE people of California approved the Central Valley Project Act they agreed to buy a water and power project for $170,000,000. When the federal government took over, it expected to spend about the same amount.

Now the latest official estimate of cost of the project is $384,-314,000. This is considerably more than $170,000,000. To be exact, it is $214,314,000 more. Alarming as the increase is, it does not indicate any bureaucratic lunacy in handling dollars. For one thing, the state's plans were changed. Several features of the project were enlarged: Shasta Dam was raised and its reservoir made 50 percent bigger; the Friant-Kern Canal was designed for greater capacity; the state plan to reverse the flow of the San Joaquin River by pumping plants was discarded and the more expensive Delta-Mendota Canal was substituted; a steam-electric generating plant was added.

These expansions hiked the cost. But the big reason for the soaring cost is that prices of men and materials went up sharply between 1933, when the cost estimates were made, and 1947, when prices were at a high point. So, even the $384,000,000 figure remains an estimate; it can go either up or down. There is some indication it may go up to $400,000,000.

. This is the 1947 itemized statement of the estimated costs:

Shasta Dam and reservoir	$114,652,000
Shasta power plant	18,309,200
Keswick Dam and reservoir	8,171,000
Keswick power plant	6,892,000
Delta Cross Channel	11,839,000
Contra Costa Canal	5,439,300
Delta-Mendota Canal	71,175,000
Friant Dam and reservoir	20,461,000

Madera Canal ....$ 2,575,000
Friant-Kern Canal   36,834,000
Tracy steam-electric plant   26,144,000
Transmission lines   50,289,000
Water rights, etc.   8,457,500
Contra Costa distribution system........   3,074,000
                                        _____
      Total $384,314,000

Until recently there had been no indication as to how much of this total would have to be paid back to the federal government. There had been no allocation of costs to the various functions of the project: navigation, flood control, irrigation, repulsion of salt water in the Delta, municipal and industrial water, wild-life benefits, recreation, and commercial power. Early in 1947, however, a report on the allocation and probable repayment of costs was submitted to Congress by the Department of Interior. This document foresees full payment for the project by the year 2009. This allocation of costs was presented:

FUNCTIONS TO WHICH COSTS MAY PROPERLY BE ALLOCATED
Navigation ....$ 18,083,000
Flood control   31,444,000
Irrigation (including salinity repulsion) 199,661,100
Contra Costa distribution system   3,074,600
Canal capacity for future water   18,815,900
Municipal water   9,091,800
Commercial power 104,143,600
                                         _____
      Total $384,314,000

The federal government will pay for flood control and navigation features of the project—$49,527,000. This is an outright gift. Thus, the actual amount which will have to be repaid to the government is $334,787,000.

The $199,661,100 which the irrigation features will cost is to be repaid without interest. Actually, it is far more than water users can pay, as will be shown, and power revenues will repay the bulk of it. The $3,074,600 for the Contra Costa distribution system will be repaid by water users in 40 years; it will carry no interest. The allocation for canal capacity for future water will be paid by users of that future-delivery water. If the water is not delivered, however, the cost of additional capacity will be paid from other project revenues. Costs allocated to municipal and industrial water will be paid with 3 percent interest. The cost of the commercial power installation also will carry 3 percent interest.

The allocation report assumes that all water features of the project will be completed by 1950 and in full use by 1965. It assumes that electrical generating capacity will be installed by 1951, transmission lines will be completed by 1955, and full utilization of the power features will be reached by 1965. It projects repayment schedules to the year 2009—or 44 years after the project is complete and in full operation.

Money to repay the federal government will come from four sources: sale of water to irrigators; sale of commercial power; sale of water for municipal and industrial uses; through a 40-year repayment contract for the Contra Costa distribution system (which really is not a part of the initial features of the project). Revenue from sales of power and municipal water will more than pay off the costs allocated to them. The "profit" will go to pay off the irrigation costs. Revenues from the repayment contract for the Contra Costa system will exactly meet the cost obligation.

Water for irrigation will be delivered at rates sufficient to cover operation, maintenance, and replacement costs "and a fixed charge, the total determined on the basis of farm benefits of water and of the estimated ability of water users to pay over a protracted period." A breakdown of repayment probabilities is offered in the allocation report:

Irrigation

Irrigation water from the Central Valley Project will serve a wide variety of agricultural purposes. Some will go directly to lands not previously under irrigation; some will serve as supplemental surface water to lands now irrigated but with inadequate or precarious supplies; some will be used mainly to replenish lowering ground water tables in areas largely or exclusively dependent on ground water for irrigation. The products from the land receiving water will cover the entire range of a remarkably diverse agriculture in the different sections of the valley, from citrus, deciduous fruits, and truck, to hay, dairy and livestock. Benefits from the use of irrigation will therefore vary greatly from area to area, and from one use to another; the cost of delivering water to different areas will likewise vary greatly.

The report shows that farm benefits per acre-foot of water vary from $3.00 to $15.00 depending on the soil and type of farming. It strikes an average benefit figure, $6.50, deducts the probable cost of distribution from main canals of $2.35 an acre-foot, and arrives at a "reasonable" canalside or riverbank price of $4.15 per acre-foot for Class I, firm, dependable water. For Class II water, a reasonable price is set at $2.15 per acre-foot. But:

> Even conservative estimates of benefits or value of irrigation water may constitute over-estimates of the amounts that can be or will be paid, however, unless allowance is made for special factors which frequently adversely affect the collection of revenues for provision of irrigation water supply. A principal factor in this connection is established capitalization into land values of the irrigation increment without the costs thereof having been retired, with the result that the actual operator is frequently burdened with excessive capital costs. There is likewise always a possibility of rising costs or unusual losses. Furthermore, it is reasonable to assume that the direct benefit to the farmer for the use of water should be substantially higher than the total price he must pay for it.

So, instead of setting the average price at $4.15 and $2.15 for Class I and II water, "an allowance is made of approximately one-third of the estimated benefit, which would establish a weighted average price of Class I water at $2.70 and of Class II water at $1.45." Both prices are for canalside or riverbank delivery.

The report then says:

> Under the proposed schedule of rates based on estimates of benefits and of the amounts irrigators may reasonably be expected to pay, under circumstances of full development and operation of the authorized project, irriga-

tors would annually pay a total of $4,329,965 for canal-side water, whereof $2,702,984 will be needed for operation and maintenance and replacement charges, and $1,626,981 will apply to repay the capital costs allocated to irrigation.

As we shall see later, the actual contribution from irrigation will be substantially smaller than this annual payment.

Commercial Power

The electrical energy not needed for project pumping works will be sold at rates sufficient to repay the costs allocated to power, plus 3 percent interest. The report states:

An average rate for sale of commercial power for the pay-out period has been fixed at the level necessary to repay the allocation to commercial power, plus 3 per cent on the outstanding balance, within 50 years after the completion of construction of the authorized power features. The rate as derived is 4.6 mills.* It is assumed that present contractual arrangements will prevail through 1949. [The Pacific Gas and Electric contract.] The payout period average rate of 4.6 mills per kilowatt hour is assumed to apply thereafter, although all power facilities are not assumed to be fully constructed until 1955. For that portion of the power used for project pumping, a charge is made of 2.5 mills as the equivalent of a proportionate share of the operation, maintenance and replacement costs borne by the joint project power facilities.

An interim power rate schedule for the Central Valley Project . . . . would realize an estimated 5.137 mills per kilowatt hour under prevailing market conditions and load factors. Both the interim schedule and the projected average rate are substantially below existing rates within the project service area, and because of this and because of the steadily increasing demand for power it is reasonable to assume that the 4.6 mill rate can be maintained as an average for the 50-year period within which allocated costs will be repaid with 3 per cent interest . . . .

Municipal and Industrial Water

It is not possible to make a precise determination of the amount of project water that will be supplied to municipal and industrial uses. Care-

---

* This is qualified in the report by this statement: "The average rate employed in the pay-out table to test repayment probability is actually .03 mills less than this, or 4.57 mills."

ful survey of the present and potential demand indicates, however, that the initial demand for about 25,000 acre-feet in 1950 will probably rise to about 68,000 acre-feet annually when full development of the authorized features is attained in 1965. A rate of $10 per acre-foot has been assumed in this report for water for these purposes. This rate may be judged by comparison with prevailing rates in areas adjacent to those where sales are contemplated. The principal alternative source sells water on a rate schedule varying from $52.27 to $95.83 per acre-foot within its district, depending on the amount used and exclusive of meter service charges. This water is treated, but the cost of treatment will not exceed $10 per acre-foot. It is estimated that, under full operation of the authorized project, gross annual revenues from the sale of municipal and industrial water will amount to $680,000 whereof $119,070 will be necessary to support operation, maintenance and replacement costs, and $560,930 will be available for application to capital costs. This will be sufficient to repay the allocated costs during the project repayment period, plus 3 per cent interest on the unpaid balance, and to meet an appropriate share of other fixed costs of the project water supply.

Contra Costa Distribution System

The Contra Costa distribution system, the estimated cost of which is $3,074,600, will distribute project water from the Contra Costa Canal to some 22,000 acres in Contra Costa County . . . . will be the subject of a separate repayment contract executed under authority of Section 9 (*d*) of the Reclamation Project Act. It is estimated on the basis of present construction costs that repayment in 40 years will involve a total cost of water at the farm headgate of from $5.25 to $6.00 per acre-foot, including all operation and maintenance charges and payment likewise of the projected rate for Central Valley Project water. This total cost per acre-foot is to be compared with estimated benefits of approximately $20 per acre, the area being suburban, cultivation intensive, and order of use high . . . .

Canal Capacity for Future Water

When the Delta Cross Channel, the Delta-Mendota Canal, and the Contra Costa Canal were designed, they were given a capacity to carry more water than is immediately available. It is planned that additional reservoirs will store water which ultimately will be carried in these canals. The report says:

When such water is made available it probably can be distributed at rates sufficient to provide, in addition to operation, maintenance and replacement expenses, repayment of the $18,815,900 allocated to the canal capacity provided for it. Early requirements for the additional water are evident and authorization to construct the necessary reservoirs is expected in the near future. Should the proposed reservoirs not be constructed or the revenue from supplying the additional water not be sufficient to repay the cost, such repayment can be made within a few years from the net revenues available from the other project functions subsequent to complete repayment of the costs allocated to them.

Using these probabilities and the revenue figures listed above, the report looks ahead to the years 2004 and 2005. By 2004, the gross income from the sale of irrigation water (at the maximum weighted average rates of $2.70 for Class I water and $1.45 for Class II water) would amount to $220,638,144. After deducting expenses for operation, maintenance, and replacement ($148,132,-332), the net income from irrigation water sales would be $72,-505,812. The report says:

> . . . . this sum, together with the financial assistance from other project functions within the same period of time . . . . would be sufficient to repay completely the capital costs allocated to irrigation. Under these circumstances, the net revenue applicable to repayment of the reimbursable capital costs of the project would amount, by the year 2004 for the project water services, and by the year 2005 for commercial power, to the sums shown in the right hand column . . . . below:

TABLE III

	Allocation	Applicable Net Revenues
Irrigation	$199,661,100	$ 72,505,812
Contra Costa distribution system...	3,074,600	3,074,600
Municipal water	9,091,800	27,424,212
Commercial power	104,143,600	214,479,257
Totals	$315,971,100	$317,483,881
Surplus		$ 1,512,781

At the rate of $1,626,981 a year, irrigation water revenues thus would pay off $72,505,812 toward the cost of the irrigation features of the project by 2004. The Bureau of Reclamation, however, does not expect irrigators to pay this much. The report states:

Foreseeing that the farmers' ability to pay for irrigation water may be reduced below the levels which now appear wholly reasonable and probable, provision for the reduction of rates below the maximum will be included in this contract under which irrigation water will be provided. In consideration of the terms of the water service contracts, which will provide for the annual determination of water rates based on current operation, maintenance and replacement costs, and on the water users' ability to pay in the particular year, an allowance of approximately $23,000,000 is made for such contingencies. In this event, the amount available for repayment of construction costs will probably not be sufficient to repay the previously stated sum of $72,505,812 by the year 2004, and continuing payments of similar water rates until the year 2009 will be necessary in order to accomplish full project repayment.

Under these conditions, net irrigation revenues through the year 2008 will have amounted to $54,272,989 and this sum, together with the financial assistance received from other project functions through the same period, $146,770,539, will leave $3,386,672 of the irrigation allocation of $199,661,100 remaining to be paid in the year 2009. This balance of $3,386,672 can be met by application of the annual net irrigation revenues ($1,197,886) plus $2,188,786 from the net power revenues, for the year 2009, bringing the final repayment from irrigation revenues to a total of $55,470,875.

The total amounts repaid, through the year 2009, for all functions will be by commercial power $227,757,693, by irrigation $55,470,875, by municipal and industrial water $29,667,932 and by the Contra Costa distribution system $3,074,600, leaving a surplus in that year of $2,068,694 from net revenues from commercial power and municipal and industrial water.

In tabulated form, here is a statement of allocation of costs and repayment in the year 2009:

	Cost Allocation	Probable Repayment
Nonreimbursable		
Navigation	$ 18,083,000	
Flood control	31,444,000	
Total nonreimbursable	$ 49,527,000	

Reimbursable	Cost Allocation	Probable Repayment
Irrigation (including salinity repulsion) . . .	$199,661,100	$ 55,470,875
Contra Costa distribution system	3,074,600	3,074,600
Municipal and industrial water	9,091,800	29,667,932
Commercial power	104,143,600	227,757,693
Total reimbursable	$315,971,100	$315,971,100
Canal capacity for future use	18,815,900	18,815,900*
Total reimbursable cost of project.	$334,787,000	$334,787,000
Total nonreimbursable cost of project. .	49,527,000	
Total cost of project	$384,314,000	

* To be repaid by water users when water from additional storage is available. According to the report: "The allocation of $18,815,900 is only about three times the amount of net revenue ($5,455,366) estimated on the basis of less favorable assumptions regarding irrigation water revenues. In the event additional storage capacity is not made available, this allocation can be repaid by the year 2012 by the application thereto of the total net revenue from the project after other costs have been returned."

Thus will the Central Valley Project be paid off—forty-four years after the full project as authorized is being fully used.

Obviously, the irrigationist is getting a colossal bargain. These figures show that 61 percent of the capital costs of the project allocated to irrigation are to be paid off out of power revenues and another 11 percent by revenues from sale of water for municipal and industrial use. But it was not long after the allocation report was sent to Congress that the Bureau of Reclamation mimeographs were churning out statements showing that these figures, generous as they are, do not begin to tell the whole story of the benefits received by irrigationists.

Said Richard Boke, regional director of the Bureau: "Because of the immense aid given by power revenues, Central Valley farmers using the project's irrigation supply will have to repay only $55,000,000 of the almost $200,000,000 listed as the cost of the irrigation works. It is not difficult to show what CVP water would have cost if it were not for this help from power, and the farmers themselves had to repay, through their water rates, all irrigation costs." He presented this table:

	Class I Water (Dependable supply)	Class II Water (Seasonal supply)
Average price per acre-foot farmers will actually pay	$2.70	$1.45
Price if power revenues were eliminated	4.24	2.28
Price if power for project had to be bought commercially, instead of supplied by Shasta power plant	5.27	2.83

"Assistance to farmers from power revenues," he said, "is not the only subsidy to irrigation . . . . Canal-side prices for CVP water would have to be very much higher if it were not for the fact that money to build irrigation features is provided by the Federal Government without interest." He showed how on this table:

	Class I Water	Class II Water
Actual average price per acre-foot	$2.70	$1.45
Price if money drew 1⅞ percent (average rate the government pays on its bonds)	4.34	2.33
Price if money drew 3 percent (as on federal power projects)	5.45	2.98
Price if money drew 5 percent (average for irrigation district bonds)	7.98	4.28

Then he added together the two subsidies, power assistance and interest-free money, and came up with this table:

	Class I Water	Class II Water
Actual average price	$ 2.70	$1.45
Price at 1⅞ percent money	6.91	3.72
Price at 3 percent money	8.11	4.36
Price at 5 percent money	10.65	5.67

The Bureau of Reclamation now proposes to collect the irrigators' money through contracts with irrigation districts or municipal utility districts. Methods of collecting repayment funds are outlined in the Reclamation Project Act of 1939. Two kinds of contracts are authorized and the Bureau proposes to use both of them. In contracting for sale of Central Valley water, the Bureau will use the so-called 9 (e) form, which is considerably more flexible than the 9 (d) contract, the straight, 40-year repayment agreement. Contract 9 (e) will be used to assure repayment of the major features of the project; contract 9 (d) will provide for repayment for construction of works to distribute water from the main canalside to the individual's land. In the final Central Valley pattern, the United States will own the major features of the project; local districts will own their own distribution systems to carry the water from government canals to their members. The repayment contract for the Contra Costa distribution system, for instance, will be form 9 (d) providing for repayment of its construction cost within 40 years in 40 equal installments. Water users also will be paying at the same time, their share of the operation, maintenance, and replacement costs of the main Central Valley features plus a certain amount for repayment of the capital cost of the main features.

Present plans for repayment of capital costs are different from the original scheme. At first it was proposed that the United States contract with the California State Water Project Authority (set up in the Central Valley Project Act) for payment:

"Negotiations are in progress with the State constituted water project authority for the repayment of all funds under the terms of the reclamation laws and by means of power revenues from plants included in the development," said the Bureau of Reclamation in 1936.

Similar statements were made by the Bureau in justifying its applications for funds between 1936 and 1940. In 1941, the wording was changed drastically:

Repayment.—The Central Valley project is being constructed by the Bureau of Reclamation and repayments will be provided for under contracts with persons, firms and corporations, to be hereafter made pursuant to the reclamation law . . . . and from revenues derived from sale of surplus power to be generated at Shasta Dam.

No mention of the state, no mention of the Water Project Authority. Secretary Ickes climaxed this shift in a letter to Governor Olson in 1939, saying that his department could not contract with the Water Project Authority because the Authority had no power to assess property of water users and no power to create liens against their property. ". . . . It is, therefore, very doubtful whether it could be the contracting agency for the purchase of the principal part of the water supply to be made available by this project."

Under the 9 (*d*) contract, capital costs must be repaid in 40 annual installments following, in most cases, a development period of ten years. During the development period payment of the capital cost can be deferred. A Bureau of Reclamation bulletin to field officials had this to say:

Under arrangements of this type, the district or other contracting organization assumed full obligation for the repayment of capital costs within the stipulated period, and fulfillment of the contract constituted purchase by that organization from the United States of the irrigation works involved.

It should be noted in passing that contracts drawn under this authority have only rarely been fully observed or enforced, particularly in respect to the repayment period. Conditions over which neither the Bureau on the one hand nor the water users or their organizations on the other could prevent—such conditions as the irrigation increment raising land prices with a change of operators before construction costs were repaid, or serious deflation in agricultural prices—have commonly made it extremely difficult or impossible for farmers to pay off the capital obligation within the contract period.

In contrast to arrangements of this kind, Section 9 (*e*) authorizes the sale of water—the sale of water as distinguished from a contract to repay capital costs—at rates sufficient to cover appropriate operation and maintenance charges and in addition to this return to the United States an amount equal to the capital costs allocated to irrigation within a period that is less than the useful lifetime of the project . . . .

In essence, it allows for the pricing of the project commodities (water and power) according to the costs of production (amortization of capital costs plus operation and maintenance) according to the market (ability and willingness to pay). This amounts, in effect, to an adaptation of standard business practice.

This is Section 9 (*e*) which will rule on sales of Central Valley water:

In lieu of entering into a repayment contract pursuant to the provisions of subsection (*d*) of this section to cover that part of the cost of the construction of works connected with water supply and allocated to irrigation, the Secretary (of the Interior) in his discretion, may enter into either short- or long-term contracts to furnish water for irrigation purposes. Each such contract shall be for such a period not to exceed forty years, and at such rates as in the secretary's judgment will produce revenues at least sufficient to cover an appropriate share of the annual operation and maintenance cost and an appropriate share of such fixed charges as the Secretary deems proper, due consideration being given to that part of the cost of construction of work connected with water supply and allocated to irrigation; and shall require payment of said rates each year in advance of delivery of water for said year. In the event such contracts are made for furnishing water for irrigation purposes, the costs of any irrigation distribution works constructed by the United States in connection with the new project, new division of a project, or supplemental works on a project, shall be covered by a repayment contract entered into pursuant to said subsection (*d*).

The allocation report referred to above said:

The very complex nature of the project, caused by the interrelationship of the authorized features makes necessary a high degree of flexibility with regard to water and cost allocations, operations and contracts. Because of the complexity of the water exchange plan which forms the basis of the project, there can not be any direct, exclusive, and unaltering relationship between individual water users or individual contracting organizations on the one hand, and all of the integral project features involved in the supply of water, on the other hand. The fact that one of the most important functions of the project is the provision of supplemental water for the recharge of badly depleted ground-water supplies illustrates again the necessity of flexibility in all allocations and contracts, as adjustment of the amounts of water required will be necessary from time to time to achieve complete utilization of water supplies. Other adjustments will be necessary over a long period as additional features are added to the project providing new water supplies until the project reaches a state of equilibrium. For these reasons, it is planned that water for irrigation will be furnished under the provisions of Section 9 (e) of the Reclamation Project Act of 1939 on a canal-side and river-bank basis.

It is important that a clear distinction be observed between the central features of the project which will provide common services, and the irrigation water distribution systems which serve a single contracting unit. As already indicated, water furnished by the project will be delivered to water users' organizations on a canal-side or river-bank basis. The contractual terms under which this water is furnished will both reflect and form a part of the financial structure and operational arrangements of the central group of common features which provide the project supply of water (and power). The centralized operation of the Central Valley Project ends at the point where water is delivered on a canal-side or river-bank basis.

Whatever supplementary distribution systems for irrigation water are necessary or desirable . . . . will be the subject of individual and separate repayment contracts executed under authority of Section 9 (d) . . . . and will have no direct relationship to the central operation, control, and financial accounting of the Central Valley Project . . . .

Under terms of section 9 (e), the Bureau proposes to service Central Valley water to the lands which need it most. Studies of the land and water supply in an irrigation or municipal utility district will be made before a contract is entered into to determine the quantity of water needed. These studies are made by Bureau engineers with officials and technicians of the districts.

Contracts drawn under 9 (e) specify the maximum charge which will be made for Class I and II water during the life of the contract. The Secretary of the Interior, however, may reduce the rate in years of poor crop returns or low prices. In the contract signed by the Southern San Joaquin Municipal Utility District, the maximum price set for Class I water is $3.50 per acre-foot and $1.50 per acre-foot for Class II water. As noted above, this is the only contract signed by the Bureau and it is the contract which is being fought by Senator Downey and the Irrigation Districts Association.

Downey has five major objections to contracts similar to the Southern San Joaquin Municipal Utility District agreement. Downey has promised a Senatorial investigation. The contract, he says, "is designed to place the Federal Government in perpetual owner-ship and control of all water from the Central Valley project." The first and most important objection to it, he reported, is that it will foster "almost endless litigation between irrigation districts and the large and small land owners within the districts which might well wreck the economy of the Central Valley and throw upon the small farmers the entire financial burden of the Central Valley Project."

The other objections he listed as follows:

1. No water rights whatever are acquired by irrigation district through the purchase of water, thus, in effect, violating the long established principle of joining water rights to the specific lands they serve.

2. An irrigation district accepting such a contract gets no credit toward repayment of the costs of constructing the project as contemplated by the Federal Reclamation Act.

3. At the expiration of a 39-year contract the irrigation district would be compelled to seek another contract under such terms as the Bureau of Reclamation would choose to offer; no permanent rights, as above indicated, having been acquired.

4. The Bureau of Reclamation as a result of such a policy would remain in the Central Valley in perpetuity as the owner of the project and all its water supply, controlling the agriculture and industrial economy through its control of water resources.

A similar discourse was offered to the Irrigation Districts Association of California by its counsel. He gave these reasons why irrigation and other districts in California should not execute water contracts with the United States for water to be delivered by districts to lands within their boundaries if such contracts contain acreage limitations or provisions for operations to be carried on under rules and regulations of a Federal agency:

1. In general, the right to water in California is vested in those who have by appropriation or otherwise acquired rights thereto or the water belongs to the State of California.

2. The United States does not own the water or water rights generally but seeks to withhold water on theory that the use of works built by the United States gives right to dictate not only the use of the water but the purposes and acreage for which it may be used.

3. Neither districts by contract nor State Legislature by legislation can legally deprive landowners of the use of the lands or their rights to water.

4. Proposed contracts with the United States would require approval of the Districts Securities Commission and it is submitted the Commission could not approve contracts depriving landowners of existing property or water rights.

5. Landowners may not lawfully be coerced into signing contracts with acreage limitations or submitting to be governed by rules and regulations of a Federal agency and by this process have vested rights taken or jeopardized.

6. Theory of Federal control of acreage or use of land in private ownership not in harmony with original intent or past practices and any effort now of Federal control of water and electrical power through threat or refusal of water is unconstitutional.

7. The whole philosophy of communal and socialistic control of land acreage and use of water and electric energy as proposed is not only unsound in principle but in direct violation of the rights of California and individual property owners.

Without attempting even to outline the complexities of water rights in California, a brief look at how the Bureau of Reclamation plans to proceed is in order.

The Bureau explains that there are two kinds of water involved in the Central Valley Project. There is, first, pre-project water— the water normally available to water users along any stream before construction of the project. Water rights already are held on this normal flow and the Bureau is bound by law and its own policy to respect those rights. Second, there is what the Bureau calls "project water." This is the water which becomes available because of the construction of dams and reservoirs and canals.

Under the law a water user cannot be deprived of the water he is entitled to under his right. On the Sacramento, for instance, the rights of water users along its banks must be satisfied before any water can be diverted into the San Joaquin Valley. The water to be diverted is project water which was dammed and stored instead of being allowed to run off through the Golden Gate or to flood the land in the spring runoff.

Now this would be a simple matter if rights were clear-cut in relation to the available water. However, there are a multitude of water-right claims. In the aggregate, these claims cover more water than is available. To seek a balance and to avoid infringing on bona fide rights, the Bureau takes three steps: (1) a specific water right is recognized; (2) it is determined just how much water is involved in the right; (3) the right is satisfied.

To schedule delivery of project water, the Bureau must know how much water must be serviced first to satisfy water rights. The Bureau is seeking agreements with water users to determine the scope of their rights. The Bureau, after consulting available records, makes an offer to a holder of a water right to deliver a certain quantity of water to satisfy the right. Usually this offer of water is somewhat larger than the amount which has been available under the right in the past. It is "free water." The Bureau makes no charge for it because it does not belong to the Bureau.

If the water-right holder is not satisfied with the offer, the matter will be decided in the courts. This is a last resort (because the litigation is slow and usually costly) but it is inevitable if the water user and the Bureau cannot agree. Once the right is determined, either by agreement or by the courts, the Bureau is committed to satisfy the right. Satisfaction of the right, in most cases, merely will entail delivery of free water to the holder of the right.

There is a further complication, however. Since the courts may award water rights which in the aggregate would claim more than the normal flow of a stream, the Bureau may have to buy a portion of the rights—a portion of the right over and above the historical normal delivery of water. In any event, no water user will receive less free water than he did before the project was built and, the Bureau says, he probably will receive more because of stream regulation.

While only one long-term water service contract has been signed, others are in process. Water so far made available by the project is being sold on a temporary basis to the Madera Irrigation District, the Contra Costa Water District, and others. The Madera Irrigation District has indicated that it has serious objections to the standard water-service contract, which as we have noted, contains provisions for the enforcement of the 160-acre limitation.

Because of its failure to negotiate either repayment or water-service contracts until recently, many farmers in the Central Valley believe the Bureau will be caught with "its goods on the shelf." That is, the project will be completed but contracts for disposal of the water and power will not have been signed. If that comes to pass, the Bureau, they say, will have to dispose of its wares on the buyers' terms—junking, if necessary, the 160-acre limitation and making other concessions simply to avoid wasting the water.

Reclamation law provides that repayment contracts must be signed before construction of projects begins. These contracts were not signed in advance of construction of the Central Valley Project —the project is past the halfway mark and only one contract has been signed. The Bureau explains the lack of contracts by saying that the federal government took over the project in the Depression: the important thing, at that time, was to get construction under way to provide jobs for the jobless. In the record, I have found nothing to support the statement, yet it is undoubtedly true. Certain it is that Congress, knowing the repayment contracts were not signed, continued to give approval to the project and to vote great sums of money for its furtherance.

There is nothing sinister in the Bureau's lack of contracts. It is probable, however, that many officials within the Bureau now regard failure to negotiate contracts a great mistake in administration.

XII. Throw the Rascals Out

CHARLES G. JOHNSON is the treasurer of the state of California. As such, he is the senior member of the Central Valley Project Authority, set up in the 1933 Central Valley Project Act. He is a tall man with a ruddy face, a cigar, a shock of white hair, and a fine deep voice. From time to time he raises this voice to protest against what he terms the federal encroachment on the sovereignty of the state of California. Although he is fighting mainly for the waning powers of the Central Valley Project Authority, his battle is the same as those groups and persons who believe the state should control and operate the project just as soon as the Bureau of Reclamation gets through building it.

He admits that the Central Valley Project Authority seems to have lost its identity "in the whirlpool of federal activities." "We have always been imposed on and more or less snubbed by these ranters and knotheads who always sneak in on activities of this sort," he says. Johnson declares that California has legal title to the Central Valley Project. He contends that the state conceded to the federal government only the right to build the project with the understanding that the state would repay those costs of construction, except for the part necessary for flood control and navigation. "It was through the Authority that the federal government was first prevailed upon to take over the Central Valley," he says. "And the thought all along has been that they were building the project for California and that California would take it over when it was completed. We don't want to give control of the most fertile section of the state to Washington. That takes away from the sovereignty of the state."

In an official statement, Johnson recalled some pertinent history:

Immediately following the executive authorization of the Project as a
Federal undertaking in 1935, consultations between representatives of the
State Water Project Authority and the Bureau of Reclamation were carried
on for several months directed to the negotiation and execution of the contract between the Authority and the United States providing for repayment of the reimbursable costs by the State and for the operation and
maintenance of the project upon its completion by the State through the
Water Project Authority.

These consultations reveal that it was the full intention of the officials
of the United States Bureau of Reclamation at that time that such a contract
would be executed. However, pending the execution of such a formal contract, and in order to expedite the working out of final construction plans
and getting construction started, the Water Project Authority entered into
a contract on March 25, 1936, which contained a special provision setting
forth the contemplation that at the earliest practical date a contract would
be entered into between the Authority and the United States providing for,
but not limited to, operation and maintenance by the Authority of the
project upon assurance of satisfactory liquidation agreement to the United
States, of the cost thereof and further assurance by the Authority of securing appropriate contracts for the disposal of water and power.

. . . . the record indicates that at the time and for a considerable
period following the execution of the contract dated March 25, 1936, between the United States and the Authority, it was the intention (1) that a
formal contract would be entered into at some appropriate time between the
United States and the Authority providing for repayment and operation
and maintenance of the project by the state: (2) that in line therewith contracts relating to repayment including those covering sale of water and
power would run directly between the Authority and local agencies pur-
chasing water and power with such contracts subject to the approval of the
Secretary of the Interior; and (3) that in the meantime construction would
proceed on all units of the project as rapidly as funds were made available
therefor by appropriation or otherwise.

. . . . The contractual relationship initiated in 1936 between the Authority and the Bureau was modified to some extent in supplemental contracts executed on March 13, 1937, and November 8, 1937, with respect to
the contemplated execution of a formal contract providing for operation
and maintenance and repayment by the state; and in the supplemental contract dated January 17, 1939, there was no provision covering such con-

templated future contract. The contractual relationship was terminated on August 31, 1939, upon completion of investigations provided for in a final supplemental contract dated June 30, 1939.

It appears that with the passage of the Reclamation Project Act of 1939, the Secretary of the Interior and the Bureau of Reclamation had reached a decision (reflected by the cessation of contractual relationship between the Authority and the United States in 1939) to depart entirely from its original intention of executing a formal contract between the State of California through the Water Project Authority and the United States providing for operation and maintenance and repayment of reimbursable costs of the project by the State . . . .

The first contract between the Bureau and the Water Authority providing for co-operative investigations into some phases of the project included this sentence:

This contract is entered into in contemplation that a future contract will be entered into between the parties hereto, providing, among other matters, for the operation and maintenance by the Authority of the project or units thereof; for payment by the Authority to the United States for expenditures incurred in connection with the project and the securing of contracts by the Authority for the disposal of facilities to be made available by the project.

This wording was significantly changed, however, in a supplemental contract dated March 13, 1937. This time the sentence read: "This contract is entered into in the contemplation that, *if permitted by law,* a further contract will be entered into, etc. . . . ." Other supplemental contracts also carried the phrase, "if permitted by law," and in the final supplemental contract no reference was made to any future contract. The Bureau of Reclamation states that the Reclamation Act of June 22, 1936, "made it legally impossible, from the standpoint of the Bureau and the Department of Interior, for it to contract with the Authority for repayment."

Governor Olson, in a letter to Secretary Ickes in February of 1939 proposed that the United States enter into a contract with the Water Project Authority providing for state operation, maintenance, and repayment for the project. Ickes replied:

The Central Valley project is a Federal undertaking to be administered in accordance with the Reclamation Law. You suggest that the Federal Government look to the California State Authority for repayment of its investment, both in water and power facilities. While the special act authorizing the Central Valley project makes it possible for the Secretary of the Interior to contract with the State Authority, there is the underlying requirement of the Federal Reclamation laws as construed and applied by this Department, especially with respect to the principal part of the supply of irrigation water made available from a project, that repayment contracts shall be made only with agencies which have the power directly to assess and to create liens on the property of the water users. As I understand it, the Authority does not have this power, and it is, therefore, very doubtful whether it could be the contracting agency for the purchase of the principal part of the water supply to be made available by this project.

As we have seen, the Reclamation Act of 1939 gave the Bureau of Reclamation an alternative method of collecting money for repayment of the federal investment in the Central Valley Project. Since passage of that Act, the Bureau has bent its efforts toward getting water service, rather than repayment, contracts.

Nevertheless, says Johnson, the Water Authority "regardless of the apparent plans of the Bureau of Reclamation to maintain control of the project upon its completion and to operate and maintain it . . . . is taking steps preparatory to entering into negotiations with the Secretary of the Interior for the State's taking over the operation and maintenance of the project upon its completion in accordance with the original intention when the project was undertaken by the Federal Government."

Another letter, Ickes-to-Olson, outlined Interior policy regarding Central Valley. It was written after passage of the Reclamation Act of 1939—on January 18, 1940, to be exact:

. . . . I said that at a later date I would outline the principles which would clearly mark out the respective spheres in which the United States and the State of California might work in the operation of the Central Valley project.

The Bureau of Reclamation has the responsibility for the operation of the projects which it builds. It is the policy of the Department of Interior and of its Bureau of Reclamation to operate and maintain features of a complex reclamation project which serve in common several interests, or which serve multiple purposes. It is the policy to delegate to local irrigation interests the operation and maintenance of features of projects which serve them directly with water, provided proper organizations, thoroughly representative of all the local interests involved, are in a position to assume and to discharge the responsibility thus imposed.

Applying these policies to the Central Valley project, the Bureau of Reclamation will operate, for example, such features as Shasta Dam, reservoir, and power plant; the afterbay (Keswick) and power plant, if any, which may be constructed; and Friant Dam and reservoir.

Further application of these policies will mean that the United States will operate, at least temporarily, the cross channel diversion works, the West side pumping system, the Contra Costa Canal; the Madera Canal; and the Friant-Kern Canal. After a developmental period for each of these units, however, it may, under conditions satisfactory to the Secretary of the Interior and to the water users, transfer the operation of one or all of these features to local agencies in accordance with regular policy, if and when suitable local agencies are prepared to assume the operation and maintenance responsibilities. For example, the Madera Irrigation District may wish to and may qualify to operate and maintain the Madera Canal; the irrigation district in the locality may wish to and may qualify to operate and maintain the Contra Costa Canal; a board of control may be organized and may qualify to operate and maintain the Friant-Kern Canal, or some other arrangement with locally organized and responsible agencies may be made, etc. Some of the possibilities enumerated in this paragraph may be remote; some of them may follow naturally once service is begun by the particular feature of the project which is involved.

You are undoubtedly aware of the fact that in the sale of electric energy the Reclamation Law requires that a preference be given to public agencies. The preference is given in the right to buy and not in price schedules, since the Bureau of Reclamation must return to the United States the cost of its projects and therefore has a responsibility of obtaining a fair return in the sale of power.

In the sale of Central Valley power, the State, or an agency of the State acting in the interests of a group of public agencies having power outlets, would under suitable conditions, be admirably qualified to receive the preference given in the law. The State of California, I feel, has a responsibility in connection with the Central Valley project. This responsibility in part at least, might be discharged by the State's making itself ready to act as a power distributor or ready to act in the interests of public power distributors. The interest of the Department of Interior is to gain the widest possible public benefits from the project, and if it furthered this interest, I would be glad to make a contract with the State or a proper authority of the State for disposal of the Central Valley power . . . .

It is clearly evident that, should the Central Valley project power be marketed to or through public agencies, the need will have been created for a standby power plant of sufficient capacity to insure continuous service. A steam plant at Antioch has been proposed for that purpose. When this plant is needed, I shall advocate its construction by the United States, together with the construction of necessary transmission lines from Shasta Dam.

I shall consider the State or its authorized agency ready to negotiate with the United States for the purchase of power from the project when it has suitable market for power, I should, however, consider the State in the preferential market for power only to the extent to which it was prepared to market that power directly to consumers or among public power agencies.

You may judge from the above paragraph that if the State is to take all of the power which will be available, it will be necessary to organize and prepare public utility districts, or other proper organizations, in addition to those now existing within economical transmission distance of Shasta Dam . . . . This responsibility, it seems to me, devolves principally upon the State. This brings up the question of financing the local power districts. On this point it seems clear that the State should prepare itself to finance these districts, or by legislation should permit them adequately to finance themselves.

The Legislature, however, as we have seen, refused to provide a method for state financing of public utility districts and killed efforts to thaw the $170,000,000 in revenue bonds authorized by the 1933 Central Valley Project Act. For a time after the Legislature had acted, there was talk of a Federal Authority, modeled on the Tennessee Valley Authority for the Central Valley. Such an authority was proposed by Governor Olson, and President Roosevelt thought it a good idea. Secretary Ickes, however, and a majority of the California Congressional delegation did not favor the idea and it was never pushed, although a bill was introduced in Congress providing for the creation of nine such regional authorities, including one for the Central Valley. The California Grange was enthusiastic about the proposal but the Authority idea did not gain any substantial support otherwise. Nothing much has been said about an Authority for the last year or so. The California

State Chamber of Commerce and the California Farm Bureau Federation both opposed the Authority idea.

Said the Commerce Chamber's magazine, *California:*

Opposition to the creation of any Federal water authority in California is based upon these grounds:

1. Vested water rights, heretofore secure to private owners under State laws, would be subject to condemnation by the Authority at its option.

2. Federal authorities like the TVA are a dangerous welding of economic control and political power which threaten interference in social and cultural activities.

3. No proposed Federal regional authority is answerable to Congress for the expenditure of its revenues and they are, therefore, dangerous instruments of government.

When we surrender control over the spending of public money, we surrendered control of government.

Said the Farm Bureau:

California Farm Bureau Federation opposes all such dictatorial proposals and insists upon the maximum control of the useful waters of any area by the people applying such waters to a beneficial use, and we hereby call upon our duly elected state officials to assume leadership in preventing the creation of any so-called "authority" in California.

It is to be assumed that, with a Republican majority in Congress, the authority idea will be pigeonholed for a time at least.

The State Chamber of Commerce has led the fight to regain the project for the state. Its spokesman declared at the California Water Conference in late 1945:

The State Chamber of Commerce recommends that management and control of the Central Valley project and all of its facilities which are properly State functions (irrigation and power) be restored to the State of California, the amount and method of payment therefor to be determined by negotiation.

State control and management of the Project is in accord with the general understanding ever since the project was established. In testimony before United States Senate hearings, prior to 1942, representatives of the U.S. Bureau of Reclamation clearly implied, and the State of California understood, that the project after completion would be controlled and operated by the State Authority.

We believe that this is the only way in which we can escape from the orbit of social planning and the loss of State's rights, for the Central Valley Project potentially is more than a plan for irrigation, flood and salinity control, navigation and the generation of electric power. Wrapped up in the same package is the power to influence greatly, sometimes to determine, where and how large numbers of inhabitants of the great valleys of California shall live, and whether business therein shall be privately or publicly owned and privately or publicly operated; as well as the power to influence, if not to determine, who shall be the owners of those agricultural lands in the valleys, the usefulness of which depends on irrigation.

The principal reason for insisting that the irrigation and power phases of the Central Valley Project shall be directed by California and not Washington is to make sure that issues affecting our social and economic system will be determined by the citizens of California through democratic processes, and not by the Board of Directors of a Federal Government corporation or by a proconsul from Washington . . . .

The State Chamber of Commerce recommends that adequate State legislation be adopted in order to establish an effective State Water Board with authority to represent the State in securing the enactment of required Federal legislation and to negotiate with the Federal Government for terms to accomplish the restoration of the Central Valley Project to the State of California . . . .

California had this to say about state control:

Under the State Chamber's program, the irrigation and power features of the Central Valley Project would be under the control of the State, but flood control, navigation and salinity control would remain as Federal responsibilities. This is the normal division of responsibilities between State and Federal Governments on projects of this type . . . . The creation of a strong State water board empowered to follow a plan of home control and development of water resources is necessary to prevent loss of local control over water and power—the two basic resources which underlie all economic development in California.

Prior to negotiations with the Federal Government, it would be possible to give only a general indication as to the cost to California if the State should assume control of the Central Valley Project. The State need not necessarily make any great expenditure. The project was authorized as a Federal Reclamation Project to be built by the U.S. Reclamation Service with money appropriated by Congress. After completion of the project, according to Reclamation Law the costs of the irrigation and power features are to be paid back to the Federal Government out of revenues from the sale of water and power in forty annual payments. Water is interest free, but the power features bear three per cent interest. Other costs of the project allocated to flood control, navigation, salinity control and fish and wildlife are not reimbursable costs and are, under any circumstances, gifts from the Federal Government. Very few reclamation projects have actually paid back to the Government the amounts which are reimbursable.

Both these statements follow the policy laid down by the Board of Directors of the Chamber of Commerce in May of 1945. The policy recommended that the Chamber oppose creation of any Federal Regional Authority having jurisdiction of any of the streams of California; support the principle that title and control of the Central Valley Project and all facilities which are properly state functions (in a footnote, it was explained that these state functions meant irrigation and power features of the project); flood control, navigation, and salinity control, said the footnote, are federal responsibilities — and should be restored to the state; support of legislation to accomplish this end.

In a letter to a San Francisco newspaper, Ickes commented at length on the Chamber of Commerce water policy. Although Ickes is no longer Secretary of the Interior, his remains a strong voice:

. . . . Of course, I well know the State Chamber of Commerce's record on the Central Valley Project. Originally it opposed the project outright in the early water and power act campaigns in California, but suddenly climbed on the band wagon after the people of California voted their approval of the project at the special election in December 1933. In the years that followed almost everyone in California, including even the State Chamber, paid vocal tribute to the Central Valley Project when it was a matter of interesting the Federal Government in it and obtaining money for its development. In recent years, however, with the Federal Government now committed to the program and the two main dams completed by the Bureau of Reclamation, the attitude of the State Chamber and some other special interests in California has changed from one of acclaim of the project's merits to claiming the project's benefits for their own exclusive profit. It is the age-old battle over who is to cash in on the unearned increment in land values created by a public investment.

I have looked over the names of the distinguished Californians responsible for the State Chamber's recommendations. Many of them are familiar.

The source of the recommendations convinces me that, regardless of their purport, their principal objective is to avoid application to the Central Valley of California of the long-established reclamation policy of the Congress which provides for the distribution of the benefits of great irrigation projects among the many and which prevents speculation in lands by the few. Certain interests would deny to California the manifold advantages of Federal reclamation, including its statutory preference to public agencies in the use of by-product power in order to retain for themselves a certain freedom for exploitation. They do not, I know, represent even a large minority of the people of California. However, they have certain advantages. They are well organized. They have money to spend in the employment of able counsel and on trips to Washington for appearances before Congressional committees. Against this array, sound public policy which favors continuation of the existing course of Federal reclamation has a hard road to travel.

The State Chamber's statement recommends restoration to the State of California of those Central Valley Project features that are "properly State functions," which a footnote alleges to be irrigation and power. The statement attempts, somewhat crudely, to show that the Bureau of Reclamation agreed to participate in the project only as a construction agency, and that it was "the general understanding both by the Federal agency in charge (U.S. Bureau of Reclamation) and the State Water Project Authority up until 1942 . . . . that the State of California would exercise control of the operation of the irrigation and power features of the Central Valley Project, after completion."

Well, let's look at the record. First, let me say that my Department and its Bureau of Reclamation always have recognized and still admire the fine work of engineering investigation done by the State Division of Water Resources under its capable chief, State Engineer Edward Hyatt, in the decade preceding the adoption of the project by the Federal Government. But I wish to point out that the Bureau of Reclamation was active in the Central Valley of California, too, prior to 1935. In fact, the Bureau's investigations into the water problems of the Central Valley began in 1902, the year the reclamation law was passed, and included no less than 14 studies and reports down through the years in proposed irrigation and power development in the Central Valley. One of the reports led to construction of the Orland Reclamation Project in Glenn and Colusa counties. In 1930, at the request of the State, which agreed to pay half the cost of the investigation, the Bureau undertook a three-year study of the Central Valley project, leading to a favorable report that I was glad to release publicly in July 1933.

About that time the State was making strenuous efforts to finance the project through the Federal Public Works Administration under an application for a grant and loan originally filed in September 1933. These efforts were unsuccessful because it was concluded that the net revenues of the project would be insufficient, under that type of financing, to assure repayment of the loan with interest at 4 per cent.

Then came the appeals to the Bureau of Reclamation which at that time was headed by Commissioner Elwood Mead, himself a Californian. Dr. Mead assured Mr. Hyatt from the start that if the Bureau accepted the responsibility of building the project, it would not relinquish its operation and management to the State. Nevertheless, it was agreed that we should proceed under the more favorable financial terms of the reclamation law, offering interest-free money for irrigation, and the project accordingly was included in the Bureau's application to the President for Emergency Relief funds. Californians en masse, from the Governor down, acclaimed President Roosevelt's action of September 10, 1935, allocating money to the Bureau of Reclamation to begin construction of the Central Valley Project "in accordance with the reclamation law." A coincident step under the law was to submit a Finding of Feasibility to the President. I don't mind revealing to you that the Finding of Feasibility on the Central Valley project which I submitted on November 26 and the President approved on December 2, 1935—making the project from that day forward a Federal Reclamation project—was prepared in draft form by State Engineer Hyatt of California with the assistance of John C. Page of the Bureau of Reclamation.

The very first Congressional appropriation for the project, passed June 22, 1936, placed it under the limitations of the reclamation law; and subsequently the Congress has reaffirmed its intent that the project be carried forward to fulfillment on the broadest objectives of that law, in 12 additional acts relating to the project passed every year down to and including 1945.

The Bureau's plans to operate and manage the Central Valley project after its completion, in accordance with these expressions of the will of the Congress, have remained consistent through the years and have been publicly proclaimed many times—as in my letter to the Governor of April 13, 1939: Commissioner Page's address at the Friant Dam celebration on November 5, 1939; and again in my letter to the Governor of January 18, 1940.

The State Chamber is misinformed on the history of the original proposal that the Bureau contract with the Water Project Authority for repayment of its investment. Ever since the act of June 22, 1936, we have considered this legally impossible, inasmuch as the Authority has not property-assessment powers as required by the reclamation law. As early as August 26, 1936, the Bureau so advised the Authority, and I confirmed this position, definitely and officially, in my letter to the Governor of April 13, 1939. The Bureau is proceeding on the plan that has been held for ten years, which is, to negotiate water and power repayment contracts with the local irrigation and utility districts qualified under State law.

Certainly there is no basis for the State Chamber's complaint that this involves "a completely new and unacceptable plan of Federal management and control along the lines of a Tennessee Valley Authority."

I do not wish to dwell at length on all the false assumptions and unwarranted conclusions contained in the State Chamber's statement, but there are three or four additional claims that I can not ignore.

For instance, it certainly is naive for the State Chamber to expect the Federal Government to hand over to the State the two revenue-producing facilities—irrigation and power—while retaining responsibility for flood control, navigation, salinity control, and fish and wildlife development which the State Chamber says "are not reimbursable costs and are, under any circumstances, gifts from the Federal Government." Apparently the State Chamber would like to have the entire project as a gift from the Federal Government, for it supports its argument for the proposed transfer with the amazing statement: "The State need not necessarily make any great expenditure."

I might add that irrigation and power development have been recognized responsibilities of the Federal Government for many decades, in just as good historical standing as flood control and navigation; and so far as salinity control is concerned, the only Federal authority that I know of for assuming that responsibility in the Central Valley of California is contained in the Secretary of Interior's approved Finding of Feasibility which the State Chamber would now abrogate.

I know of no possible alternative method of financing the project, under either Federal or State law, with anything near so favorable terms of repayment as those of the reclamation law. But I can only ascribe to ignorance of the law or willful misrepresentation the State Chamber's assumption that Federal appropriations for power, like those for irrigation on reclamation projects, are repayable "in 40 annual installments, interest free." This form of Federal Subsidy granted to reclamation water users on family-sized farms in the arid West never has been, and should not be, extended to power users.

Incidentally, the Federal Reclamation repayment record, which the State Chamber tosses aside with the remark that "very few" projects have paid back their reimbursable cost, stands today at 97.3 per cent of all the construction charges due and payable since 1902 . . . .

The Chamber apparently is hopeful that the state would be able to get interest-free money from the federal government after it took over the project. The attitude of the Department of Interior (at least while Ickes was Secretary, and there has been no indication of a change of tune) was outlined in a letter from Ickes to Governor Warren on March 7, 1945:

The question of whether the State of California is to assume the responsibilities of financing the construction of the Central Valley Project has been placed before you by a recently organized State group . . . .

Naturally the activities in relation to the Central Valley of such a group of well-known Californians interests me, since the Bureau of Reclamation of the Department of the Interior has an investment of $157,180,000 in the Central Valley project, and has plans for its completion which would involve additional expenditure of more than $200,000,000 during the postwar period, in order that all of the farmers of present and potentially irrigated lands might be assured of adequate water permanently.

In addition, the Bureau has tentative plans that might result in the construction in the Central Valley after the war of works requiring hundreds of millions more. The Reclamation Law, of course, has provisions that have proved very useful in the development of the West, including the clause which enables advancement of Federal funds without collection of interest charges on the capital outlay. I assume, of course, that the State would wish to protect the project in the manner of these provisions in its legislation and with its credits and funds . . . .

If the State has arrived at a financial position where it is ready to reimburse the United States Treasury for expenditures already made in behalf of the people of California, and is further prepared to guarantee the additional financing necessary to complete the project within a reasonable number of years, the Department of Interior is prepared to withdraw from the project. Before we hand back these responsibilities to the State, however, we feel that sufficient evidence should be presented to prove the willingness and ability of Californians to shoulder the burdens of this great enterprise . . . .

I would very much like to have your views on this, because the Bureau of Reclamation has made many commitments in regard to further development, and because the doubts which have been raised by the proposal to have the State again assume the responsibilities of constructing the Central Valley Project necessarily make us think twice before making further commitments, at least, until the present uncertainty is resolved. Do you think the State is now prepared to resume full responsibility for the Project?

Governor Warren's answer to this letter was not made public. Warren has taken no position on the return-the-project-to-the-state program. "There can not be a simple 'yes' or 'no' answer to the question of State operation," he has said. "If we ask the Federal Government to come in here and build Shasta and Friant and the other works with its own money, we have to realize the Federal Government has something to say about the project. We can't eat our pie and have it, too."

An effort to get Congressional approval of a return of the project to California was made March 23, 1945, when House Joint Resolution 139 was introduced. This resolution would have set up a "Central Valley Commission" of five members, including the Commissioner of Reclamation, a representative of the Corps of Engineers, and three others. This Commission would have been empowered to determine reimbursable costs of the project. It provided that at any time within three years after the adoption of the joint resolution by the Senate and the House, the state of California could elect to reimburse the United States for the irrigation and power features of the project. Reimbursement was to be "in the manner provided in the reclamation laws for repayment of construction costs," i.e., in 40 annual installments, the money to be interest-free as to the irrigation costs. This joint resolution, however, did not pass.

In light of the Chamber of Commerce's plea for local control, echoed by the Farm Bureau, the attitude of the Madera Irrigation District is significant. The statement was made by an M.I.D. spokesman at the California Water Conference in late 1945:

A third point referred to by conference speakers was that of Federal versus State control of the Central Valley project. In spite of the arguments which have been offered as to why the project should be transferred to the State, the Directors of Madera Irrigation District are unconvinced as to the advantages to be gained by such a course, and as a matter of fact advocates of such a transfer have not been very specific as to how the project would be operated or maintained, nor just what would be the basis of repayment under State jurisdiction.

Under the Federal Reclamation law the procedure seems fairly well outlined and the basis of payment established; namely, interest-free money with 40 years to pay out. This district also expects to invoke the provisions of the Federal law under which it will be possible to finance construction of a lateral system on the same basis. We see no particular advantage in any switch in operation and maintenance of Friant Dam and reservoir and Madera Canal from Federal to State auspices. This district expects to buy water from the project at the side of the Madera Canal and below those points to have exclusive jurisdiction over the disposition of the water and affairs of the district. We feel that Bureau operatives are competent men who know their business, as it is assumed State operatives would be if they were in control—there is no good reason to assume that one agency will do any better job than the other in that respect.

It has been claimed by proponents that under State jurisdiction and State law the troublesome excess land restrictions would be removed. Discussions between the State and Federal Governments do not seem to have proceeded far enough to give any assurance of this. It seems not impossible that if the Federal Government did turn the project to the State there might still be attached certain obligations to continue policies which the Federal Government considered to be in the interest of public welfare. Certainly there has been no indication that there may not.

The point has also been made that as a Federal undertaking, the Central Valley project will always be under the domination of politicians and bureaucrats in Washington. It is not a comfortable feeling to assume that a project of this magnitude will always be subject to such jurisdiction. Rather, it is felt that it will proceed and be administered on its merits as a project in the interest of the public good. If, however, it is considered that the project is fated to be dominated by political considerations only, it cannot be overlooked that similar activities exist at Sacramento as at Washington and in as virulent and active a form. The board of directors of Madera Irrigation District are not in agreement that transfer of the project from Federal to State control would necessarily eliminate these influences.

At the same conference, State Senator Oliver Carter, had this to say:

Some people have said, "Let the people of California take over." Well, if we are willing to pay for it, if we are willing to put up the money, then I say let the State of California take it over; but I mean we have to be willing to finance the project. We have to pay for that which has already been constructed and then we will have to be willing to put up the money to finish the project, otherwise we better quit talking about State projects.

All this talk about taking it over and letting the State take it over and pay for it on an easy payment plan, you are just talking through your hat, because Congressmen from New York and Congressmen from Louisiana or Congressmen from the Middle West are not going to give California anything. We have to conform to the pattern laid down by Congress in order to get Federal money. If we are to get Federal money we have to abide by Federal law. We delude ourselves if we think we can use Federal money without the application of Federal law . . . .

XIII. Sportsmen, Arise!

EATED ON a trestle across the Sacramento River at Balls Ferry is a man. He watches a slot beneath his feet. Every time a fish swims through the slot the man clicks a counter: right hand, big fish; left hand, little fish. This seems an odd pursuit, even for a government employee, but actually the man is doing important work. He is counting salmon, checking the upriver migration of the fish as they make their way from the sea to gravel spawning beds in the upper Sacramento and its tributaries.

Everybody knows the romantic story of the salmon. How it starts life in a fresh-water stream, goes down to the sea where in four or five years it gains maturity, and then, guided by some super-special sense, it battles its way upriver, escaping the nets and hooks of the fishermen, leaping over falls and other obstacles until it comes to the stream where it was born. There it mates and dies and the wondrous cycle begins again. All true. But hooks and nets seem to be the least of the migrating salmon's worry. Low water, water of the wrong temperature, water from foreign streams, and dams all conspire against the completion of the salmon's cycle.

The fish watcher on the trestle, clicking off the arriving salmon, is one of many men who are concerned with the salmon of the Sacramento and San Joaquin rivers. For the Central Valley Project and the works of the Corps of Engineers involve dams. Dams block streams; dams also block fish fighting their way upstream. Reservoirs behind the dams spread the water and allow it to be warmed by the sun; diversion canals can suck fish into their current and away from their natural habitat.

Shasta Dam provided the first difficult problem in relation to salmon in the Central Valley Project. It blocked off the spawning areas in the upper reaches of the Pit, McCloud, and Sacramento

175

rivers. More than $2,000,000 has been spent in an attempt to undo the harm which Shasta did to the salmon run. No adequate measurement of the worth of the $2,000,000 salmon salvage work has so far been made but the spending of $2,000,000 indicates the extent and the importance of the fishery problem.

As part of the project, the Bureau of Reclamation has provided an elaborate system of trapping salmon near Keswick Dam. It transports mature fish to other streams where they may spawn in natural gravel beds. Other adult fish are taken to a hatchery on Battle Creek where their eggs are hatched artificially. How successful this hatchery will be cannot be determined at this time. The California Division of Fish and Game says: "Judging from past records of the success of hatcheries, it is neither economically feasible nor biologically sound to attempt to substitute artificial for natural propagation where suitable conditions for natural propagation can be maintained." The Coleman Hatchery on Battle Creek has a capacity for 52,000,000 eggs but has not yet handled anywhere near that number in any one year.

Sportswriters rejoiced in the summer of 1947 when three-year-old salmon returned to the Coleman hatchery after spending their lives at sea. This return of the salmon to the only home they knew indicated that the hatchery program was working out well. The salmon had been marked before being released from the hatchery as fingerlings.

Salmon fishermen, both commercial and sport fishermen, are most concerned about two proposed structures. One is the Delta Cross Channel of the Central Valley Project. The second is the dam either at Table Mountain or Iron Canyon which the Corps of Engineers has been authorized to build. Local interests, as we have seen, are opposed to the Table Mountain–Iron Canyon project. The Bureau is studying a system of dams on the tributaries of the Sacramento which would eliminate the need—at least for many years—for a dam at the Table Mountain–Iron Canyon site on the main river. The Army, however, has rejected the tributary plan as too expensive. It is believed that the tributary dam system would have

a beneficial effect on the salmon run: it would eliminate an insur-
mountable barrier on the main river and would provide "live"
streams in the tributary channels during the spawning season and
for the period when the small, newly-hatched fry mature before
heading for the ocean.

The California Division of Fish and Game, in a special report,
states that salmon originating in the streams of the Central Valley
(the ones caught by commercial and sport fishermen) have an annual value of $1,300,000. The proportion of the run which origi-
nates above the site of the Table Mountain Dam (spawning in Clear
Creek, Cow Creek, Cottonwood creeks, and in the main river) is
worth $520,000 a year, says the report. "It is, therefore, of para-
mount importance that the effect of dams on fishery resources be
considered on the same basis as irrigation, power, flood control, and
salinity control in studying the economy of the basin-wide, multiple-
purpose projects." The pessimistic Division also declares: "In
addition to salmon and steelhead, shad and striped bass may be
seriously affected by the proposed dams . . . . The striped bass
alone supports a large sports fishery and was the principal species
sought by over 200,000 anglers who fished in the Central Valley
area in 1941."

The Division, observing that "Development of methods of over-
coming the adverse effect of dams and diversions on anadromous
fishes (such as salmon) has but recently been undertaken and results to date give no guarantee of success."

People who are interested in the salmon run as a means of livelihood, as a sport, and as a national resource, believe this is the least
that should be done:

Dams should be located as far upstream as feasible to avoid destruction
of spawning grounds. The transfer of runs to other streams is a poor substitute for the maintenance of original spawning areas.

Adequate flows must be maintained below dams:

a) To permit the upstream migration of adults.

b) To provide water for maintenance of spring-run fish in good condition over the summer.

c) To provide water during the spawning, hatching, and growing periods.

d) To permit the young salmon to perform their seaward migration.

The Division report continues:

It is essential . . . . that there be no artificial reduction in the flow from any dam from the beginning of the spawning period to the end of the period of emergence of young fish from the gravel. Variation from high to low flows will cause the loss of large numbers of eggs since spawning is usually concentrated along the stream margins which are dried up with any drop in flow.

The adults must have free access to the spawning grounds . . . . Streams should not be blocked by canal crossings . . . .

All mixing of waters from different streams through direct discharge from canals above the point where mixing naturally occurs should be kept at a minimum. Canals that dump directly into stream beds, mixing water supplies, are believed to be major hazards to fish life.

Adequate protection should be provided during construction periods . . . . to prevent any man-made catastrophe which might eliminate for all time a portion of, or a whole, annual cycle of salmon.

Planning, design and construction of temporary fish ladders, traps, lifts, tank trucks, or other facilities should be well in advance of the time they are actually required . . . .

Studies should be initiated to determine the need for screens and racks at all points where losses of either young or adults may occur in diversions . . . .

As a general principle of fish protection, consideration should be given by the engineers, in planning dams, to the levels at which water will be withdrawn from the reservoirs. These must be as low as possible in order that cool water may be discharged through them. Fish life in general and salmon in particular, require cool water. Water drawn from the warmer upper layers of reservoirs during holding, spawning, or incubation periods will cause heavy losses if the temperatures exceed the tolerance levels of the fish . . . .

It has been pretty well determined that construction of either a high or low-level dam at Table Mountain or at the alternative Iron Canyon site will effectively block the salmon run. If this dam is built, 40 percent of the salmon which normally spawn above Table Mountain will have no place to spawn; presumably they will die frustrated, without completing their cycle, unless something is done about it. Several plans are under study.

The California Division of Fish and Game has this to say about Table Mountain Dam:

It is understood that only a "tight" dam is now planned for this site. Earlier, consideration was given to construction of an open-type round-head, buttress dam that would store water only when flows exceeded 24,000 cubic feet per second. At flows lower than this, salmon could pass through to spawning grounds upstream. Even the latter type dam would have serious effects on salmon by (1) flooding out spawning grounds, (2) stranding seaward migrants as forebay levels fell in the reservoir, and (3) interrupting the migrations of adults and young fish during storage of flood waters.

Other plans propose an initial low dam to be followed later by the construction of a high dam at Table Mountain. In terms of fishery protection, both the initial and ultimate dams will have equally bad effects on salmon and steelhead runs except that the low dam (pool elevation 400 feet above sea level) will not flood out the new Coleman Salmon Hatchery on lower Battle Creek now being used in the Shasta program. It will flood the Balls Ferry rack and trap. Even though the low dam will not flood out the hatchery, it is questionable whether it will still be usable. The high dam will put all these facilities under 60 to 70 feet of water.

In view of the serious losses in the fisheries that may result from the construction of Table Mountain Dam, a reexamination of the economics of the entire project is recommended. The dam will completely nullify the present maintenance program now in operation below Shasta Dam, on which nearly $2,000,000 has already been expended. Furthermore, from a preliminary examination, the suggested methods for maintaining the runs appear to offer little hope of success.

The present annual value of salmon, exclusive of steelhead, originating in the upper Sacramento above Table Mountain is estimated to be $520,000. This is derived directly from the observed and estimated sizes of runs spawning in the different streams . . . . This area accounts for approximately 40 per cent of the total Central Valley salmon run. In addition to the loss of this annual income to the State, Table Mountain Dam will prevent full, future potential development of salmon run to the upper Sacramento River. The annual value of this potential increase is estimated to be in the order of $140,000 . . . .

A maximum run of 150,000 salmon migrate past Table Mountain dam site into the upper river. Of these, 125,000 compose the fall run, and the remaining 25,000 the spring run. The fall run peaks in late October, and the spring run about June 1.

One of the gravest dangers to salmon from construction of Table Mountain Dam is the problem of water temperatures. Water stored in Shasta Reservoir will be warmed considerably there. Released to flow into Table Mountain Reservoir, it would be warmed again, and might very well reach temperatures in excess of those tolerated by either young or adult salmon. These dangers would be more pronounced in the years of low run-off when the discharge from Shasta and Table Mountain reservoirs would be principally from the upper, warmer layers.

The temperature problem would also be present in the plan to divert water at or below Table Mountain to rehabilitate tributaries entering the Sacramento below it. The water would have to be carried considerable distances in open ditches and, even though it was drawn off the bottom of the reservoir, its suitability for salmon would be limited to its maximum temperature.

The following proposals have been advanced as offering possible solution of the salmon problem (or part of it) created by Table Mountain Dam. Fishery investigators are in agreement that none of them will prevent serious damage to the resource.

1. The salmon runs blocked at Table Mountain Dam might be maintained through artificial propagation. This idea is erroneous. To handle a run of 150,000 adult salmon would require hatcheries of unprecedented capacities, and to date no salmon run of commercial size has ever been maintained successfully by artificial propagation. All the hatcheries have done so far is to supplement natural spawning. In addition, there are no streams or springs in the vicinity of Table Mountain having the quantity or quality of water needed to supply a hatchery or hatcheries of the required capacity. The run now passing Table Mountain dam site can not be maintained by hatcheries alone.

2. The runs might be maintained by a combination of artificial propagation and natural spawning as in the present Shasta maintenance program. This might be accomplished by diverting Battle Creek around the forebay of Table Mountain reservoir and constructing another hatchery with rearing and holding areas near Table Mountain Dam. This would be expensive, and might not be justified in light of economic and biological studies.

3. Water might be diverted from a low dam immediately below Table Mountain Dam to rehabilitate a number of intermittent tributaries. The economic, engineering, and biological feasibility of this plan remains to be determined.

4. All spring run salmon might be trapped below Table Mountain Dam

and transferred to Mill Creek and Deer Creek for natural spawning. Only detailed studies would determine the practicability of this plan.

5. It has been suggested that fishing for resident game fish in Table Mountain Reservoir would more than counter-balance the loss of salmon and steelhead runs to the upper Sacramento River. Reservoirs with highly fluctuating forebay levels are poor producers of fish. The periodic drying up of the richer, food-producing, shallow water areas by seasonal storage and release of water seriously reduces production of fish. The history of most such reservoirs in terms of angling is one of diminishing returns. In most California reservoirs, the fishing has not compensated for the loss of runs of salmon and steelhead; and it is exceedingly doubtful that it would do so in this case.

In addition the system of dams on the tributaries has been suggested. These dams for flood control, irrigation, and river regulation would supposedly aid the propagation of salmon in the old-fashioned way. But the Army demurs:

Certain local interests have raised strong objections to the Iron Canyon project* on the grounds that the dam inundates about 1,850 acres of present irrigated lands and blocks off the remaining migratory fish spawning areas on the upper Sacramento River. Accordingly, investigations have been made to determine whether a combination of smaller reservoirs on the tributary streams entering the Sacramento River between Keswick Dam and Chico Landing could be economically substituted for the flood control storage proposed at the Iron Canyon site. Such studies indicate that, if foundation conditions are satisfactory, a combination of fourteen alternative reservoirs, located on twelve tributaries, with a combined storage capacity of not less than 800,000 acre feet might be substituted for the Iron Canyon project at an estimated first cost of not less than $70,000,000 or about $50,000,000 more than the cost of equivalent storage at Iron Canyon. The difference in storage requirements between the two plans to fulfill the same flood control accomplishments is due to the fact that storage at the Iron Canyon site is more strategically located than the storage at the individual alternate sites for the control of floods that might originate on various upstream subdrainage areas. The relative benefits between the main stream and tributary storage plans do not justify the increased investment necessitated by the latter plan, even if the tributary storage dams are

---

* Recall that the Army intends to substitute the Iron Canyon site for the Table Mountain site. In this discussion, however, there is little difference between the two sites.

credited with saving the whole Sacramento River migratory fish run, estimated to have a capitalized value of about $15,000,000 . . . .

The Corps of Engineers says further, in its comprehensive report:

The contemplated reservoir projects on the major tributaries of Sacramento and San Joaquin Rivers are proposed to be operated so as to maintain increased low water flows which would beneficially affect existing and potential fish life. The principal projects of this type are the Big Bend and Bidwell Bar Reservoirs on Feather River, the Bullards Bar Reservoir on Yuba River, the Folsom Reservoir on American River, the Nashville Reservoir on Cosumnes River, the New Melones Reservoir on Stanislaus River, and the New Don Pedro project on the Tuolumne River.* Other projects, more particularly the Iron Canyon Dam in upper Sacramento River, will block off existing spawning areas which, unless compensated for, will result in the loss of existing fish runs. Analysis of preliminary information contained in a joint report by the U.S. Fish and Wildlife Service and the California State Division of Fish and Game, dated December 27, 1944, indicates that, with proper sequence construction of the proposed reservoirs, any detrimental effect on upper Sacramento River run by the Iron Canyon project might be more than compensated for by building up new runs on the major tributaries of Sacramento and San Joaquin Rivers upon which new multiple-purpose storage projects are proposed. Such analysis further indicates that the gross benefits to existing and potential fish life creditable to the proposed reservoirs on such tributaries would be at least $700,000 annually, while the damage to existing fish life resulting from the proposed Iron Canyon project might be as much as $500,000 annually. Although, due to limited and incomplete data, no final determination can be made at this time, indications are that with a proper sequence of construction a net fish benefit of not less than $200,000 annually might be creditable to the reservoirs proposed herein. Accordingly this amount has been used as a measure of the fish benefits creditable to the proposed comprehensive plan.

Dr. Richard Van Cleve, chief of the Bureau of Marine Fisheries of the California Division of Fish and Game, was criticized before the 1945 California Water Conference for his failure to present facts to back up his statements about the habits of salmon and the effects of irrigation and flood-control works on them. Said his critic:

---

* Which will be discussed below.

Dr. Van Cleve's claims of the calamitous effect on the fish (by construction at Table Mountain or Iron Canyon) can be briefly paraphrased as follows: (*a*) that proper temperatures cannot be maintained either behind Iron Canyon Dam or below, and the spring fish will therefore not survive the summer; (*b*) that the entire salmon run above the dam will be destroyed; and (*c*) that this run has a value of from $560,000 to $2,000,000.

He asserts . . . . "The water stored behind Iron Canyon Dam will be warmed by the high summer temperatures . . . . Therefore I can not see how proper temperatures can be maintained." To support this statement he offers no supporting statistics or data of any kind. Surely Shasta Dam must have offered a testing field for the doctor's theory; but he offers not one fact based upon experience. And from the information received by the U.S. Army Engineers the reason for his omission is plain: The argument was proven contrary to the fact at Shasta Reservoir this year . . . .

Dr. Van Cleve thinks that all dams annihilate fish—and apparently he urges that all progress in the form of flood control, irrigation or power developments must stop.

A similar rowdydow is in progress over the Delta Cross Channel in relation to salmon and other fish. The Delta Channel will extend 50 miles from the northern to the southern edge of the Sacramento–San Joaquin Delta and will carry surplus Sacramento water to the pump lifts. The Sacramento water will supply the Contra Costa and Delta-Mendota Canals. The present plan is for an "open" channel: existing channels will be dredged to enlarge capacity and a diversion dam which will turn the Sacramento water into the proper channels. The water will be sucked south by pumps. The Division of Fish and Game and the United States Wildlife Service had this comment on the channel:

This channel, if constructed, will raise many entirely new and complicated problems concerned with the safe passage of fish both down and upstream. An open type of channel would probably result in heavy losses of young salmon no matter what type of screening might be devised. Losses also would result from interference with normal migratory routes, confusion to fish caused by new directions of flow, and by mixing waters from different drainage basins. A closed type of channel is essential to prevent the loss of salmon runs from intercepted streams.

The San Francisco Tyee Club (Tyee is another name for the

King or Chinook salmon which make up the greater part of the Sacramento–San Joaquin salmon run) is very worried about the Delta Cross Channel. The Club declares:

You don't have to be an expert on salmon or striped bass to see what will happen to these species if the Bureau's proposals are put over. Full operation of the channel calls for the diversion of 10,000 cubic feet per second from the Sacramento River near Hood. This water is to be pumped over the levee into Snodgrass Slough which lies nearby. A series of deepened channels will theoretically carry about 4,600 second feet of this water as far as the pump lifts on the south side of the delta not far from the town of Tracy—6,400 second feet will be used to control salinity and keep the water in the delta area fresh.

What effect will this exchange of Sacramento River water in the upper delta area have on migrating adult salmon? It is probable that the Sacramento River runs will be led up into Snodgrass Slough instead of up the Sacramento River Channel. We are informed that this might be corrected through special ladders that it is hoped would lead the fish around the pumps and back into the main river. However, what will be the effect on the San Joaquin runs which will have to negotiate a considerable section of that river in water that is predominantly Sacramento River water and which is flowing upstream?

Admittedly, the salmon have ground for confusion. "It certainly looks," said the Tyee Club, "as though the Bureau of Reclamation had been burning the midnight oil for some time trying to think up the toughest possible test for the salmon's homing abilities." And that is not the whole story:

In addition to the harmful effects that the open-type channel across the delta will have on the adult salmon, it will kill all of the downstream salmon migrants as well as all the young striped bass and shad that have to use any channel other than the main Sacramento to get to the sea. We will assume that the Bureau will provide a foolproof system of screening the pump intakes from the main Sacramento River.

On the southern side of the Sacramento levees, however, it will be a different story. It is known that the young salmon heading for the sea will in general follow the downstream flows. They will have to develop new habits if they are to get through the delta area. There will be a heavy resultant flow across the lower ends of all rivers south of the Cosumnes toward the pump lifts near Tracy . . . . The result will be that all young salmon coming out of the San Joaquin River, and this will include those of the San Joaquin proper, the Merced, Stanislaus, and worse yet, from the Tuolumne, as well as a good share of those coming down the Mokelumne and Cosumnes Rivers and all small striped bass and shad in this area will be diverted to the pumps and from there into the West Side ditch and into the fields.

The Tyee Club contends that pump intakes cannot be effectively screened to keep out sea-bound salmon as small as 30 millimeters. And:

There is no possibility of building a by-pass. The reason is that the nearest place where the currents really flow toward the sea and where fish would not be attracted right back to the pumps is about 40 miles away. Even engineers will admit that 40 miles is a long fish by-pass, especially when there is practically no drop in water levels and when it is through an area where high temperatures are the rule in the spring and summer. Even if such a by-pass could be built, it would have to be cooled to keep the fish alive.

The Tyee Club believes that the only solution to the problem is to build a closed conduit for the Delta Cross Channel. Such a closed channel would be a great deal more expensive than the open-type channel. The proposed cost of the open channel is $9,600,000, and the Bureau estimates that a closed channel would cost somewhere around $35,000,000. The Tyee Club, however, believes that the extra cost of the closed channel would be justified. Says the club:

In order to save a capital investment of between 15 and 20 millions, they [the Bureau] propose to destroy a self-perpetuating resource worth over $5,000,000 annually. This just does not make sense. Moreover, we are informed on good authority that there is no assurance that the open-type channel will succeed in delivering water of the required purity to the lower delta. Is the Bureau of Reclamation willing to gamble on a channel that may not work and which will certainly kill off most of the Central Valley's salmon that are left after the Army Engineers get through with them?

The Bureau, harried by the fishermen, is making studies for a closed-type channel but in its comprehensive report on the basin, the official word, it is still planning an open-type conduit.

While the fishermen worry, duck hunters are hopeful that the water and reservoirs of the Central Valley Project will be beneficial to the welfare of their quarry. The reservoirs will provide resting grounds for the migratory ducks and geese but will not be ideal for this purpose because the lack of food-fluctuating levels of the reservoirs will make it impossible for natural food to flourish. The water to be provided for duck refuges and for growing food to feed the migrants will be a benefit, however. The Preliminary Report on Waterfowl Management Requirements in Relation to the Central Valley Project concludes that the project can materially aid the management program by providing sufficient water to establish proper waterfowl habitat in the Sacramento and San Joaquin valleys. The report says that approximately 4,000,000 ducks are taken annually in California and assigns a value of $20,000,000 to these birds, exclusive of the value of the intangible items of health and recreation of the duck hunter.

Recreation benefits are hard to measure. But it is certain that anywhere in the hot interior valleys, water is a welcome and cheering factor. The reservoirs which are proposed under the comprehensive plans of both the Bureau and the Army Engineers will provide places where people can have fun. Because most of the dams are planned for the foothills, their reservoirs will be readily accessible to the people of the valleys. In addition, stream regulation probably will maintain live streams for a longer period than at present. A dried-up river is no fun; a river running past a sandy beach is an invitation to a picnic on a hot night.

Boating and angling will be practicable on almost every reservoir planned. The National Park Service, in co-operation with the Bureau of Reclamation already is planning facilities for Shasta Reservoir and Millerton Lake behind Friant Dam. The purpose is not to make the reservoirs into National Parks. Rather it is to see that the lakes are made usable within their limitations. Reservoirs, because of their fluctuating water levels, are not ideal spots for fishing or boating, and the receding water line leaves something to be desired in the way of beauty. But during the periods of high water, which will last in most cases until late in the spring, much good use can be had of the lakes formed by the dams. Thousands of black bass already have been taken from Millerton Lake, much to the gratification of the men and women who like to kill black bass close to their homes. The dams themselves have a recreational value. Thousands of people visit the dams every year just to see a dam. This is particularly true of Hoover and Shasta; the giant structures lend themselves well to picture-postcard memories. The National Park Service is proceeding along sound lines. It simply wants to explore every recreational possibility offered by the water-power structures. By careful surveys, the potential recreational benefits are charted. Then it is up to the people to come along and have a time for themselves. Fullest recreational benefits will be realized when and if the comprehensive plans are completed. The prospective reservoirs will increase the water area of California by 300,000 acres, most of which will be usable for local residents. Then the fun begins. Anyone who has ever lived in the oven valleys knows that whenever there is cool water available, it's a party.

XIV. A New Set of Dreams

FROM NOW ON this thing gets complicated. The Central Valley Project—tremendous as it is—with its three dams, five canals, and three power plants is still only the beginning of a proposed program to control and conserve the water of the interior valleys. The Bureau of Reclamation has plans for an ultimate project which will cost more than $2,000,000,000. That estimate is based on 1940 prices and so is very low indeed. Including the initial features of the project, the ultimate plan calls for construction of forty dams and reservoirs, twenty-eight hydroelectric plants, and eleven main canals.

This ultimate project is designed to make water available to nearly 3,000,000 acres of land not now irrigated. In addition, it will provide a sure supply of water for 2,000,000 acres which are now partially irrigated but for which there is insufficient water, and another 400,000 acres which are under full irrigation but now suffer severe shortages of water in dry years. It will protect 360,000 acres of Delta land from salt-water intrusion from San Francisco Bay. It will provide 450,000 acre-feet annually for cities on San Francisco Bay, plus 300,000 acre-feet annually for other urban, domestic and industrial uses, duck clubs, and game refuges. Incidentally, these allocations for urban use may be too low: if California's cities continue to grow as they have, they will need much more of the Sierra's water than that. And the project, to keep the big figures rolling, will generate 8,100,000,000 kilowatt-hours of electrical energy a year.

Conservation of water which is now wasted will be the aim and the greatest boon of this ultimate project. Historically, over nine million acre-feet of water run out to sea every year. Wasted. When (and if) the ultimate project is completed, it is estimated that only

600,000 acre-feet of water will escape unused to the ocean. Every important stream will have its reservoir and the held waters will be put to work on cropland.

This will cost big money, but the Bureau of Reclamation finds that the benefits will far outweigh the costs. The Bureau figures that benefits will total $275,003,000 a year. Like this:

Supplemental irrigation	$ 30,220,000
Salinity control	1,600,000
New irrigation	197,880,000
Municipal water	8,040,000
Flood control	7,949,000
Navigation	1,314,000
Commercial power	28,000,000
Total	$275,003,000

Operation, maintenance, and replacements will cost $29,350,-000 a year. Interest and amortization of the capital costs, on the basis of fifty years at 3 percent, will come to $70,380,000 annually —the total yearly costs: $99,730,000. Which gives, the Bureau says, a benefit-to-cost ratio of 2.7 to 1.

Any discussion of the ultimate plan is difficult for a variety of reasons. First, there are many dams and canals and power plants to be talked about; the number alone is confusing. Second, these projects are not to be built all at once. There is a three-step time schedule: immediate completion of the initial features of the project; second, a 1945–60 schedule, and a third stage of construction for the more distant future. Third, some of these projects are not even on paper as yet; they are estimates of dreams, assays of needs and ways to meet those needs. Fourth, the Bureau has included certain works which already have been authorized for construction by the Army Engineers. And fifth, the Bureau may have thought of several new projects by the time this chapter appears in print.

The safest thing to do is to cling fast to the idea that the Central Valley Project is designed to move water from north to south; from areas where there is more than enough water to places where there is not enough. With the help of maps, it is possible to indicate the great scope of the plan. The numbers on the maps, incidentally, refer to the construction stages: 1—for immediate; 2—for the 1945–60 stage; and 3—for the ultimate, some-day stage. Careful now.

From the north to the south, then, starting at the extreme north: A dam and reservoir will be constructed at the Fairview site on the Trinity River. This will allow storage of 1,200,000 acre-feet. The reservoir will regulate the Trinity River, but more important, it will allow exportation of Trinity watershed water into the Central Valley. This will be accomplished by a tunnel, nine miles downstream from the Fairview Dam. This tunnel will pour about 700,000 acre-feet of Trinity water into the Sacramento every year.

Shasta and Keswick dams, of course, are to be completed as quickly as possible. And their power plants, too. Because Shasta Dam only partially regulates the flow of the Sacramento, a new reservoir some day will be necessary somewhere below Shasta. The dam at Table Mountain has been proposed. The plans call for an immense reservoir of 5,600,000 acre-feet, largest contemplated in the Central Valley system. As we have seen, this site is the subject of considerable controversy because it would mean flooding of lands now irrigated and would have a serious effect on salmon propagation. The Bureau says:

Studies indicate that water supplies to meet future requirements for many years can be secured from other projects and that construction of this large reservoir at the Table Mountain site, with consequent flooding of valuable agricultural land and damage to the fishery resources of the Central Valley, can not be justified at present. Until such time as it can be shown that the benefits from the project far outweigh the damages that would result, construction of the large Table Mountain reservoir should be deferred. If ultimately constructed, a power plant would be installed at the dam and an after-bay dam and power plant would be provided at the Iron Canyon Dam site, 13 miles downstream.

Meanwhile, as we have seen, the Army Engineers have been

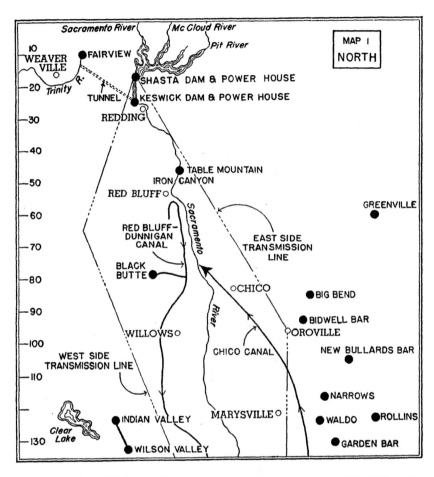

A SCHEMATIC VIEW OF THE ULTIMATE DEVELOPMENT OF THE CEN-
TRAL VALLEY PROJECT—NORTHERN SECTION. THE SCALE
ON THE LEFT INDICATES MILEAGE FROM NORTH TO
SOUTH. FOR THE CENTRAL SECTION SEE PAGE
195, AND FOR THE SOUTHERN SECTION
SEE PAGE 200.

authorized to build a low-level dam at Table Mountain. We have
seen, too, that the Army apparently prefers the Iron Canyon site
for the low-level dam. Such a dam, as contemplated by the Army,
would serve as an afterbay in the event a high-level dam is ever constructed at Table Mountain.

The experts seem to agree, at least, that the Sacramento will
have to be reregulated below Shasta if it is to be controlled as to
floods and used to the maximum for water conservation. The Bureau is studying a plan to build fourteen dams on streams tributary to the Sacramento below Shasta, seeking a means to eliminate
the immediate need for a low-level dam at Iron Canyon and to protect the salmon run. The Bureau asserts:

Although the benefits from the tributary plan would have certain advantages, the power output at the main stream site would be much larger than
would be possible at the few tributary reservoirs where power installation
might be economically justified. Also the single reservoir on the main
stream would provide more positive flood protection than the several tributary reservoirs which would control only a portion of the drainage area. It
would also more completely conserve the run-off entering the river below
Shasta Dam and be valuable for the re-regulation of power releases from
the Shasta and Keswick Dams and the potential importations from the
Trinity River. The construction, operation, and maintenance costs for the
tributary reservoirs would be considerably greater than the cost for a similar amount of storage on the main stream.

A new reservoir, Black Butte on Stony Creek, would be built to
give more water to the existing Orland Reclamation Project and
provide flood control. This dam would be of earth-fill construction,
117 feet high, and would impound 160,000 acre-feet.

South, still on the west side of the valley, two Coast Range
streams also would be improved. These streams, by construction
of dams and a tunnel, would be tied in to the Monticello Project
(see below). On the north fork of Cache Creek, the Indian Valley
Dam would be built and on the main stem of the Cache, Wilson Valley Dam is planned. Water stored by these dams would be available for irrigation of the land of Yolo County above Woodland and

a great measure of flood control would be achieved. Indian Valley is planned as an earth-fill dam, 208 feet high, with a reservoir capacity of 250,000 acre-feet; Wilson Valley Dam plans have not been completed but it is estimated that it would furnish irrigation water for 175,000 acres now dry.

The important streams rise in the Sierra: the Feather, Yuba, and Bear rivers and these, too, will be co-ordinated into the Central Valley power and water system.

Feather River enters the Sacramento below Marysville. It has the largest runoff of any Sierra stream. The Bureau tentatively plans to build two reservoirs—Bidwell Bar on the middle fork of the Feather and Big Bend on the north fork. Bidwell Bar Reservoir will have a capacity of 1,200,000 acre-feet behind its concrete dam. A power plant is planned at Bidwell Bar Dam and another at the Elbow afterbay which would reregulate the water released from Bidwell Bar. Big Bend would have a reservoir of 1,000,000 acre-feet and a power installation. A smaller reservoir (833,000 acre-feet) is planned at Greenville on Indian Creek, a headwater tributary of the Feather's north fork.

On the Yuba, two projects are contemplated. New Bullards Bar Dam and Reservoir is planned for the north fork of the stream and Narrows Reservoir will be built on the main stream. New Bullards Bar will have a capacity of 675,000 acre-feet and Narrows 500,000. On Dry Creek, seven miles south of the Yuba, Waldo Dam and Reservoir will be built with a capacity of 202,000 acre-feet. On the Bear River, Rollins Reservoir, a small one (60,000 acre-feet) will be built primarily as a storage reservoir for mining debris with a little left over for irrigation. Garden Bar will be built 27 miles down the same stream. This will be a 200,000-acre-foot job.

Now, what happens to this water? It goes like this: A great canal will be built down the west side of the Sacramento Valley, from Red Bluff to Dunnigan, near Woodland. This 115-mile canal will carry Sacramento River water to irrigable lands which are now dry-farmed. Lands above the canal will be served by laterals fed by pumps. Another canal will be built from the Feather River near Oroville to Chico Landing on the Sacramento. This 43-mile canal has a couple of justifications. It will service lands along its route with water from the Feather. What water is not used for irrigation will reach the Sacramento at Chico Landing and go into the main stream where, at times, it will help meet navigation requirements which otherwise would have to be met by releases from Shasta or Table Mountain Reservoir.

As for power: generating plants will be included at Fairview (40,000 kilowatts), at Tower House (60,000), and Spring Creek (70,000) on the Trinity River diversion works; at Table Mountain (200,000), and Iron Canyon (40,000), at Big Bend (200,000); Kennedy (35,000), on the north fork of the Feather; Bidwell Bar (104,000), Oroville (40,000) on the Feather, and at Elbow afterbay (20,000) also on the Feather. New Bullards Bar (60,000), New Colgate (50,000) on the north Yuba River; Narrows (70,000) and Garden Bar (4,000) complete the power-generating works in this northern section of the Sacramento Valley. To get the power to market, the Bureau plans two high-capacity transmission lines, one on the east side and one on the west side of the Sacramento. The eastern link is almost completed. The western line is only started and there will be many fights about it. In addition, there will be a grid of lower-capacity transmission lines which will serve the territory the main lines pass through. The whole power system, then, will be co-ordinated so that the most effective amounts of both water and power can be realized.

This is the same show, second act, and it deals with the central section of the two valleys—an arbitrary line drawn simply because this thing has to be broken up. Remember that the whole idea of this project is to move water from north to south. And realize that man has never before moved water so far to serve his needs.

Generally speaking, the Coast Range streams do not add a great deal to the project. One stream, however, Putah Creek, is extremely important to the project. On this stream, the Bureau proposes to build Monticello Dam whose reservoir will hold 1,600,000 acre-feet. The Monticello project ties in closely with the Wilson and

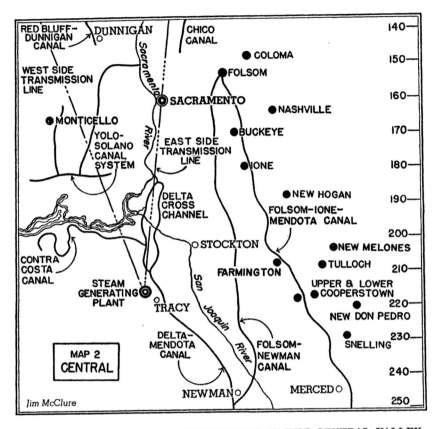

MAP OF THE ULTIMATE DEVELOPMENT OF THE CENTRAL VALLEY
PROJECT—CENTRAL SECTION. MILEAGE SCALE AT RIGHT.

Indian Valley dams. Monticello would store the water of Putah Creek and also water from Cache Creek which would be diverted by tunnel from Clear Lake to Soda Creek and thence to the Putah. Monticello, the Bureau says, would provide water for 100,000 acres of land now unirrigated, furnish 20,000,000 gallons of water a day for municipal and industrial use at Vallejo (which needs it badly), Benicia Arsenal, Suisun, Fairfield, and other towns. It is designed to provide flood control for rampaging Putah Creek.

The Bureau plans to build a dam 275 feet high at Monticello. Originally, the Bureau wanted a dam 300 feet high which would have impounded 2,200,000 acre-feet of water in the reservoir. The state objected, however, and the 1,600,000 acre-foot reservoir has been agreed on. Ranchers of the Berryessa Valley, whose lands will be flooded by the reservoir actively are opposing the project. A bill has been introduced in Congress seeking funds for the work which has been approved by the Interior Department.

A canal system would be built to put Putah Creek water on the land. One canal would run north and one south from Putah Creek to Cordelia. A second canal, to the east, would parallel Putah South Canal and would end at Montezuma Slough. Ultimately a third canal would take water from the Sacramento River at Knights Landing and carry it south and into the Fairfield area.

South of Monticello are the Delta Cross Channel, which carries Sacramento River water through the island maze of the Delta to the intake pumps of the Delta-Mendota Canal and the Contra Costa Canal which is now complete. The Delta-Mendota Canal, Contra Costa Canal, and Delta Cross Channel are all parts of the initial features of the project.

On the east side of the Sacramento Valley, on the Sierra streams, the project hits high gear again. In this central section, 12 dams are planned and their reservoirs will contribute heavily to the San Joaquin Valley acres.

In the north, the first dam planned is Coloma, which will have a reservoir of 800,000 acre-feet on the American River. Below Coloma, near Folsom, is the site for Folsom Dam, one of the key units of the Bureau's plan and one of the most controversial of the dam projects.

Folsom would be an earth-fill and concrete dam, backing up a reservoir of 1,000,000 acre-feet—a figure now agreed on by the Bureau, the Army, and the state of California. Folsom would provide needed flood control for the American River—a stream which can get very rowdy when full—excellent recreational facilities near Sacramento, and irrigation and power.

A 550,000 acre-foot reservoir is planned at Nashville on the Cosumnes, and on Laguna Creek, Buckeye Dam will be built with a capacity of 437,000 acre-feet. Ione Reservoir on Dry Creek, a tributary of the Mokelumne River, is designed for a capacity of 1,137,000 acre-feet.

New Hogan on the Calaveras River is an enlargement of an existing reservoir and its ultimate capacity will be 325,000 acre-feet. Littlejohn Creek, east of Stockton, will be dammed at Farmington to provide a reservoir of 100,000 acre-feet. New Melones is planned for the Stanislaus River substituting for an existing reservoir. New capacity will be 1,100,000 acre-feet. Tulloch Dam and Reservoir, on the same stream, is designed as an afterbay for Melones.

Storage at New Melones would be supplemented by Upper and Lower Cooperstown reservoirs on Dry Creek which lies between the Stanislaus and Tuolumne rivers. The Turlock and Modesto Irrigation districts are planning erection of the New Don Pedro Dam on the Tuolumne which would create a reservoir submerging the present Don Pedro Dam. It would have a capacity of 1,100,000 acre-feet. Surplus flow of the Merced River would be diverted to Dry Creek (what, another?) between the Merced and the Tuolumne for storage in the 241,000 acre-foot Snelling Reservoir.

What happens to this water? First of all, local needs are taken care of and the local lands are irrigated. But there will be a surplus of water available for export to the west side of the San Joaquin. This will be accomplished by several canals and by an intricate integration of these twelve dams. These are the main canals:

The Folsom-Newman Canal will run 132 miles from the American River just below Folsom Dam directly south across Sacramento, San Joaquin, and Stanislaus counties to the Delta-Mendota Canal. This surplus water would then be carried either to the Mendota pool in the San Joaquin River or, alternatively, to the proposed San Luis Reservoir on the high land to the west of the Delta-Mendota Canal.

The Folsom-Ione-Mendota Canal would carry water from Folsom Reservoir 30 miles south to the Ione Reservoir. From Ione the canal will run 136 miles south to the Mendota pool. Both of these canals will have connections with the Sacramento so that Sacramento River water can be transported in them when needed in dry years. The Delta-Mendota Canal requires a pump lift of 200 feet from the Sacramento while the Folsom-Newman Canal requires only a hundred-foot lift for American River water. And the Folsom-Ione-Mendota Canal can deliver water from east-side Sierra streams, including the American, to the Mendota pool by gravity. A considerable saving in pumping costs would result from the use of the Folsom-Newman and Folsom-Ione-Mendota Canals. Operation of a portion of the Delta-Mendota Canal would be necessary at all times, however, to serve the lands lying between the Delta and the point where the east-side canals join the Delta-Mendota line. Meanwhile, the Folsom-Ione-Mendota Canal will gather the excess waters of the streams between the American and Merced rivers for storage in Ione Reservoir. And when Ione is full, there will be available storage capacity in Farmington and Buckeye.

And as for power, these power-generating plants are planned: Coloma (40,000 kilowatts), Salmon Falls (12,000) on the south fork of the American, Folsom (60,000), Folsom Canal (18,000) on the Folsom-Ione Canal, Sloughhouse (16,000) on the Folsom-Newman Canal, Nashville (18,000), New Melones (48,000), Tulloch (20,000), and New Don Pedro (60,000).

And, very important, the steam generating plant is in this central section. It will be somewhere near the Delta. This generating plant will be the stabilizing unit—it will stabilize the power produced by the hydro plants. The transmission lines converge on it and radiate from it. It is the heart of the power part of the project. It will have a rated capacity of 240,000 kilowatts.

That takes care of the central section. So far we have built twenty-eight dams and many miles of canals and transmission lines. And, in effect, we have almost completed the transfer of the northern waters from the Sacramento, Feather, and American systems to the San Joaquin Valley. The southern section, which comes next, completes this transfer and also moves water of the San Joaquin River on its unnatural southward course.

And still we go south, first on the west side of the San Joaquin Valley where the land is so fabulously fertile and where there is so little water.

In this section the line of the Delta-Mendota Canal is completed and the Sacramento River water is delivered to the Mendota pool at the great bend of the San Joaquin River as it starts north to the Bay. Angling in from the northeast is the line of the Folsom-Ione-Mendota Canal which also deposits its water into the San Joaquin at Mendota.

Completely dependent on these canals is the San Luis Reservoir on dribbling San Luis Creek. This reservoir is to be filled with northern water via pumps from the Delta-Mendota Canal. And when it is in operation, the San Luis storage will feed the San Luis–West Side Canal which skirts the foothills on the western rim of the valley. The canal will carry water to fill the Avenal Gap Reservoir which also is on a dry stream; the water will be raised by pumps from canal to reservoir. Water from the 240,000-acre-foot Avenal Gap Reservoir will be used in the Lost Hills section of the valley.

Now for the east side of the San Joaquin. Buchanan Dam, a slab and buttress design, will be built on the Chowchilla River to provide a reservoir of 70,000 acre-feet. This project is still under study. South a piece is the Hidden Reservoir site on the Fresno River. This earth-fill dam, still under study will provide a reservoir of 90,000 acre-feet.

Then there is Friant, a major key in the entire project. Friant

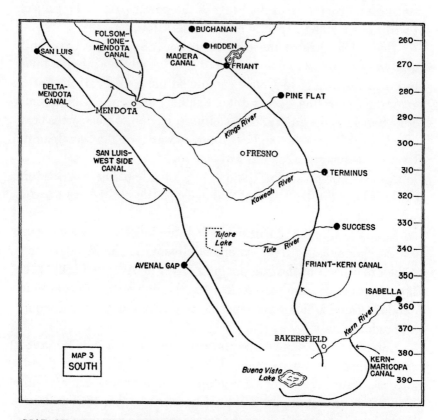

MAP OF THE ULTIMATE DEVELOPMENT OF THE CENTRAL VALLEY
PROJECT—SOUTHERN SECTION. MILEAGE SCALE AT RIGHT.

Reservoir, feeding two main canals, diverts the water of the San Joaquin. The water which is taken from the San Joaquin at Friant is replaced lower down on the stream by the Sacramento River water. Friant is almost complete. Its drum gates have been installed and the valves which will complete the structure are being worked on.

The Bureau proposes to build a 388-foot concrete dam on the Kings River 30 miles east of Fresno to create a reservoir of 1,000,-000-acre-feet capacity. As noted earlier, however, Pine Flat has been authorized for construction by the Army Engineers and they, in fact, are already at work. The Bureau, game to the last, still is in there pitching for Pine Flat. The Bureau has asked for clarification of the Pine Flat situation. It appears, however, that the Army has a good headstart and clarification may come too late, if at all. The Army project contemplates a reservoir of 1,000,000 acre-feet but would not immediately provide power-generating facilities.

Although the Army has authorization for the three remaining southern dams, the Bureau also lists them as part of the Central Valley Project. These dams are Terminus on the Kaweah, Success on the Tule, and Isabella on the Kern. Terminus would be an earth-fill structure impounding 145,000 acre-feet. Terminus, like Isabella and Success, is designed to provide increased supplies of gravity-flow irrigation water. Success, an earth-fill dam, would back up a reservoir of 115,000 acre-feet at an estimated cost of between seven and eight million dollars. Isabella is planned as an earth-fill dam about 40 miles northeast of Bakersfield. It will create a reservoir of 550,000 acre-feet. The Army has been given a $1,000,000 appropriation to start work on Isabella.

Now, what happens to the water? The San Joaquin River water, stopped at Friant from its normal course, is distributed through the Madera Canal north to the Madera Irrigation District. But the bulk of the water will go, via the great Friant-Kern Canal, south through the dry lands to Bakersfield. This canal crosses the Kings, Tule, Kaweah, and Kern rivers. At present, the unregulated water of the Kaweah, Tule, and Kern rivers find their way either into the two valley "lakes," Buena Vista Lake and Tulare Lake, sump areas on the valley floor. These lakes are not regularly equipped with water and only to the extent that water is available. They yield amazing crops.

Water from the Friant-Kern Canal can be pumped to bench-lands above the line of the canal as well as distributed by gravity to the lower-lying lands. Pumping is expensive, however. The Bureau proposes that a water exchange be effected whereby the waters of the Kaweah, Tule, and Kern could be used on these high lands. Lands normally irrigated with the water of these streams could be serviced from the Friant-Kern Canal—thus eliminating the need of the expensive pumping from the Friant-Kern Canal to the higher benchlands. Because the water of these streams is wholly utilized, this water-exchange agreement would have to be worked out to the satisfaction of those people who now hold the water rights.

An example of how this water-exchange plan could work is of-fered by the proposed Arvin-Edison development. This calls for digging the 55-mile Kern-Maricopa Canal. Says the Bureau:

The Arvin-Edison project would be constructed to provide a much-needed supplemental water supply for the irrigation of lands in the Arvin-Edison Water Storage District. This district includes about 100,000 acres of irrigable land southeast of Bakersfield and above the existing canals diverting from the Kern River. The present highly productive irrigation development, somewhat in excess of 36,000 acres, relies entirely on pump-ing from ground water. Natural replenishment of these underground reser-voirs, largely from minor streams entering the area, is inadequate even for present demands. This has resulted in a rapid and continuing lowering of ground water levels.

Kern River is the closest major stream to the district, but the entire flow of this river is now utilized except in years of high runoff. Therefore, in order to obtain an adequate supplemental supply the district will have to import water from the Central Valley Project through the Friant-Kern Canal. Direct use of the water from the Friant-Kern Canal would require a pump lift of about 300 feet. This pumping would not be necessary, how-ever, if water from the Friant-Kern Canal could be exchanged for Kern River water, allowing the latter to be diverted to the Arvin-Edison area by gravity. Such an exchange could only be made by agreement among all the affected interests including the owners of water rights on Kern River . . . .

As for power, these southern dams are not too important. Pine Flat, under the Bureau's plans, would have a generating capacity of 45,000 kilowatts and a power plant at Hot Springs on the Kern would have a capacity of 3,500 kilowatts.

In passing, although we have noted some of them, these are the dams which the Army has been authorized to build and which are listed as part of the Central Valley Project by the Bureau: Iron Canyon, Black Butte, Folsom, New Don Pedro, New Melones, New Hogan, Farmington, Pine Flat, Terminus, Success, and Isabella. Included in the Army's future program are Bidwell Bar and the Elbow afterbay, Big Bend, Bullards Bar, and Garden Bar. Also on the Army's list already recommended for construction are Indian Valley, Nashville, and Buchanan, as well as several other smaller dams which would serve the single purpose of flood control alone.

Now back to the Bureau. When (and if) this long list of dams and reservoirs is constructed, it is estimated that 20,000,000 acre-feet of water can be put on the land or used for urban-industrial purposes. At present, approximately 9,650,000 acre-feet is available from these same sources. This great increase in usable water will be accomplished primarily by the elimination of waste—by cutting the amount of the runoff into the sea.

The table on page 204 explains this water supply and the use and loss of water in the Central Valley Basin.

And as for power: the generating system provided at the multiple-purpose dams plus additional steam generating capacity ultimately will produce 9,000,000,000 kilowatt-hours of energy annually. Of this amount, 10 percent will be lost in transmission, leaving an effective production of 8,100,000,000 kilowatt-hours to be used for operating project pumps and to be sold to wholesale customers for resale.

For pumping, approximately 2,500,000,000 kilowatt-hours

WATER SUPPLY AND USE AND LOSS OF WATER,
CENTRAL VALLEY BASIN

(Annual means in acre-feet)

	Historical Conditions	Future Conditions, Including Historical	Change Resulting from Comprehensive Plan
Estimated Available Supply			
Natural runoff 18,400,000		18,400,000	
Draft from carry-over storage....... 1,000,000		2,400,000	+ 1,400,000
Trinity River importation		700,000	+ 700,000
Total supply 19,400,000		21,500,000	+ 2,100,000
Estimated Use and Loss			
Use:			
Irrigation use 7,450,000		16,600,000	+ 9,150,000
Municipal and miscellaneous uses... 300,000		1,000,000	+ 700,000
Outflow for salinity repulsion 1,900,000		2,400,000	+ 500,000
Total use 9,650,000		20,000,000	+10,350,000
Loss:			
Evaporation loss 350,000		900,000	550,000
Waste or ocean 9,400,000		600,000	− 8,800,000
Total loss 9,750,000		1,500,000	− 8,250,000
Total use and loss 19,400,000		21,500,000	2,100,000

will be used, leaving 5,600,000,000 to be sold. Transmission lines would be provided to get this power to the places where it is to be used. The Bureau says:

The power to be generated at the Shasta and Keswick plants will require a minimum of three 230-kilovolt circuits with a capacity of 150,000 kilowatts each to transmit the output to load centers. The plan provides for extending the present 230-kilovolt line south from Oroville to Sacramento and to a central distributing point in the Delta region. Two other circuits are to be constructed along the west side of the Sacramento Valley to the same terminal substation .... Other 230-kilovolt lines will eventually be needed to inter-connect with plants to the south of the Delta location and for supplying power to project pumping plants. Lines north of Shasta will some day be necessary .... From future power plants which will probably be built along the west slope of the Sierra Nevada, transmission facilities will be needed to carry the output to points of connection with existing transmission facilities for co-ordination and planned utilization. The marketing of power on a low-cost basis is dependent upon some such network of lines being available.

At this point it is sufficient to note that a great deal of power can be made available, through the ultimate Central Valley Project, for California's growth. Few dispute the opinion that California's population and industrial centers will grow. California is now growing too fast for dispute.

Development of hydroelectric power—supplemented by steam-generating facilities—is imperative if industry is to be served. That is true because California has a limited supply of thermal energy. Its stores of oil and natural gas will not last forever and the state has no coal presently available. Cheap hydro power is California's only hope for a stable industrial economy alongside her agricultural economy which itself needs great quantities of power.

Briefly, these are the new dreams, the new plans. They will cost a great deal of money—actually no one knows how much—and they will take many years to construct. When they are built, however, one of man's greatest undertakings will have been accomplished and that day when California's water will not be wasted will have been reached. The water, instead of running sterile to the sea, will go to work on the thirsty land.

XV. A Busy Year and a Dry One

DULY RECORDED in the beginning was the observation that the Central Valley thing was a continuing fight. And all the time I have been sitting here at the typewriter, the fight has been going on. In writing the earlier chapters, it was necessary to have an arbitrary stopping point; this point was approximately February 1, 1947. Now is the time to catch up and see what has been happening since then.

For 1947 was a busy year for the Central Valley Project. Almost from the beginning of the year certain aspects of the project were under fire. Senator Downey made a terrible fuss about his bill to repeal the 160-acre limitation and a House hearing was held on the same matter. And, more important, the Congress, with an economy-minded Republican majority, took some lusty swings at the Central Valley budget—and almost made them stick.

When the Republican majority announced its intention of chiseling six billion dollars from President Truman's budget, it was apparent that reclamation projects, among other items, would suffer. President Truman included $20,000,000 in his budget for the Central Valley Project. And Governor Warren went to Washington to ask that this allotment be doubled; he said the Central Valley Project needed at least $40,000,000 for the work to go forward satisfactorily.

Warren had the apparent backing of the California delegation until the chips were down. All the California Republicans in the House of Representatives, however, voted in favor of the six-billion-dollar cut.

On April 20, the appropriations subcommittee of the House recommended a 65 percent reduction in the Truman recommendation. In other words, the committee said it thought $6,900,000 was all that should be spent on the project during the 1947–48 fiscal year.

The outcry was terrific.

Michael W. Straus, the commissioner of reclamation, shouted that the committee's action would slow work on the project. He said it would take 27 years to finish the thing if the budget cut were allowed to stand.

Secretary of the Interior Julius Krug said that the funds allowed would not even permit a minimum economic rate of construction. He said it would be more courageous to shut down the project altogether. And, he said, the government would lose about $2,000,-000 a year in power revenues if Congress accepted the committee's denial of funds for transmission lines. And, he added, farmers in the project area could not possibly hold out until 1964 for project water.

Governor Warren, who had returned to Sacramento, said he was "shocked" by the committee action and declared he would go to Washington again to protest.

Representative Franck Havenner, of California, called the appropriation "a miserable pittance."

Richard Welch, of California, chairman of the House Public Lands Committee called a meeting of the delegations of the seventeen Western states to talk about the cuts in the reclamation budget.

Senator Wayne Morse, of Oregon, a Republican, declared that any Congressman who voted for the drastic reclamation cuts should be defeated.

Senator Hatch said he agreed.

But the outcry was not loud enough. And the West was not strong enough. On April 25, the House passed 307 to 30 an appropriation bill embodying most of the drastic cuts. The House twice defeated motions on the floor which would have given the Central Valley Project the $20,000,000 President Truman had asked. And only three of California's Republicans in the House (there are 14) voted with the Democrats to return the bill to committee. Eight of nine Democrats voted for this measure—all except Sheppard, a member of the Appropriations Committee.

Ruth Finney, Scripps-Howard writer who has watched the progress of the project in Congress many years, called the bill "the most devastating bill ever prepared to harm the west." But all the California representatives except Havenner, Douglas, King, Miller, Holifield, and Welch voted for final passage of the measure.

Governor Warren went to the radio to tell Californians just how serious the cut in appropriations was and then went to Seattle to confer with other Western governors about what to do. On May 7, this governors' conference gave its verdict: These reclamation projects are vital to the nation's welfare and are beyond partisan considerations. The governors declared that reclamation projects are not inconsistent with an economy program because the money is ultimately repaid to the government.

On May 10, Warren was back in Washington before the Senate Appropriations Subcommittee. Again he asked for a $40,000,000 appropriation. As for the House appropriation, he declared it was "totally inadequate." "Our people," he said, "are going to pay back every dollar of this project's cost."

The Senate loosened the purse strings a little and voted an appropriation of $10,016,288 for the project. This figure included funds for transmission lines not included in the House bill. And finally, the Senate-House conference committee agreed on the final figure: $9,141,288 for the Central Valley Project. Like this:

Joint (irrigation, power–flood-control) facilities at Shasta Dam.$ 690,000
Irrigation facilities 5,622,028
Shasta power plant 427,800
Keswick Dam 100,740
Keswick power plant 218,040
Transmission line, from Oroville to Sacramento.............. 256,680
Transmission line, from Shasta powerhouse to Shasta substation 1,500,000
Transmission line, Contra Costa extension 118,000
Transmission line, Keswick to Shasta substation.............. 160,000
Substation, Contra Costa 48,000

During the House hearings, Representative Robert Jones, chairman of the subcommittee, said again and again that the Central Valley Project (and other reclamation projects) would not be hurt by the cuts his committee made. He based his statement on the fact that certain uncommitted funds were in the hands of the Bureau, available for continued work on the project. Jones was right: the Bureau had a carry-over of $21,000,000, part of which was already committed to contracts. The carry-over permitted the work to continue.

The Republican attitude was never made entirely clear, except that the party was anxious to achieve some measure of economy in its first return to Congressional power. Then, too, Republicans seemed convinced that the Bureau had enough money for Central Valley. The fact that Central Valley funds would have been exhausted by the end of the fiscal year did not make much difference in Congress. There would be time enough, in 1948, they intimated, to provide additional funds—and 1948 is an election year when big appropriations build votes as well as canals and transmission lines.

Congress, however, found that it could not wait for 1948. In December of 1947, it voted a supplemental appropriation of $11,405,000 for the Central Valley Project. Thus the Congress got credit for economy and the project got money to continue building.

During the hearings before both the House and Senate committees, James B. Black of the Pacific Gas & Electric Co. was at the same old stand singing the same old refrain noted in chapter ix. The P. G. & E., he repeated, was willing to build all the power lines necessary to move Central Valley power to market. For the government to build the lines, he said, would be wasteful duplication.

But this time Black had powerful opposition—from Governor Warren and Senator Knowland. Their opposition was effective. Although only token funds were voted for transmission lines, the appropriations had the effect of committing the Congress to completion of the east-side line from Shasta to the Delta via Oroville and Sacramento. And further, through the efforts of Knowland and Warren, the Congress was, in effect, bound to construct the west-side line, the line Black particularly does not want built. It came about this way:

Although only $1,500,000 was appropriated for construction of a link between Shasta powerhouse and the Shasta substation 25 miles away, Senator Knowland said (and he was not contradicted) that he considered this link to be the start of the west side line.

In the conference between the Senate and the House, House committeemen tried to have the Senators remove all language pertaining to the west-side line. They contended that the money should be spent to build the Shasta–Shasta-substation line along "the most direct route." Knowland would not agree. Although, in the final bill, there was no mention of the west-side line, conferees said it was their understanding that the funds were provided for start of the west-side line.

Said Representative Leroy Johnson (California) on the House floor: "We hope this is only the beginninng of the steps to be taken in the extension of this line down the west side of the valley to the booster pumps at Tracy so that we may have an integrated system of power in connection with the Shasta Dam project," and Finney noted that no representative arose to contradict him or state an opposition view.

Although the battle of the transmission lines is far from over, the original commitment by the Congress for the west-side line is a major victory over the P. G. & E.

While the appropriations wrangle was in progress, there were three moves made on the problem of the 160-acre limitation. Hearings were held on the Downey-Knowland bill which would have repealed the limitation from the Central Valley Project and projects in Texas and Colorado. The Subcommittee on Irrigation of the House Public Lands Committee, held hearings on a similar bill. And in California, an attempt was made in the Legislature to pass state laws which would have blocked enforcement of the limitation.

Downey did his level best to convince everyone that the 160-

acre limitation was "unworkable." During the hearings which lasted sixteen days and which take 1,329 pages to record, Downey acted in the role of prosecuting attorney and his target was the Bureau of Reclamation. Downey threw a lot of angry language around. And the hearings brought to everyone's attention the affair Downey was having with the Di Giorgio Fruit Corporation, one of the large landowners of the Southern San Joaquin Valley. Downey clearly was head over heels about Di Giorgio and did nothing to hide his crush.

Downey's line before the committee was that it would be unfair, unethical, and "governmentally dishonest" to enforce the limitation. Such a course, he said, would destroy big ranches built up in good faith. Downey repeated his familiar argument that the limitation on water would mean that the burden of project costs would be borne by small farmers. This water, said Downey, would replenish the underground water table by seepage and then the large landowner would be able to pump it onto his lands without paying for it. Since control of this seepage in the underground reservoirs is impossible, he said, the only way to see that the large landowners pay their share of project costs is to remove the limitation and let them buy project water for all their land—not just 160 or 320 acres.

This contention was bolstered by Edward Hyatt, California's state engineer. Underground water flow cannot be controlled, he said. "When water is made available to non-excess lands, it is unavoidably made available to excess lands," he said. "It is therefore idle to prohibit delivery of underground water to excess lands." And Downey pointed out that there is no way a large landowner can be prevented from pumping water which lies under his own land—whether this water comes from the Central Valley Project or not.

William E. Warne, assistant reclamation commissioner, however, took the Bureau line, which was also presented by Commissioner Straus, Secretary of the Interior Krug, and others:

"It seems to be that there is a basic fallacy in this argument for repeal. If a big landowner can get underground water without coming into the project, they why does he want the limit repealed?"

And Straus summed up his views: "I simply think these large and corporate landowners in the Central Valley want interest-free water and the present law blocks them just as it was designed by Congress to do, so they are out to kill the law." Straus admitted that enforcement of the limitation would be difficult but said that 97 percent compliance already had been achieved on reclamation projects and continued:

"I submit that no lawmaking body would for a minute consider nullification of the anti-trust laws that protect the public from monopoly because of a few violations. Neither would laws against murder, thievery and the thousand and one other criminal code violations be torn from the statute books because there is not 100 percent compliance."

Actually, the hearings were a repetition of earlier hearings on the same matter. Over all there seemed to be some implication that the Communists were plotting against the Republic and battling to keep the water limitation in the law. This ghost was laid, appropriately enough, by Father William J. Gibbons, a director of the National Catholic Rural Life Conference. He told the committee:

The efforts of the large landowners to fasten the term socialistic or communistic upon the restrictive provisions adopted by our Congress for the purpose of widely distributing private property are repudiated by the National Catholic Rural Life Conference. The conference, in fact, is convinced that no more dangerous collectivistic tendency exists, short of communism, than the present concentration of productive property. The practices of land monopolists destroy the spirit of private enterprise and reduce our rural population to the status of proletarian agricultural workers. No surer preparation for state capitalism was ever devised than this progressive concentration of wealth in the hands of the few.

Downey, pursuing his infatuation with Di Giorgio, hailed the operation of this 12,300-acre ranch time and again. When Secretary Krug was on the stand, Downey asked him: "Mr. Di Giorgio has 5,200 stockholders . . . . among his stockholders are many veterans. Well, then, isn't the benefit of this water being spread widely among those 5,200?"

Said Krug: "No . . . . I am certain that the Congress did not have in mind that the reclamation benefits received from these great projects would be spread to our people through their owning stock certificates in some corporate farm. The entire history of the Reclamation Act is the opposite."

The hearing finally dragged to a close, after Downey had taken his licks at all the Bureau people he could think of. In passing he handed Krug a bad couple of hours, apparently for the fun of it because it did not seem to advance the hearings greatly. Downey summoned the full committee for his two-hour summation in support of the bill (most of the time only one or two committee members were present). Downey's parting blast at the Bureau was this: "I want to characterize the attitude of the Bureau as mendacious, dishonest, and misleading. Its purpose is to propagandize." And he predicted again that the Bureau's policies would drive the small farmer off the land. "This is a matter of religious ideology to the people of the Reclamation Bureau. The Bureau is willing to sacrifice not only dollars but the small farmers on the altars of ideology." At the end, Senator Ecton, the only committeeman who heard the entire hearings, was a tired and confused man. It was clear that he did not quite understand why the small farmer would have to give up his land. "If this matter is as you put it, the Secretary of Interior ought to be in here fighting for your bill, but he isn't. That's what makes it so confusing."

Congressman Welch took the Public Lands Committee to California during the fall and held hearings on the limitation. The committee visited Shasta Dam, and so on, held a two-hour hearing on the water limitation in Sacramento, and devoted a full day to the subject at Fresno. Once again the same arguments were put on the record. More than four hundred people appeared at the hearing. The afternoon session was conducted by a lone committee member—the rest of the committee went home. Although there was no ready solution, this Congressman, Fred Crawford of Michigan, admonished the crowd just before adjournment: "You people in California had better get together on this matter before Congress has to act on it."

Meanwhile the California Assembly defeated two bills which would have prevented application of the limitation within the Central Valley Project and, secondly, would have reaffirmed the fact that the federal government cannot deprive landowners of their water rights as guaranteed under the State Water Code. Governor Warren opposed the bills. He said they "represented almost a declaration of war on the Government so far as the Reclamation Service is concerned." At the same time, he once again said he favored the small-farm idea but did not think the 160-acre limitation was workable in the Central Valley. Warren hoped some middle ground could be found for a solution.

There was another bitter fight (what, another?) over the Rockwell Bill. This measure was introduced through the efforts of the National Reclamation Association. Ostensibly, it was designed to end, by legislation, a controversy regarding the use of interest money derived from power. A ruling of the Solicitor General, in interpreting the Reclamation Act of 1939, had held that the entire amount of interest on power facilities on reclamation projects —i.e., 3 percent—was applicable to help pay the costs of the irrigation features and thus reduce the final cost of water to the farmer.

From the earliest days of reclamation, power has been called upon to help pay for irrigation. The law clearly permits the Bureau (but not the Army Engineers) to make use of *net power revenues*, over and above amortization and interest, for that purpose. The solicitor's opinion tossed the interest component, too, into the irrigation pot.

This opinion was attacked by various groups, notably private power interests, but was never brought to court. Opponents of the ruling held that the interest earned on money advanced for power installation should be returned to the Treasury.

In the fall of 1946, however, the National Reclamation Association appointed a study committee empowered to draw up a bill which would defeat the opinion by legislation. Such a bill was drawn and introduced by Robert Rockwell of Colorado. This bill, among other things, would have set power rates as high as the traffic would bear.

The Bureau of Reclamation considered the bill a vicious one and promised to denounce it and fight it. William Lempke of South Dakota thereupon introduced another bill. Both bills were heard simultaneously. Within a couple of days the original Rockwell bill was abandoned; a second was introduced and the hearings continued. After three days the second Rockwell bill, pretty well eviscerated, was combined with the Lempke bill and as such was unanimously reported by the committee. It is now before Congress.

The present form of the Rockwell bill is very different from the first version. It has been endorsed—as a whole—by the Bureau of Reclamation. It provides that the amortization period for power facilities shall be 78 years instead of 50; it reduces interest on power loans from 3 percent to 2½ percent and, very important, it makes silt control, fish and wild life, and recreation features nonreimbursable costs—just like flood control.

The bill provides that only one-fifth of the interest component —one-half of 1 percent—shall go to aid irrigation features of projects. The other 2 percent will be paid directly into the Treasury.

Thus, although the amount of interest money which goes directly to aid irrigation is cut, the over-all effect of the present bill is extremely favorable to reclamation. By extending the period of amortization for power works, power rates can be lowered. Making silt control, fish and wild life, and recreation nonreimbursable means that the farmer will save still more money. Instead of being a bill designed to raise public power rates, the revised bill does just the opposite. It has a good chance of passage. The Bureau, through Michael Straus, while endorsing the present bill made it clear that the endorsement was for the bill "in its entirety." In other words, if Congress amends it on the floor, the Bureau will probably fight the amendments.

In all of the whooping over the cuts in the Central Valley appropriation, another appropriation went almost unnoticed; the Army Engineers were given $1,000,000 to start work on Isabella Dam, and an additional $1,750,000 to continue work on Pine Flat. This highlighted the fact that the important fight in the next few years will be between the Army Engineers and the Bureau to see who builds what in the Central Valley. As noted earlier, the Army has already begun construction of Pine Flat Dam on the Kings, a project which the Bureau lists in its Central Valley Project.

But the big fight now is centering on Folsom Dam on the American River. The Army has authorization to construct this work and the state, the Bureau, and the Engineers have agreed that the reservoir should be 1,000,000 acre-feet. There the agreement ends. Sacramento interests want the Folsom Dam very badly. They want it primarily for flood control because they know that if the Sacramento and the American rivers ever crest at the same time at the same point, Sacramento will be under water. But, if the dam is constructed by the Army, its value as an irrigation dam will be largely nullified because power revenues will not be available to subsidize the irrigation works. Net power receipts from power plants built by the Army must be returned to the Treasury—thus they cannot be used to help pay the expense of canals. Sacramento wants the dam very badly, so badly, in fact, that the traditional roles of the city's newspapers have been reversed. The *Sacramento Bee*, traditional friend of the Bureau, is plunking for Army construction, on the theory that the Army has a head start and the best chance to get funds to complete the work. The *Sacramento Union*, on the other hand, is wholly on the Bureau's side because it realizes the need for irrigation facilities. The Sacramento Chamber of Commerce's attitude is: get the dam; let the Army build it; then we'll get the law changed so that power revenues can be used as a subsidy for irrigation.

During the summer, there was an interesting development in the Folsom fight. Representatives Miller and Engle of California introduced a bill which would include Folsom Dam and Reservoir in the Central Valley Project. If that bill should pass, the dam would be reauthorized as a reclamation project and would be paid for like other reclamation projects, and power revenues would aid irrigation. The bill has another interesting feature, however. It would tie the Folsom water conservation directly to the urban counties of the San Francisco Bay area, Contra Costa, Alameda, and Santa Clara. It provides for canals and power lines to move American River water to the cities on the shore of the Bay, where already the water shortage is becoming a problem, particularly in such places as Richmond and San Jose.

The Folsom dispute is interesting because never before has the Army built a California irrigation dam and its history in power development is almost nil. There is some indication that Congress, very conscious of the Army which has just finished a successful war, may be inclined to make the Engineers the building agency for all government agencies. This would keep an awful lot of colonels at work.

Actually, the Congress is to blame for the confusion that exists between the Army and the Bureau. The law is confusing and causes overlapping of authorities and that leads to bitterness. The Army, of course, would be delighted to get into the irrigation business. An exhibit posted by the Army at the State Fair late in the fall of 1947 bragged happily, after pointing out the flood-control merits, that its projects would impound 4,500,000 acre-feet of dependable storage of irrigation water.

In the next few years look for the 160-acre limitation fight to drift out of the public mind; look for an intensification of the fight between the Army and the Bureau to build the dams.

Meanwhile, the shouting and the fighting notwithstanding, the Central Valley Project is being built. Contra Costa Canal is finished; so is Madera. Six miles of the Friant-Kern Canal have been finished and by the end of the fiscal year the canal will be completed to Pozo Creek, twenty miles north of the Kern River, which will mean that it is an operating unit even though it will not be wholly complete. The Friant-Kern Canal, of course, cannot be a firm operating unit until completion of the Delta-Mendota Canal but it will be able to deliver Class II water before that time. Twenty-five miles of the Delta-Mendota Canal are under contract and contracts have been let for the pumping plant and the gigantic pumps for the lift from the Delta into the canal. Contracts for additional mileage of the canal will be let from time to time. Work is progressing in the powerhouses at Shasta and Keswick. And work has started on the west-side power line and is continuing on the east-side link.

Nature served warning in the winters of 1946–47 and 1947–48 that the dry years may be just ahead. It was a winter of light rains, the beginning of a dry "cycle" which may make the need for the project more apparent than ever. And in this dry year, when the water levels fell in the lakes behind the dams, a power shortage developed. Then the water-and-power relationship was gravely illustrated; without full development of California's streams California will have flood and drought and California will not have enough power to support her growing industrial complex. Nothing could be surer and simpler than that.

XVI. Picture Book

WHEN THE engineers set out to build the Central Valley Project, they set out to change the look and nature of California—although they may not have known it at the time.

When you start giant machines eating into the earth and snaking along for hundreds of miles forming canals behind them, when you pour ton after ton of concrete for seven or eight years, when you set 10,000 men to work, when you string poles and wire along the valley floor, you have done more than build a mechanical thing. You have given the land itself a new look and a new promise of life.

The Central Valley Project is a relatively simple plan. It will move water from the north, where there is too much, to the south, where there is not enough. It will provide the means to move water farther than man has ever moved it before. It will help to conquer floods. It will help to moisten fertile land which is now barren or in limited production because there is not enough water. It will open vast areas of new land—for new farm families to use and protect. In the land of the frontier, it will create a new frontier.

Hundreds of millions of dollars have been spent. Millions more will be spent. But money alone cannot do the job. This is more than a money project. Thousands of men have worked on the project with their hearts and hands and minds. Men have been killed and men have been seriously injured in the course of the work. In spite of high water, bad weather, delays of one kind or another, the immense chore was accomplished. The men were equal to the task and their work was done with precision, with pride, and with a flair.

Words can explain the project, can describe it and help to bring an understanding of the problems around it. Pictures, perhaps, can give a better idea of the look of the changing land and the men who did the job. Here, in brief, is a pictorial description of the project, of the work going forward on the various elements of the project, and the final promise of water on the land.

No one can describe the complexities of the valley to another's satisfaction. Nor can pictures do the whole job. They can help suggest, however, the sturdy vigor and the rich productiveness of this land and its people.

~~~~~~~~~~~~~~~~~~~~~~~~~~~~

The majority of the following pictures were taken by Bureau of Reclamation photographers under the direction of Ben Glaha. The dust jacket also is a Bureau photo. The flood picture on page 221 is used through the courtesy of Edward Hyatt, California State Engineer. The aerial view of finished Shasta Dam was taken by Jon Frederic Stanton.

In the southern San Joaquin Valley, orchards died and men left the land. The battle was lost to drought.

And in the Sacramento Valley, floods swept the fertile fields and homes.

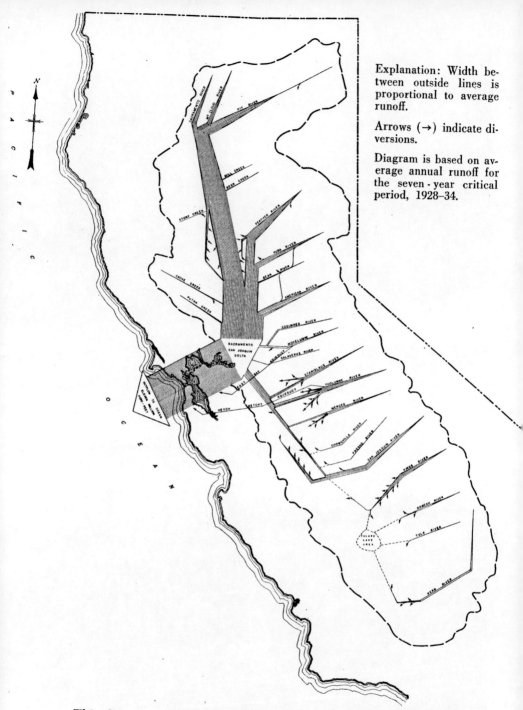

Explanation: Width between outside lines is proportional to average runoff.

Arrows (→) indicate diversions.

Diagram is based on average annual runoff for the seven-year critical period, 1928–34.

This diagram shows where the water of the Central Valley comes from and where it goes—out to sea through the Golden Gate. Eleven million acre-feet of water run to waste in the sea during an average year.

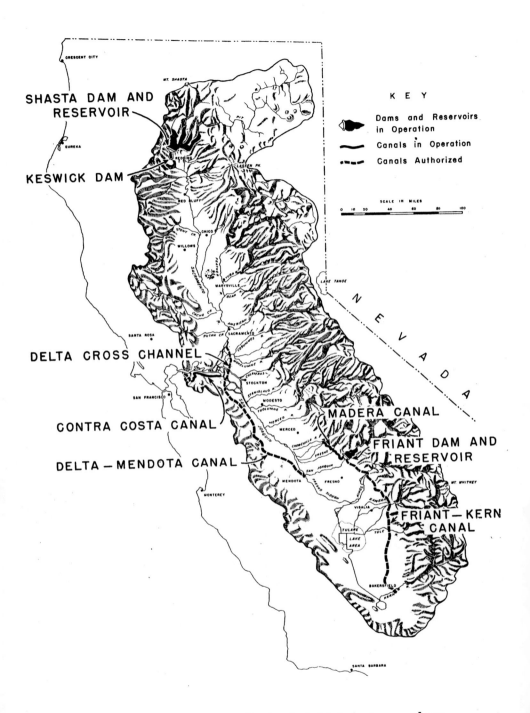

These are the Central Valley Project's initial features—three dams, five canals, powerhouses, and transmission lines—devices to get water and power to the places they are needed most.

THE PLAN

Building a water and power project is a big job. You start with a need and a dream and work toward a plan. Long before the first steam shovel lumbers up to the job, long before the first dynamite blast raises a yellow-red cloud of dust, many men have been at work to perfect the plan. In California, more than twenty years of planning went into the Central Valley Project, under Edward Hyatt, state engineer. The flow of streams had to be measured year after year. Surveyors hiked the hills searching for dam sites; diamond drillers sent their bits into the hard subsoil, feeling for the rock foundations for dams. Chemists and hydraulic engineers and designers labored with their retorts and slide rules. The names—the ones you read about in the papers—reflect leadership: Ed Hyatt, Julius Krug, Harry Truman, Earl Warren, Harold Ickes, Robert Bradford Marshall, Michael Straus—and John Savage, the man who designed Shasta Dam and most of the other great dams of the country. But you need more than leadership. You need many men of skills and courage to transform leadership's ideas into plans from which a project can be built. You need a great variety of men to do a great variety of jobs.

A stream gauger. Wet work, but necessary for the planning:
how much water, when, and where.

Surveyors plot the canyon of Putah Creek, doing the field
work for Monticello Dam.

Land classification: to find out what kind of land it is and what water will do for it.

Test borings brought up by diamond drills show the composition of the underground. These were made at Friant Dam site.

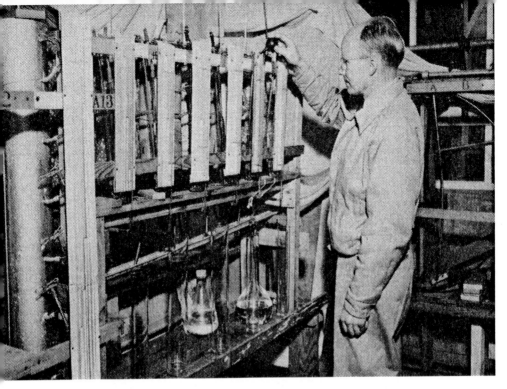

Soil analysis: in the Denver laboratories of the Bureau of Reclamation, a chemist tests the valley land for quality.

Trial run: in the Denver laboratory, engineers have built a scale model of the Delta to see just what happens in the tangled waterway.

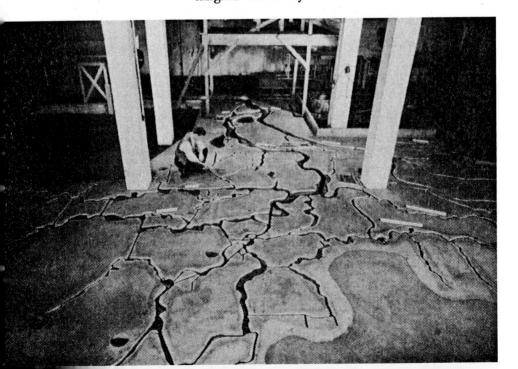

THE JOB

When the plan is done and the contract let, you call in the men who do the work. At Shasta, they called in Francis Trenholm Crowe, the "Westerner from Maine." Frank Crowe had spent a lifetime in the river canyons of the West building dams—"I never bellied up to a desk in my life," he said. Shasta was his nineteenth big Western dam—Hoover his biggest job.

He was a highballer, a boss who wanted the job done quick and right. (Frank Crowe died shortly after finishing Shasta twenty-six months ahead of schedule.) "I bring my organization to the job," said big Frank Crowe. "It's just like a circus crew. They drift apart when the job is done but they come back as soon as a new one opens up." Some of them hated Crowe's guts and some had a tough sort of love for the guy.

Frank Crowe's boys did the work. He drove them, insisting the work must be fast and good. The hard-rock men, the powder men, the muckers, the men who swung the buckets on the big power shovels, the truck drivers, carpenters, dozers, worked and cursed in the red dust, under the stifling sun, worked in the red mud and in the cold rain. With Frank Crowe roaring and swearing his orders, they built Shasta. "Hell, that's what we came up here for," said Crowe.

When hills have to be moved, you need drillers in the mass . . . .

. . . . and alone against the sky.

You need grease monkeys to keep the big shovels in
working trim.

And welders to keep the big wheels rolling.

To bridge a lake and move a highway, the high steel men
take over.

The forms have to be strong and tough and so do the men.

Sand blasts clean the surface of the new-laid concrete.

Welders put the gigantic penstocks together—water for the powerhouse.

THE TOWER

This spraddle-legged steel tower was the key to construction of Shasta Dam. Erected on a hillside about 200 feet above the river, its bare steel rests on foundations sunk a hundred feet down. The tower itself stands 465 feet high. From this head tower, Frank Crowe strung cables to seven movable tail towers on the sides of the canyon. From these cables he dropped the 16-ton buckets of concrete to the spot they were needed on the job. "That tower cost $600,000 before we put any machinery in it," said Crowe. "But it was two and a half million dollars cheaper than any other way of doing the job." From the radiating cableways, 6,500,000 cubic yards of concrete were poured—from the first bucket to the last. Now that the water has risen around the tower, the parts remaining above the water will be salvaged.

The river and the tower. Near the tower is the cylindrical concrete batching plant where the concrete for the job was mixed.

The tower in action. From the radiating cables dropped the buckets of concrete—eight cubic yards at a time.

The conveyor belt brought the sand and gravel to the batching plant. The dam begins to grow, section by section.

Driver Frank Crowe keeps the work going around the clock—
year after year.

The hard-hat brigade starts the long descent from the face of the
dam at change of shift.

In the foreground, the growing powerhouse. The powerhouse is as tall as a 15-story building, a block long, but it is dwarfed by the dam itself.

The dam was built in sections and then connected into a solid monolith—the second largest in the world.

. . . . the river narrows.

The river's licked—"pinned down, shoulders to the mat," in the words of Frank Crowe.

THE FINISHED DAM

"Look at that Shasta Dam," said Frank Crowe. "That dam will stand there forever holding back the river. And that powerhouse will keep right on turning out juice until somebody discovers how to make power out of sunlight." Shasta is the second highest dam (Hoover is higher) and the second largest in bulk (Grand Coulee is more massive). "Old Shasta's about the secondest dam there is," said a workman. But when the water one day tops the spillway it will flow from a height three times that of Niagara Falls.

Shasta is the key. But the other parts of the project have their great importance. Keswick Dam, nine miles down the stream from Shasta, forms an afterbay for Shasta and will generate its share of power. Friant Dam on the San Joaquin, although not as spectacular as Shasta, still is a man-sized dam and it is the key to the southern half of the project. From this dam, high on its concrete face, flow the Madera and Friant-Kern Canals and give it its reason for being.

Shasta, Keswick, and Friant, the great dams, and their canals and powerhouses will solve, in a measure, the most acute water problems of the Central Valley. Around them other dams and canals will be built in the future. Some day there will be an integrated, water-power system which will dwarf any other project yet built. Then California's water will not run to waste into the sea. Then California's industries will have power aplenty.

The finished dam—the highest structure in California—602 feet from bedrock to the 3,500-foot roadway on the crest.

This is unfinished Keswick . . . . the work was stalled by the war.

Friant Dam on the San Joaquin, low and serene against the hills. It dams the river for the needs of the southern valley.

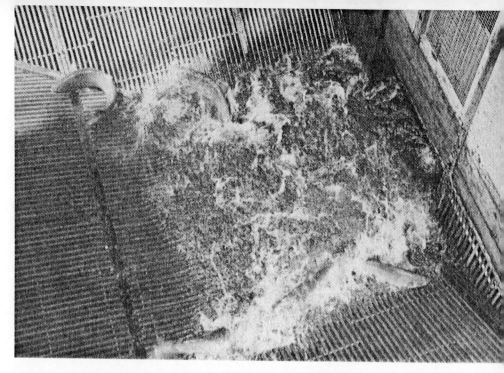

Fishermen work on the project, too. Salmon are trapped at Keswick, transported in trucks for natural spawning, or taken to the hatchery.

At the hatchery, after a proper time, the fingerlings thrive. They are marked and set loose to make their way to the sea.

The changing face of the land: the Westley wasteway, a unit of the Delta-Mendota Canal, cuts across the flat valley near Tracy.

This is the leisurely beginning of the Friant-Kern Canal. It has more than a hundred miles to go, rimming the eastern edge of the valley.

In the switchyard—the complex adjuncts of hydro-power generated at Shasta powerhouse.

This is the end product: the water reaches the land in a potato field in Kern County. Without the water there would be no potatoes.

This is the end product: the water reaches the productive groves. Without the water, the orchard dies and men leave the land.

This is the end product: golden-green grapes laid in the sun to dry into raisins in the lush vineyards of the San Joaquin.

This is the end product: acres of figs soak up the sun in a San Joaquin Valley orchard. Water makes the valley go.

This is the source of the wealth and prosperity of California. This is the inexhaustible resource—the Sierra snow pack. From it comes the water and the power which have made California great. The idea is to prevent any of this power and water from being wasted.

XVII. Epilogue

THIS GREAT interior basin is the country of only two seasons—the wet and the dry. In the fall the first rains bring out an improbable green fuzz on the brown-red hills and the fields are green all winter. And in the winter, the valleys lie dormant for a few months, sponging up the rains and lying under a thick, gray tule fog. The sodden winter valleys gulp down the water against the sure time when the summer sun will suck the moisture from the earth and bleach the grasses and sere the land. Here there is enough water but it comes at the wrong times and in the wrong places. Enough water, but too much·of it goes to waste. Enough water if man can catch it and save it for the land.

The vistas and patterns of this land are not uniform. The great valley lies flat and dun-colored in the summer, but the pattern varies from the tweed of a cotton field to the green baize of alfalfa. The unwary traveler, lulled by miles of flatness and the monotony of orchards and vineyards, hop fields and rice paddy, does not at once see the productiveness of the land. But anything that grows, grows here.

At Arvin there is a field of potatoes where the low vines stretch away to the low hills—for how many miles?—and it seems there can not be so many potatoes. And in the field there is an occasional man, his overalls bleached light blue by many washings and by the sharp valley sun. He wears a spiky straw hat and he carries a shovel. With the shovel he directs a slow-moving furrow of water to the plants. He is the last man in the chain of irrigation. His job puts the water directly on the fertile earth.

At Arena there is a way station where the melon farmers bring their crops to load them on trains. And when the melons ripen the

Arena crossroads are lined with trucks as far as you can see and each truck is piled high with glossy, green melons. Where are the people who can eat all these melons? Or near Manteca you might see a mile-long train of slat-sided gondola cars piled with twisted, beige sugar beets on the way to the refinery. How many million beets are in that trainload and where are the people who will eat all that sugar?

Near Strathmore the narrow concrete road is lined by orange groves and the groves are fringed with gray-leaved olive trees. In the summer stillness and brightness (between the silent groves) you can hear the steady beat or whir of pumps bringing water to the trees. And far down the measured rows there is a cloud of dust raised by the man and the tractor working in the soil.

This is the land of the agricultural baronies, the stockades of great wealth in the valleys. Near Merced, the California Packing Corporation cultivates a fabulous peach orchard. And the people of Calpak are management and they are a sufficiency. Management son marries management daughter and they mingle little with the town and not at all with the men who work the soil. There are others: Di Giorgio works his empire further south, 12,000 acres of excess profits tax; Arakelian's empire is in grapes and wine; Anderson-Clayton's Silver Creek Ranch (when Russell Giffen owned it, he called its 42,000 acres "a family-sized farm") is in cotton and melons; there are many: the Kern County Land and Water Company, the Bear Creek orchards in figs, El Solyo, the Merritt Ranch.

But the great majority of the farmers are the little ones. Their kinship with the baronies is remote. They are hard-working men, quick to recognize improvements in techniques, quick to seize mechanical aids for the chores. They are far removed from the sharecropper, the agricultural peon. The land is theirs, their farms are businesses. They walk and work in the grandeur of the valley and they are conscious of their land and know its moods.

A land of seedless grapes, of oil wells, of desert alkali patches. Cotton clings to the tumbleweeds at the edge of the roads, reminders of the chicken-wire trucks which carry it to the gins in the fall. White-face cattle dot the far-away pasture and lie in the scanty shade of the windmill and water tank. At every crossroads there is a congress of solemn, upright milk cans awaiting the truck from the creamery.

Sleek cows move slowly in the irrigated pastures near Cottonwood. And near Gridley the farmers keep a sharp watch (and shotguns cocked) against the migrant ducks which can strip their fields of rice. Cattle graze on the sallow badlands near Oroville where volcanic outcroppings peak and blacken the yellow valley floor. Great pumps reach into the Sacramento River and boost the water over the levees onto the low bottom lands where asparagus and tomatoes flourish.

This is the land of the long-legged jackrabbit and the clumsy meadow lark. The land where the rattlesnakes lie in the rocks where the hills begin, where the gray mourning doves scatter from the white patches of Jimson weed and the sharp call of the quail is heard in the foothill brush.

In this valley there is no consciousness of the mountains. The Sierra is hidden behind a constant veil of cloud and haze and the flatness of the valley floor is dominant. But once in a while the haze breaks to show the surprising, jagged, snow-covered peaks. Mostly the mountains lie behind the haze, and the rounded, yellow foothills, patched with granite clumps and somber green chaparral, seem like the real mountains against the valley.

The towns are exactly alike and they are connected by the railroads and the highways. They are hot-weather towns and their people go about in cotton dresses and shirt sleeves and in the summer the women leave for the mountains or the coast, if they are rich enough, and the men stay home to sweat it out. There is a sharp division between the right side and the wrong side of the tracks in these towns—on the one side the respectable businesses and residential section, on the other the Chinatown, the skid rows where the Mexicans, Hindus, and Okies find their hovels and their entertainment.

The division between man and master is sharp. The rancher here in this land is too ambitious. His economy is based on more than he can do himself. He cannot harvest his crops alone or with the help of his family. He must hire migrants to do his work, and his terrible dependence on this floating labor makes him distrust and dislike the men who work for him. Money for cultivation, fertilizer, irrigation water, and all the other attentions to the land the farmer pays out because there is no escape. But he cannot harvest his crops alone and the laborers' bill, which is high, stands between him and his final return and he feels victimized by the workmen he needs so badly. He needs men to prune his oranges, pick his grapes and lay them tenderly in field trays to dry in the sun; he needs hands to pick his peaches and apricots, to cut them in halves for drying; he needs women to peel peaches and tomatoes in the canneries. The women and children go into the fields to pick cotton, to help wherever hands are needed. The tents and trailers of these migratory workers crowd the farmer's unused plots of land.

And these farmers distrust even the rain. Rains in the valleys always do some damage. The rains mean the end of the long growing season in the fall; then it damages the late tomatoes and the cotton and the rice. And the rains of spring, needed as they are, sometimes knock the almond blossoms from the trees, and when there is too much rain the ranchers complain that the pasturage is without nourishment for their herds.

But the real fear is reserved for the dry years. As much as he dreads the untimely rain, the farmer really knows that the year when the rain does not fall is his year of danger. Then his risks are increased immeasurably and his year becomes a gamble from beginning to end. He, more than the city dweller, knows the relationship between the Sierra's sharp peak and the furrowed fields of the valley.

The city dweller, however, is becoming more and more conscious of the place of water in his life. In the dry winter of 1947–48 the rains came very late—so late that many feared they would not come at all. In many parts of the state—Benicia, Santa Clara

County, Vallejo, Santa Barbara—the situation was critical. In some, it was a jail offense to wash an automobile or water a lawn.

And along with the shortage of rainfall there developed a major shortage of power. Certain industries had their power supply curtailed; clocks ran slow throughout the state when the alternating current was cut from 60 to 59 cycles; the P. G. & E. called for help in billboards and newspaper advertisements.

In the past it was gold that came from the fabulous Sierra streams to bring men wealth. Now from those same hills, from those same streams, comes the one inexhaustible resource, the one sure wealth of the state. The rancher knows and the city dweller is coming to realize that the snow on the Sierra and the rain of California's gray winters are the future.

How the water is used will determine what California is to be.

Index

257

Printed in the United States
1048200003B/160